BUSINESS SCHOOL
ESSAYS THAT MADE A
DIFFERENCE

The
Princeton
Review

Business School
Essays that Made a
Difference

Nedda Gilbert

Random House, Inc.
New York
www.PrincetonReview.com

The Princeton Review, Inc.
2315 Broadway
New York, NY 10024
E-mail: bookeditor@review.com

ISBN-13 978-0-375-76569-8
ISBN   0-375-76569-7

VP—Publisher: Robert Franek
Editor: Lisa Marie Rovito
Designer and Production Manager: Scott Harris
Production Editor: Christine LaRubio

Manufactured in the United States of America.

9   8   7   6   5   4   3   2   1

ACKNOWLEDGMENTS

A book such as this is truly a collaborative effort. Many of the ideas and insights presented here belong not to me, but to the extraordinary business school admissions individuals who generously agreed to share their insights and essays with me.

I am particularly indebted to three schools for jumping into this project from the get-go. Their can-do attitude made the success of this project much more probable.

At Babson College, sincere thanks goes to Kate Klepper, Director of MBA Admissions, Olin Graduate School of Business.

At the University of Chicago's Graduate School of Business, I am especially grateful to Don Martin, Director of Admissions, and to Allan Friedman, Director of Executive Communications.

At the Tuck School of Business, my deepest thanks go to Kiki Keating, Director of Public Relations, and to Kristine Laca, Director of Admissions.

Thanks also go to Rose Martinelli, Director of Admission at the Wharton School of Business, for always being willing to dialogue and help. She challenged me to examine all sides of the issues here.

Other business school folks who provided thoughtful inspiration and essay materials are:

Kate Ardini, MBA Admissions Assistant and Facilitator Extraordinaire, Sloan School of Management, MIT

Glenn Berman, Director of Admissions, Rutgers Business School at Rutgers, The State University of New Jersey

Pamela Black-Colton, Assistant Dean for MBA Admissions and Administration, William E. Simon Graduate School of Business Administration, University of Rochester

Ute Frey, Haas School of Business, University of California—Berkeley

Rod Garcia, MBA Admissions Director, Sloan School of Management, MIT

Daniel Garza, Director of Marketing, McCombs School of Business, University of Texas—Austin

Christine Gill, Director of Marketing and Admissions, Weatherhead School of Management, Case Western Reserve University

John McLaughlin, Assistant MBA Admissions Director, Sloan School of Management, MIT

Linda Meehan, Assistant Dean of Admissions, Columbia Business School, Columbia University

Mark Miester, Editor, Office of University Publication, Tulane University

Emile Pilafidis, MBA Program Director, Peter F. Drucker School of Management, Claremont Graduate University

Bill Sandefer, Director of Admissions and Financial Aid, A. B. Freeman School of Business, Tulane University

Melanie Standridge, Assistant Director of Marketing and Recruiting, Peter F. Drucker Graduate School of Management, Claremont Graduate University

Mary Spreen, Director of Admissions, Henry B. Tippie School of Management, University of Iowa

Matt W. Turner, PhD, Director of Admissions, McCombs School of Business, University of Texas—Austin

Sherry Wallace, Director, MBA Admissions, Kenan-Flagler Business School, University of North Carolina—Chapel Hill

Jeanne Wilt, Assistant Dean of Admissions and Career Development, The University of Michigan

Jenni Winslow and Lisa Guglielmi, first-year students at Haas School of Business, University of California—Berkeley

Heartfelt thanks goes to my editors who were instrumental in bringing this book to fruition: Lisa Marie Rovito, for her patience, wit, and supreme ability to turn dross into gold. I'd also like to thank Rob Franek for the opportunity to write another book. He's so good. He *is* Hollywood.

My sincere thanks to John Katzman, founder of The Princeton Review, who gave me my start and recognized that I needed freedom and flexibility to make things happen.

A small circle of friends and family also needs to be acknowledged.

My children *tried* to endure my immersion in this project. My youngest, still at home, felt my best work would be done with her at my side. Despite an arsenal of distractions, she could not be deterred from rollerblading over my toes during phone interviews. I truly could claim that this book took blood, sweat, and tears.

That said, both of my daughters desire to be famous, so here goes: Kaela and Lexi, thank you for letting me do my work. *You* make the difference in my life.

Thanks also goes to my dearest friends, Janine Molinaro and Susan Smotrich, for seeing me through several crises; my father, Dr. Irving Buchen, for providing thoughts on being a great writer; Livingston Johnson, who dropped everything to retrieve a document sent into computer oblivion; and Peter and Leslie Tilles for generously offering their home to my children so that I could write.

Final thanks go to my husband (and Harvard MBA), Paul Gilbert. I promised him I would not involve him in this book. I failed him miserably.

CONTENTS

Chapter 11

INTRODUCTION

It's never easy to write a book. This was especially the case with this one. Perhaps because I was already established as someone who writes about business schools (my first book was The Princeton Review's *The Best Business Schools*), I thought that writing a companion book would be relatively uncomplicated.

Where my first book had several chapters on how to put together a winning application, this book would elaborate on that theme by focusing solely on the essay portion of the application process.

The essays can count for up to 75 percent of your application. So critical are they in the admissions process that neither the highest test scores and grades nor the most stellar work experience can salvage a candidate with problematic essays. I reasoned that this book was sorely needed. Not only would it provide detailed information on how to write a winning essay, it would feature loads of actual b-school essays, accompanied by critiques from the admissions officers themselves on what worked and what didn't.

But life is full of surprises. In my very first phone call to a school that in years past had provided me with generous access to its inside workings, I hit a wall. This school, one of the nation's most prestigious, did not believe that real winning essays should be made public. Their concerns were several: First, publishing these essays might encourage an act of plagiarism. Second, they did not want to provide an advantage in their applicant pool to purchasers of this book. Third, they did not want to sanction essay-writing assistance. Finally, they thought students would use these essays too literally and treat them as formulaic blueprints.

I considered this school's positions seriously. These are legitimate concerns. I had equally strong concerns for *not* doing this book, though, which I'll explain a bit later.

That said, I share some of the business school's concerns about this type of book. So before advising you any further on your essays, a cautionary note is necessary.

A WORD OF WARNING

First, do not use these essays as specific templates for your own storytelling. This book shows you the depth and breadth of good essays, how mature self-awareness is expressed, and how goals and limitations are explored. They are meant to provide you with an example of how one person chose to answer a question. Use these essays to inspire you and get you on the right track.

Second, as you read through the essays, bear in mind that one lone essay did not win the applicant his or her admission. Many factors enter into an admissions decision. Each essay in this book was part of an application that included many criteria. It was the consistency throughout the application that won individuals with an essay in this book admission.

Finally, though it goes without saying, don't plagiarize the essays in this book. That's worth repeating: Do not plagiarize the essays you read in this book. We encourage you to note buzzwords, structures, and themes that you like, but draw the line at copying paragraphs, sentences, or even phrases.

Many schools have begun to hire outside consultants for the sole purpose of catching those who plagiarize, lie, and cheat in their applications. This includes catching those who hire someone to write their essays for them. The writing section of the GMAT is one of the factors used to verify that your essay writing is your own. Obviously, schools expect the essays you compose at home, which undergo many rewrites, to be superior to those undertaken on the GMAT. Still, admissions officers are skilled enough to identify troubling discrepancies. If you get busted, you won't get into b-school at all. Plus, plagiarism is simply wrong, so don't do it. Period.

Official Disclaimer!

Our editors aren't asleep on the job.

The essays in this book appear exactly as they did for business school admissions officers. We only changed the layout, and in some cases, protected the anonymity of individuals, institutions, and organizations. Because we have not edited the essays, you may find errors in spelling, punctuation, and grammar. We assure you that we found these errors as well, but we thought it would be most helpful for you to see what the business school admissions officers saw—not what they could (or should) have seen. We still recommend that you carefully proofread your own personal statement, but should you miss an error, take comfort in the fact that others (accepted applicants, even!) sometimes did too.

CHAPTER 1

BUSINESS SCHOOL ADMISSIONS:

A BRIEF OVERVIEW

Although admissions requirements vary among business schools, most rely on the following criteria: GMAT score, college GPA, work experience, your essays, letters of recommendation (academic and/or professional), an interview with an admissions representative, and your extracurriculars. The first four are generally the most heavily weighted. The more competitive the school, the less room there is for weakness in any area. Any component out of sync, such as a weak GMAT score, is potentially harmful.

Happily, the admissions process at business school is one where great emphasis is placed on getting to know you as a person. The essay component is the element that allows the schools to do just that. Your essays can refute weaknesses, fill in gaps, and in general, charmingly persuade an admissions board that you've got the right stuff. They are the single most important criteria in business school admissions.

But as we've just said, they're not the only criteria. All pieces of your application must come together to form a cohesive whole. It is the *entire application* that determines whether you win admission.

Anticipate and Coordinate

The application process is very time-consuming, so anticipating what you need to accomplish within the admissions time frame is critical. To make the best use of our advice, you should first contact each of the programs on your personal list of schools. Their standards and criteria for admission may vary, and you'll need to follow their specific guidelines. Please note that the less competitive a school is, the more easily you may be able to breeze through (or completely omit) the rigorous requirements we identify as crucial in the application process for the top programs.

In addition, business school applicants are often overwhelmed by how much they have to do to complete not only one, but several applications. Proper management of the process is essential, since there are so many factors to coordinate in each application.

You'll have to prep for the GMAT, then actually take the test, round up some writers for your recommendations, follow up with those chosen to write recommendations, make sure the recommendations are mailed in on time, have your college transcript sent, and finally, write the essays. Of course, some schools require an interview as well. What makes all of this particularly challenging is that many applicants have to fit this in among the demands of a full-time job.

We know that it takes a supreme force of will to complete even one application. As grad school applications go, a top business school's is pretty daunting. If you don't stay focused on the details and deadlines, you may drop the ball.

There are many common and incredibly embarrassing mistakes you can avoid with prudent early planning. They include allowing your recommendation writers to miss the deadline, submitting an application full of typos and grammatical errors, sending one school an essay intended for another, or forgetting to change the school name when using the same essay for several applications. Applicants who wind up cramming for the GMAT or squeezing their essay writing into several all-nighters seriously shortchange themselves.

Apply Early

The best advice is this: Plan and apply early. The former diminishes the likelihood of an accidental omission or a missed deadline. The latter increases your chances of acceptance.

The filing period ranges anywhere from six to eight months. The earlier you apply, the better your chances. There are a number of reasons for this:

1. Early on, there's plenty of space available. As the application deadline draws near, fewer spaces are left. Pretty logical, right?

2. In the beginning, admissions officers aren't yet sure how selective they can be. An early application may be judged more on its own merit than on how it stacks up against the competition. This is in your favor if the applicant pool turns out to be especially competitive.

3. By getting your application in early, you're showing strong interest.

One caveat: You might not want to be the very first one in line. It's best to be close to the front, but not absolutely first.

Rounds vs. Rolling Admissions

Applications are processed in one of two ways: rounds or rolling admissions. Schools that use rounds divide the filing period into approximately three timed cycles. Applications are batched into the round in which they are received and reviewed in competition with others in that round. A list of a b-school's round dates can be obtained by contacting their admissions office if they employ this method. Applications to schools with rolling admissions are reviewed on an ongoing basis as they are received.

GMAT and GPA

The GMAT and GPA are used in two ways. First, they're "success indicators" for the academic work you'll have to slog through if admitted—will you have the brainpower to succeed in the program? Second, they're used as benchmarks to compare each applicant to other applicants within the pool. At the more selective schools, you'll need a higher score and average to stay in the game.

The Educational Testing Service (ETS) administers the GMAT. You'll need to register to take the exam by calling 800-GMAT-NOW (800-462-8669) or by registering online at www.mba.com. Many applicants take the exam more than once to improve their scores. Test preparation is also an option for boosting your numbers—call 800-2Review (800-273-8439) for more information about The Princeton Review's GMAT courses.

Your college transcript is a major factor in the strength of your candidacy. Some schools focus more closely on the junior- and senior-year grades than the overall GPA, and most consider the reputation of your college and the difficulty of your course selections. A transcript loaded with offerings like "Environmental Appreciation" and "The Child in You" won't be valued as highly as one packed with calculus and history classes.

Letters of Recommendation

Letters of recommendation act as a reality check. Admissions committees expect them to support and reinforce what they're seeing in the rest of your application. When the information doesn't match up with the picture you've painted, it makes you look bad. Because you won't see the recommendation (it's sent in "blind"), you won't even know there's a problem. This can mean the end of your candidacy. That's why you need to take extreme care in selecting your references.

Scan each application for guidelines on choosing your references—business schools typically request an academic or professional reference. The academic reference should be someone who can evaluate your performance in an academic environment. It's better to ask an instructor, teacher's aide, or mentor who knew you well than a famous professor who barely knew your name.

The same holds true for your professional reference. Seek out individuals who can evaluate your performance on many levels. The reference will be far more credible. Finding the right person to write your professional reference, however, can be trickier. You may not wish to reveal to your boss early on that you plan on leaving, and if the dynamics of your relationship are not ideal (hey, it happens once in a while), he or she might not make an appropriate reference. If this is the case, seek out a boss at a former job or someone who was your supervisor at your current job but has since moved to another organization. Avoid friends, colleagues, and clients as references unless the school explicitly says it's okay.

Advise your writers on themes and qualities you highlighted in your application. Suggest that they include real-life examples of your performance to illustrate their points. In other words, script the recommendation as best you can. Your boss, even if he or she is your biggest fan, may not know what your recommendation should include.

A great recommendation is rarely enough to save a weak application from doom. But it might push a borderline case over to the "admit" pile. Mediocre recommendations can be damaging; an application that is strong in all other areas now has a weakness, an inconsistency.

A final warning on this topic: Procrastination is common here. Micromanage your references so that each recommendation arrives on time! If need be, provide packaging for an overnight letter, have your reference seal it up, and then ship it out yourself.

The Interview

Not all business schools attach equal value to the interview. For some, it's an essential screening tool. For others, it's used to make a final decision on those caught somewhere between "admit" and "reject." Some schools may encourage, but not require, the interview. Others make it informative, with little connection to the admissions decision.

Like the letters of recommendation, an interview may serve as a reality check to reinforce the total picture. It may also be used to fill in the blanks, particularly in borderline cases.

If an interview is offered, take it. In person, you may be an entirely more compelling candidate. You can further address weaknesses or bring dull essays to life. Most important, you can display the kinds of qualities—enthusiasm, sense of humor, maturity—that often fill in the blanks and positively sway an admissions decision.

Act quickly to schedule your interview. Admissions departments often lack the time and staff to interview every candidate who walks through their doors. You don't want your application decision delayed by several months (and placed in a more competitive round or pool) because your interview was scheduled late in the filing period.

A great interview can tip the scale in the "admit" direction. How do you know if it was great? You were calm and focused. You expressed yourself and your ideas clearly. Your interviewer invited you to go rock climbing with him next weekend. (Okay, let's just say you developed a solid personal rapport with the interviewer.)

A mediocre interview may not have much impact, unless your application is hanging on by a thread. In such a case, the person you're talking to (harsh as it may seem) is probably looking for a reason not to admit you, rather than a reason to let you in. If you feel your application may be in that hazy, marginal area, try to be extra-inspired in your interview.

Approach this meeting as you would a job interview. Dress and act the part of a professional. But at the same time, remember: You're being sized up as a person in all of your dimensions. Avoid acting stiff or like a stuffed shirt. Limit your use of business jargon. Be personable. Gear yourself up for an enjoyable conversation in which you may discuss your hobbies or recent cross-country trip. Talk about your passions or any areas in which you have achieved excellence—even something like gourmet cooking. Just avoid stunt-like gimmicks (we don't advise you to pull out a platter of peppercorn pâté sautéed in anchovy sauce). The idea is to get the interviewer thinking of you as someone who will contribute greatly to the quality of campus life. Try to be your witty, charming, natural self.

How to Blow the Interview

1. **Wear casual clothes.**

   This is an automatic ding. Wearing anything but professional attire suggests you don't know or don't want to play by the rules of the game.

2. **Bring your mom or dad. Or talk about them.**

   Business schools value maturity. If Mom or Dad takes you to the interview, or your answer to the question "Why an MBA?" begins with "Dad always told me . . . ," the interviewer is going to wonder how ready you are for the adult world of b-school.

3. **Talk about high school.**

   Again, they'll question your maturity. Stories about high school, and even college, suggest you haven't moved on to more mature, new experiences. Exceptions: Explaining a unique situation or a low GPA.

4. **Show up late.**

   This is another automatic ding at some schools. Short of a real catastrophe, you won't be excused.

5. **Say something off the wall or inappropriate.**

   No doubt, the conversation can get casual, and you may start to let your guard down. But certain things are still off-limits: profanity, ethnic jokes, allusions to sex, your romantic life, and anything else that might signal to the interviewer that the cheese fell off your cracker.

6. **Chew gum or munch on one of those new designer mints.**

   Your teacher always said, "Don't chew gum in class." The same rule applies here.

7. **Forget to write a thank-you note to your interviewer.**

   Sending a thank-you note means you know how to operate in the business world, and it goes a long way toward convincing the interviewer you belong there.

Work Experience

Business schools are particularly interested in your work history. It provides tangible evidence of your performance in the business world thus far and hints at your potential. It's one thing to show academic wherewithal as demonstrated by your grades and GMAT score, but your work experiences best demonstrate your leadership, strategic abilities, and creativity in a business environment.

Your work experience will also be examined for the following: Have you progressed enough (or too far) to benefit from a business school education? Have you advanced within your organization/career? What industry perspective will you bring to the program? It's the job of the Admissions Office to create balanced, diverse classes, so applicants hailing from under-represented fields—health care and public service, for example—may be particularly appealing.

Now that we have an understanding of what the entire application process is about, we're ready to focus on the essays.

Apply Online!

Access more than one hundred b-school applications online at www.PrincetonReview.com/mba/apply.

CHAPTER 2

THE IMPORTANCE OF THE ESSAY

An essay is any school's Rorschach test when considering your candidacy. Whether you're applying to business school, law school, or medical school, what you write says more about you than your GPA or test score.

Unlike the law or med school admissions processes, b-school admissions are unique in their request for many essays and their heavy weighting of those essays. Although grades and standardized tests are considered key benchmarks for admission, they function more as a threshold. Your stories are what close the deal one way or the other.

The Real You, Revealed and Dissected

In b-school admissions, the essays tie all the pieces of your application together. They weave a narrative of who you are and why you belong in a particular program. They provide a framework for your personal and professional activities, highlighting your choices and attitudes as well as your analytical and communication skills. They also reveal your character and integrity. That's because those onerous essay questions are designed to elicit thumbnail profiles of the *real you*, which is arguably the most heavily weighted criterion in the admissions process. For these reasons, the essays are invaluable screening tools.

At the top business schools, evaluating a candidate's character, genuine accomplishments, and potential has always been pivotal. That's because b-schools operate like micro-communities, and there is an expectation that you will work well and make connections within that community. Furthermore, the curriculum is designed so that you learn from your classmates. Therefore, each student's perspective, experience, and behavior is vital. B-school learning is also team-oriented, so a cooperative spirit (or lack thereof) says a lot about whether you're a strong fit for a particular program.

But perhaps most important, b-schools are a primary source of future business leaders. So attributes like honesty (yes, that includes what you put on your resume), leadership, and ethics matter. In the wake of Enron, WorldCom, Tyco, and other corporate scandals, they matter more than ever. You can almost hear the collective b-school groan when the latest Wall Street violator turns out to be another MBA.

Figuring out whether you'll one day prove to be a source of pride or an embarrassment to your alma mater and the business community is the gray zone in admissions. So how does a b-school attempt to get at your true character and determine your potential as a business leader?

While it may be almost impossible to make such a prediction, the essays are good indicators of character strengths and flaws. So as you compose your stories, know that you're being looked at through many different lenses.

B-School Applicants Need an Advocate

. . . and that's exactly why we decided to produce this book.

The truth is, I've always been on the side of those pinning their dreams on getting into the most highly regarded program they can, wanting to make something of themselves by going to one of the "best" programs. In fact, I've always secretly identified with those applicants.

Perhaps it's because admissions decisions can seem arbitrary, or because admissions boards wield such a degree of power in young lives. Who wouldn't need a little guidance for such a daunting task?

I had other reasons for wanting to help candidates with their essays. As we mentioned earlier, b-schools are uniquely interested in nontest-score characteristics. High on their list is emotional maturity, self-awareness, leadership ability, creativity, teamwork potential, and morality. Even the venerable Harvard Business School has a stated mission to do no less than "educate leaders who make a difference in the world." To screen for all these qualities, the schools rely on the essays. And herein lies the problem.

AN ESSAY CAN BE AN IMPERFECT SCREENER

It may be difficult for an engineer who will one day launch a new product that will transform an industry to craft a compelling self-narrative. How many great business leaders might be disqualified from getting their MBA at a top school because their writing or storytelling skills are poor, or because at this young age they don't know how to show self-awareness or articulate it in their essays?

In this way, the essays on b-school applications can be overreaching. But they're imperfect in other areas as well. When you consider the questions posed by the most selective programs, you realize that it's genuine frontline caretakers, like social and health care workers, who may best embody the value systems b-schools are looking for. It's by virtue of their chosen profession that caretakers demonstrate such value systems. On the other hand, also by virtue of their chosen profession, such redeeming qualities in would-be MBAs are often less evident.

CAUGHT BETWEEN A ROCK AND A HARD PLACE

Ironically, success and financial reward are part of the b-school hype. Indeed, many schools are judged each year on their career placement statistics (translation: the number of grads who secure high-paying positions, and how quickly they do so), so they work hard to ensure that their statistics are competitive. But an applicant who articulates too much interest in the very pot of gold the MBA dangles may be penalized for lacking the softer skills b-schools desire these days.

The truth is that the negative aspect of the MBA stereotype might at times be true; many pre-MBAs are ambitiously preoccupied with success and financial reward. But why should that be considered unattractive? As you can see, these essay questions don't necessarily play to a would-be MBA's strengths. The essay writers of today need an advocate.

So how does one navigate between posturing as a sincere do-gooder and an ambitious future financial officer?

It's a difficult challenge. The majority of b-school applicants are deeper than their stereotypes would suggest. As we said before, they are reflective, accountable, and morally sound. Finessing all that in a series of short stories with strict word limits is no easy task.

CHAPTER 3

HOW TO CRAFT YOUR ESSAYS

Hidden Agendas

Now that you know that the essays are used to check applicants for a range of qualities, it makes sense that each question on the application has a reason for being there. Even seemingly straightforward essay questions such as those in the vein of, "Why do you want the MBA? Why do you want the degree at this juncture in your life? And why here?" have an agenda.

As essay questions go, this one is fairly clear-cut. Although you'd rather do anything (including clean the bathroom) than sit down to suss out an honest and intelligible response, it seems doable. So why do so many applicants fail to answer the question successfully? Because even a straightforward question needs to be thought through.

Here's the inside line: Schools consider this essay the ballast to your candidacy. They want to see well-crafted goals for your education and career outlined here. When I explain this to applicants, it surprises them. After all, they argue, b-school is a journey, and part of the journey is not knowing what lies ahead. Would-be MBAs treat this essay as an opportunity to share their excitement about the discovery. But if you're not sure where you're headed or why, it's nearly impossible to answer such questions convincingly.

It is critical that you present well-defined goals and expectations in your essays. At the best schools, admissions committees want you to lay down a compelling rationale for why you need the MBA and why their program specifically meets your needs. If you can't do that, why should they award you one of their coveted spots? They want students who will value the resources at their program, not those in need of a two-year pit stop.

Half the battle in writing a winning essay is in knowing what the essay question is attempting to draw out, and we aim to offer some guidance in that respect. We don't want you to spend hours working on one question and completely miss the mark. Later on we'll identify and translate commonly asked essay questions. But let there be no mistake about it, equally important to the content, or the "what" of the essay, is the "how."

The "How" of an Essay Is Important

Think of your essay-writing this way: All written communication lives or dies on the "how" in its message. The way you present yourself in your essays and frame your subject is crucial to the impression you create. Ever receive an apology letter that felt warm and real (as opposed to perfunctory)? Did it have a positive impact on how you felt about the person after you read it? If it did, you saw an example of a good use of "how."

Still not sure what the "how" is? It's

- The mood and tone in your writing

- Your writing style and skill and the clarity of your thinking

- Your ability to follow directions

- The judgment you use in selecting your subject matter

- The impact you leave on the reader

Tone and mood can communicate that you are candid, warm, friendly, and a true leader by example. It can also betray negativity, inappropriateness, or a lack of maturity.

There are many variables to the "how" of anyone's writing. There is no one formula we can hand off to you. What might work for one essay or person won't necessarily work for another. The trick is to be self-aware.

Composing a Symphony, One Note at a Time

It is said that Mozart's patron, the Emperor of Austria, once uttered to Mozart, "You have too many notes in this piece." Mozart, who knew that his piece was balanced and perfect, replied, "Your Highness, which note would you like me to take out?"

Think of each essay as one note in your carefully orchestrated song. That song should sing of your capabilities, strengths, and accomplishments. As we said, it should reflect self-awareness and concern for the welfare of others and the world at large. Some of the high notes to hit are dignity, humility, perspective, morality, and wisdom. But your song should also address weak points and anticipate what details in your record might be of concern to the admissions committee.

As you compose your essays, you must determine which notes to hit, which to amplify, and which to play softly. You must orchestrate well. Every note must have a critical reason for being, complementing those that come before and those that follow.

What Your Essays Should Say about You

Applicants tend to place great emphasis on their accomplishments and strengths. But as we said before, there is more to writing an essay than this. You'll need to carefully weave evidence of these favorable qualities into your essay so you can appear in the best possible light without boasting, lying, or being mushy or corny. In other words, the trick is to navigate between maintaining a modest position and showcasing your accomplishments.

As you compose your essays, remember to remain aware of what the details of your stories actually reveal about you.

Your essays should suggest that you are:

A leader

Humble

Mature

Goal-oriented

Creative

Dignified

Intelligent

Hard-working

Concerned for others

Team-oriented

Positive, with a can-do attitude

Introspective

Moral and ethical

Accountable

Able to recognize and learn from mistakes and failure

Wise

Self-aware

Unique

Of sound mind and perspective

Your essays should avoid communicating that you are:

Arrogant

Vain

Entitled

Egotistical

Competitive

A perfectionist

Blindly ambitious

Angry or quick to blame

Immature

Overly bookish

Mediocre

Prejudiced regarding race and/or gender

A poor or boring writer

One who exercises poor judgment

One who sets unrealistic goals

Now Add Two Shakes of Salt . . .

Take the favorable qualities from the first list that best describe you, and jot those down. It's time for you to find a vehicle through which to convey your finest features.

Consider what compelling stories you have to tell and sketch them out. Reflect on what each story says about you and what kind of picture each paints. Then when you sit down with your application, you'll start to draw connections between your stories and the questions that are asked of you.

CHAPTER 4

CASE STUDIES

Many years ago I was hired by several Wall Street investment banks in New York City to assist their corporate analysts with their applications to b-school. During this time, I interacted with a wide variety of clients (and a personal referral from one such client), each with his or her own unique set of strengths, weaknesses, and circumstances.

Below you will find eight tales of business school hopefuls, whose stories may serve both as inspiration and warning. As you read them, you may identify with the applicants' challenges in completing a winning application. Their stories may also help you figure out how to best describe your experiences to showcase your most desirable qualities.

1. A Tale of Two Brothers

I met two brothers, just a year apart in age, who were both applying to Harvard. Each had exceptional credentials, although one brother had near-perfect grades and test scores and had gone to Harvard as an undergrad; the other went to Bowdoin.

At that time, one of the essay questions inquired about a favorite extracurricular activity. As both were expert skiers, skiing was an obvious choice. The two brothers were born and raised in affluence on Fifth Avenue in New York City and, unsurprisingly, they had learned to ski in glamorous locations. The Swiss Alps was the most frequented and memorable locale.

One brother made the Midwest the scene of his essay and mentioned the location only once. His story focused on the bumps on a "skull and crossbones" run he did over and over for days until he got it right. He spoke of the importance of earning performance, about always working harder than the guy next to you. This was the bedrock of everything he did— challenging himself again and again until he had mastered the task at hand. Skiing, as a metaphor for all of his pursuits, was about being the best he could be and, through sheer force of will, attaining his goals.

He also spoke of the beauty of the mountainous terrain, of his awe of nature, and the freedom he felt when speeding down vertigo-inducing runs. He made creative use of his passion and talent for skiing, and he made a compelling analogy between his core ethos of hard work and the commitment he would bring to b-school. The unique twist to his material was refreshing, and it was on message. Even though the only skiing I've ever done is down my driveway on a cafeteria tray, I could relate to his story.

The other brother chose to write about skiing in Switzerland and chronicled other ski trips abroad. His story was basically about the exhilaration of skiing. Unfortunately, this essay was predictable, and the setting in the Alps was a turn-off. In the absence of gripping insights, the venue came to be front and center. He came off as just another pampered candidate. This was the brother who had the superior grades, Harvard undergrad degree, and better test scores.

Have you guessed the ending to this story? The brother who wrote about conquering the "skull and crossbones" run won admission to Harvard Business School. The brother with the presumed edge in his academics did not.

It's important to note, though, that it was not just this one essay that earned one brother an admission and the other a rejection. It was the consistency of their themes in the remaining essays. For the brother admitted, these themes painted an appealing picture of a hard worker with leadership and teamwork abilities.

In fact, knowing both brothers, I would say the essays ultimately did reflect their true personalities. One was indeed pompous. The other was thoughtful and self-aware.

As you can see, the "how" in your writing is powerful enough to elevate you or sink you.

2. Spousal Privilege, Denied

Here's another example. An applicant I worked with had to write about the person he admired most. This was a common essay question at the time, and it stumped a lot of applicants. Most applicants assumed the subject of the essay had to be famous or powerful, which made the task more daunting. Once they decided on an individual, they were often at a loss as to what to write about.

As we've said before, knowing the agenda in a question goes a long way. This question is really asking you about the character traits and strengths you value in others, as well as in yourself, which is revealed in your selection. Whom you select is not as important as what you say about him or her, so your choices can be humble.

This particular gentleman chose to write about his wife. The moment he picked her, I knew the essay was at risk of being compromised. Would you want to work alongside someone whose view of the world ends at his front door? This essay was too intimate for a b-school application, and it demonstrated that he was inward-focused and myopic.

How does this story end? This candidate was not aiming for schools like Harvard, but nonetheless, schools that were selective. He was accepted into one of them. In spite of this acceptance, though, it would be unwise to conclude that this essay didn't impact his application negatively. The essay certainly reflected questionable judgment.

There is also tremendous variability in admissions factors to take into account. During the year in which this candidate applied, applying to b-school was not as popular as in previous years, so he was in a less competitive pool. Furthermore, many business schools have favorite hunting grounds for recruiting applicants. He worked at one of them—a prestigious Wall Street firm. He had a solid and impressive work history.

In all likelihood, the admissions board found this essay problematic but was able to overlook it in light of other redeeming factors. Nonetheless, times have changed. The demand for admittance to b-school remains high, and schools are more sensitive to issues of character. If the same person applied with the same essay now, I think an admissions board would give far more weight to this one essay, and it would be more damaging.

3. MAID IN MANHATTAN

Many years ago, community service was not the popular and accepted activity it is now. But we have become a society of do-gooders—so much so that a majority of our nation's high schools now integrate community service into their requirements. At b-schools, service through organizations like Habitat for Humanity is an equally acknowledged staple of student life. In this process, volunteerism is important because it reflects empathy and interest in others—both critical to effective leadership.

When I met this next applicant, schools were just getting jazzed about the concept of volunteerism. He was savvy enough to recognize that a volunteer activity would indeed communicate his positive attributes and put him ahead of the curve. Several of the b-school applications he was working on required an essay about the applicant's greatest accomplishments. He wanted one of those accomplishments to be his commitment to community service. The problem? He didn't have one.

Shortly thereafter he hit upon an idea. Late one night when he was burning the midnight oil, he was still at work when the cleaning crew came in. He noticed that the woman who cleaned his office spoke little English. He decided to help her learn English as a second language; he thought this might allow her to do something more than cleaning up after others. This became the subject of one of his essays on his greatest accomplishments.

If you've already learned a thing or two through these examples, you may know where I'm heading with this one.

This essay was a stretch. The concept of helping someone could have been moving, but this act of kindness seemed self-serving. Common sense says that someone who wants to go out and help others actually leaves his building to do so. Although helping this woman was noble, as a greatest accomplishment it came off like a bad Hollywood movie. The premise also seemed flimsy because of the timing; a genuine history of service to others dates back to some period of time before your application is due.

I can't tell you exactly what happened with this candidate because I lost contact with him. I do know he was struggling to come up with material for not only this essay, but also many others. He was hampered by the fact that he was relatively young, that he had only two years of work experience, and that those experiences were very typical of an investment banker. With all work and no play, and nothing truly dramatic in his life, it was a challenge to create a compelling essay.

Hey, no one said this was going to be easy.

4. THIRD-GENERATION DROPOUT

By contrast to the last tale, this next candidate had a genuinely unique background. He had worked in his family business since college, and he was a third-generation executive in a true mom-and-pop operation. As he was an only child, the legacy of this company would be in his hands.

This candidate seemed to have such rich material to work with. First, his family was in the business of wholesaling comic books, a nontraditional industry if ever there was one. (To build diversity, b-schools seek out candidates from diverse venues like this.) From the story of how his grandparents built their business from nothing to his future plans for the business, there was great opportunity for creativity in his essays. Surely there were many issues he could touch upon to describe what the MBA could offer him.

Naturally, I was surprised when I read his essay addressing why he wanted the MBA. Overall, the essay was passive. It lacked passion and focus. Nowhere was there anything about his vision for the comic book company, how the comic book industry was evolving, what the threats and opportunities in the marketplace were. He wrote nothing of the need for this company to integrate accounting principles, business strategy, or professional marketing into its practices.

Of all the candidates I had met at that point, he seemed to have the strongest, most genuine need for the MBA.

Or so it seemed. The truth was, like many family businesses, this one was embroiled in family power struggles. The "Mom" and "Pop" of this business, the applicant's grandparents, did not want to relinquish control, and his father was wrestling for dominance. This candidate might have been the next generation, but the business was in his father's hands for the time being.

As for his personal life, it was equally stalled. Friends from college had married or moved on with their professional lives. He felt out of sync and uninspired. His real reason for wanting to go to b-school was to figure out what he wanted to do with his life.

This unstated objective was unfortunately quite evident. As we said before, b-schools are not pit stops for figuring out what you want to do with yourself. If you're not clear on your professional objectives in the short and medium term, how can you select the most appropriate program to help you achieve those objectives?

It was hard for this candidate to map out a potential career plan, but he did it. He articulated it well in the rewrite of his essay, and the plan did not include a career in the field of comic books.

He applied to six schools, many of which were state programs, reasonable choices given his academics—a B average and decent test scores. He was admitted to all but one and chose to attend a school in Texas, far from his family.

5. Disabled, but Not Disadvantaged

This story is about an applicant who was injured in a farming accident when he was a child, which left him with a devastating physical handicap. Despite this handicap, he had done exceptionally well and was in a senior position at a blue-chip investment bank.

When I met him, his application was almost complete. Each essay I read was better than the last—well crafted, passionate, interesting, and reflective. I had almost no feedback for him. He had excellent test scores but only average grades, and he had done his undergrad at a little-known college in the Midwest. His target list of b-schools consisted of the most prestigious, top-tier programs.

Even today, almost every application has a personal statement essay, or what I call a bonus question. Although it's optional, I almost always encourage individuals to submit something here, as it is an invaluable opportunity to provide the admissions board with additional information. It can be used to communicate something remarkable, or it can be used to explain poor grades or test scores (this is where many applicants indeed do this, but we'll get to the "how" of that later).

Obviously, I thought this candidate could make use of the personal statement opportunity. But he was quite resolute that with what he'd communicated in his other essays, there was nothing more to say.

End of story? Almost.

You won't be surprised to learn that he was admitted to his first-choice schools. You may be surprised, however, to learn that not a single essay in any of his applications made mention of his childhood accident or of the resulting handicap. And yet an essay about this injury would go straight to the heart of character, as would a story about overcoming adversity. But this applicant did not want his essays to elicit sympathy. He had spent his whole life trying to make his handicap a nonissue, and he was admitted solely on the merits of his candidacy.

6. If at First You Don't Succeed—Grow Up

Analysts are generally hired straight out of college. They spend two years in an analyst training program, after which they are expected to matriculate at a business school or find other work. Post-MBA, they often return to the bank in a more senior capacity, but this is not a contractual agreement. These analysts are often a "safe" or "easy" admit; the banks are considered feeder programs to the schools because success in the job often correlates with success at b-school.

I worked with one applicant who was a second-year analyst at a prestigious Wall Street investment bank. She was the top-ranked analyst in her second-year program, an honor bestowed upon her for her outstanding work. She had good grades, but unfortunately just an average GMAT score. At less competitive schools, her score would not have been a problem, but she was fixated on getting into one of the nation's best programs. I couldn't blame her.

Her essays would have to promote her candidacy above the penalty of a low score. She began by addressing her GMAT score in the "personal statement" section. She explained that she had test anxiety and that despite taking the exam on two different occasions, she was unable to improve her score. Because she scored lower on the Math portion of the GMAT, she played up her success in calculating complex financial transactions for the bank. I thought she had proactively put her problematic scores into context.

Unfortunately, her other essays were predictable. They lacked introspection and passion. She was driven and ambitious—assets in her line of work, but hardly qualities that would make her an engaging dinner partner. Despite my feedback explaining that her essays were boring, her rewrites were no better. She wasn't able to tell a compelling story.

Younger applicants would generally need more years of experience to accrue the professional and emotional maturity that older applicants have. For an applicant from a feeder program like this, there is probably a discount factor. That is, schools may not expect the most inspiring essays. But in her case, the bad essays gave them no reason to admit her over the highly qualified competition.

This candidate applied to five schools and was rejected by all of them. Because I had worked with other candidates with similar backgrounds and scores, I was able to determine that her essays were the death blow. I encouraged her to reapply after she had left the bank and gained some maturity.

She spoke a little French, so she chose to attend a graduate-level, one-year foreign language immersion program involving overseas study. She became fluent in French and lived abroad. When she applied to b-school again, she composed essays that sang with excitement; they spoke of her passion for France and her experiences while there. She reapplied to three of her original b-school targets and won admission to her first-choice school, a bastion of finance. At graduation, she returned to a life of investment banking, her greatest passion.

The moral of this story is not that you have to go to Paris or change your life completely to write a great essay; it's that you have to write about something that inspires or excites you. For this woman, it took getting out of the box to find that inspiration.

A final note: Later on, it occurred to me that the b-school had truly lost out in not admitting this applicant the first time, proof again that essays are imperfect predictors. She quickly took on a leadership role at that school and became a genuine champion of the program. For the time she was there, she made a difference. Perhaps this school had underestimated how great a contribution she would have made the first time she applied.

7. A NEAR-MISSED OPPORTUNITY

Shortly thereafter, I worked with another second-year analyst at a different investment bank. She, too, was a bright star at her firm. Unfortunately, like the applicant above, her GMAT scores were mediocre.

Unsurprisingly, she had targeted top schools for admission. Her first choice was regarded as the "in" school and had just been chosen as number one by a widely read business magazine. It offered not only a great education, but also a dramatic departure from the cutthroat atmosphere of other programs, as its focus was on teamwork and other "soft skills." It was going to be extremely difficult to get into this already popular number-one program.

This applicant worried about her GMAT score, and for good reason. Like the analyst applicant we mentioned earlier, she was able to make a compelling argument for why she could manage the academic rigor of b-school and that she should not be judged by her score. She focused on portraying herself as the type of student who fit with the culture of this school. She slaved over her essays.

Unlike the other analyst, this applicant had a unique advantage: She had founded, almost single-handedly, a volunteer program aimed at getting Wall Street executives and analysts out of their offices and into community service projects. The program set new standards in this industry. It not only succeeded where others had failed (Wall Streeters are not exactly known for their kind spirits), but it also became "in" to volunteer with this program. Again, this was about fifteen years ago, before we were becoming a nation of do-gooders. At the time, this was highly novel.

You've already jumped to the punch line with this applicant. Yes, she was accepted into that number-one school. But it wasn't necassarily a slam dunk.

When the applicant first sat down to write her essays, she initially got hung up on a lot of details about her work (too much detail and techno-babble is always a mistake). In the essay that asked for a discussion of her accomplishments, she failed to articulate her volunteer program as a major achievement. I know that seems unbelievable, but this is exactly the kind of opportunity that gets missed without careful introspection and self-awareness.

Perhaps because of the intensely competitive culture in which she worked, she was overly focused on professional accomplishments. She didn't recognize what would be most valued by a b-school. Her best story nearly got buried.

After I had several discussions with her, her community service program came to be front and center in her essays. Still, she was never fully confident that this one achievement would override her GMAT score or that it would have more significance than her work history. Fortunately, her essays *did* articulate her accomplishment, and she stood out among a sea of applicants. Her essays also made it clear that she was a genuine fit with this school. Her GMAT score became a nonissue.

The epilogue to this story is that she had what it takes. She just wasn't going to showcase her best advantage until someone showed her the way.

8. The Job-Hopper

Another individual I worked with was an ex-analyst at one of the investment banks for which I was a consultant. He had attended one of my information sessions when he was a first-year analyst. Shortly after we met, he left the bank's training program because he found it rigid and limiting. He had kept my business card, and years later he phoned me.

After leaving the program, he had found a position at a smaller firm. He then went to work in finance at a service-oriented company. After that job, he was a project manager in a technology firm. By the time we spoke almost four years later, it seemed as though he had changed jobs every six months. Not only that, but the companies he had worked at were no-name firms.

Before we go on, I will give you some personal background: This applicant was born and raised in India. He had attended a selective college in America, had good grades and a solid, though not exceptional, GMAT score. He was feeling tremendous pressure from his parents, who were still in India. They did not consider business a worthy profession, so getting into a world-famous b-school was critical to earning their approval. It was equally critical to his life plan.

When he phoned me, I had been retired from my consulting work for several years, and I had just had a baby. He talked me into working with him and was very persistent, calling almost every day. To say the least, he was difficult to work with.

He was also convinced that b-schools had a bias against Indians and that it would therefore be more difficult for him to win admission. I didn't think this was true. What is in fact true is that all applicants are vulnerable to the diversity b-schools are aiming to create. But they also benefit from it.

He decided that only one school would do. I cautioned him that his chances were better if he applied to a mix of schools, but he was fixated on just one. With all that was riding on his acceptance, I worried that he was setting himself up for a letdown. His patchwork of jobs was problematic. His essay on this subject would have to compensate for a lot.

He used many essays to write movingly about his family and life in India. A socio-economic analysis he made of the Indian caste system was fascinating. He related it to behavioral expectations placed on him as a member of the elite. His mother and father, both medical doctors, were considered professional aristocrats. But because the tax rate in India at that time was around 95 percent, they were not rich. The rigidity of the caste system kept them at the upper rung of society, but ironically, they could not offer him financial support in college or thereafter. In the context of the American standard of living, he was poor. He spoke eloquently of the impact of those inconsistencies.

Now he had to answer the essay question on his professional experiences. Not all of the job switching was his doing, which gave me hope. At one organization, an entire department was eliminated; at another, the company was sold. As I've said in other sections of this book, the trick with a background like this is to focus on how you overcame adversity and what you learned about yourself.

He did speak of a personal ethos of determination and about how much he had learned, but some of this was a stretch. At many of his jobs he was overqualified—he was simply biding his time until he could figure out the next step. His work history came off less as a case of bad luck and more as a case of a young man unable to stay on a chosen path.

He was rejected from his choice school. Ever persistent, he insisted on speaking to an admissions officer to find out why he was a no-admit. The feedback was hardly surprising; the admissions board found his work background of serious concern. They found the remainder of his application and essays compelling, however, and they encouraged him to reapply.

My advice to him was to find a job he was passionate about and stay put for a year.

He did. Right on cue, many months later, he came knocking at my door. This time, his "problem" essay spoke of more stability and genuine passion. He reapplied early in his choice school's first round and got in.

There are several points to this story. First, an essay can blow your emotional cover. Genuine passion or sincerity is hard to manufacture. In this case, the insights he took away from having worked so many jobs lacked fire. Second, even an application full of great essays, such as this applicant's essays about his family, may not overcome an inherent problem.

As we've said before, there are many variables in the admissions process. At another school, perhaps one that was less selective, he would have been admitted in the first round. At this particular school, his application full of moving, well-crafted stories made an impression on the board, which probably had something to do with his being encouraged to reapply. When he did, they remembered him. Fondly.

CHAPTER 5
COMMON ESSAY QUESTIONS
(AND WHAT THEY'RE REALLY ASKING)

Creating Perfection Takes Time

"Essays are the love letter of why a student wants to attend business school."

—Julia Min,
Director of MBA Admissions at Stern School of Business,
New York University

No one ever said it was going to be easy. Depending on where you're applying and how prolific a writer you are, a b-school application will take anywhere from fifty to one hundred hours to complete. Sound excessive? Go ahead and try it. You'll probably scrap and rewrite an essay many times over. It takes time for thoughts to gestate. Indeed, it might feel like a fine wine ages faster than you write an essay.

You'll need to look at every essay question on each of your applications to determine how to optimally allocate your stories and anecdotes. One story might work well for either a leadership essay or an essay about failure. But you might have several good stories for leadership, and none for failure. Mapping out how you're going to allocate your anecdotes and stories is critical to your overall strategy.

Take a look at the essay questions from Harvard and Wharton below to get an idea of what you're up against. Keep in mind that not all schools will require you to write such exhaustive essays. The more selective a school is, the more rigid and demanding their standard for admission will be. That said, we're going to focus on the most brutal applications. They are the gold standard for essays, and their questions demand the greatest efforts.

Harvard Business School

1. Discuss an experience that has had an impact on your development as a leader. (400-word limit)

2. What are your three most substantial accomplishments, and why do you view them as such? (600-word limit)

3. Recognizing that successful leaders are able to learn from failure, discuss a situation in which you failed and what you learned. (400-word limit)

4. Discuss an ethical dilemma that you experienced firsthand. How did you manage and resolve the situation? (400-word limit)

5. Provide a candid assessment of your strengths and weaknesses. (400-word limit)

6. What are your career aspirations, and how can Harvard Business School help you to reach them? (400-word limit)

7. (Optional) Is there any other information that you believe would be helpful to the Board in understanding you better and in considering your application? Please be concise.

The Wharton School, University of Pennsylvania

1. Describe how your experiences, both professional and personal, have led to your decision to pursue an MBA at the Wharton School this year. How does this decision relate to your career goals for the future? (1,000 words)

2. Describe a situation where leadership and teamwork were critical to the outcome of a project in which you were directly involved. What did you learn from the experience and how have you applied what you learned to other situations? (1,000 words)

3. Describe a personal achievement that has had a significant impact on your life. Give specific details. What did you learn from this experience? How did it help shape your understanding of yourself and the world around you? (500 words)

4. Please tell us something else about yourself that you feel will help the Admissions Committee know you better. (500 words)

Reading Between the Lines

Being a great storyteller and gifted writer can be a major advantage to the prospective b-school student. But be forewarned: A wonderful answer to a question not asked will not help you here. We can't stress enough that you *must* answer the question.

Each school has its own set of questions. Although posed differently, all search for the same insights. Here's a list of commonly asked questions and what's behind them.

THEME 1: CAREER GOALS AND THE MBA

Describe your specific career aspirations. How will your goals be furthered by an MBA degree and by our MBA program in particular?

How do you feel the "X" school MBA degree can help you attain your specific career and personal goals for the five years after you graduate?

Discuss your career progression to date. What factors have influenced your decision to seek a general management education? Based on what you know about yourself at this time, how do you envision your career progressing after receiving the MBA degree? Please state your professional goals, and describe your plan to achieve them.

TRANSLATION:

What do I want to be when I grow up, and how will the MBA get me there?

This may be the most important essay question. It lays out the reasons why you should be given one of the cherished spots in the program. Even if your post-MBA future is tough to envision, this question must be answered.

A good way to frame this essay is to discuss how the MBA makes sense in light of your background, skills, and achievements to date. Why do you need this degree? Why now? One common reason is being stymied in your work by a lack of skills that can be gained in their program. Or you may want to use the MBA as a bridge to the next step. For example, an actress who wants an MBA to prepare for a career in theater management. The more specific, the better.

It may be easier to provide specifics by breaking your plans into short-term and long-term objectives.

Don't be afraid to present modest goals. If you're in accounting and want to stay there, say so. Deepening your expertise and broadening your perspective are solid reasons for pursuing this degree. On the other hand, feel free to indicate that you'll use the MBA to change careers; 70 percent of all students at b-school are there to do just that.

If you aspire to lofty goals, like becoming a CEO or starting your own company, be especially careful that you detail a sensible, pragmatic plan. You need to show you're realistic. No one zooms to the top. Break your progress into steps.

Finally, this essay question asks how a particular program supports your goals. Admissions committees want to know why you've selected their school. That means you not only have to know, but also show, what's special about their program and how that relates specifically to your career aspirations. Hint: Many admissions officers say they can tell how much someone wants to go to their school by how well their essays are tailored to the offerings in their program.

THEME 2: EXTRACURRICULARS AND SOCIAL INTERACTION— OUR NONWORK SIDE

What do you do for fun?

What are your principal interests outside of your job or school?

What leisure and/or community activities do you particularly enjoy? Please describe their importance in your life.

TRANSLATION:

Would we like to have you over for dinner? Do you know how to make friends? What are your special talents—the *B-school Follies* needs help. Are you well-balanced, or are you going to freak out when you get here?

B-school is not just about business, case studies, and careers. The best programs buzz with the energy of a student body that is talented and creative and that has personality. You won't be spending all your time in the library.

Are you interesting? Would you contribute to the school's vitality? Are you the kind of person other MBAs would be happy to meet? Describe activities you're involved in that might add something to the b-school community.

Are you sociable? B-school is a very social experience. Much of the work is done in groups. Weekends are full of social gatherings. Will you participate? Initiate? Get along with others? Communicate that people, not just your job, are an important part of your life.

Can you perform at a high level without being a nerd?

B-school can be tough. It's important to know when to walk away and find some fun. Do you know how to play as hard as you work?

How well-rounded are you? Business leaders have wide-angle perspectives; they take in the whole picture. How deep or broad are your interests? A warning: Don't just list what you've done. Explain how what you've done has made you unique.

THEME 3: WHOM YOU MOST ADMIRE

If you were able to choose one person from the business world, past or present, to be your personal professor throughout the MBA program, who would this person be and why?

Describe the characteristics of an exceptional manager, using an example of someone whom you have observed or with whom you have worked. Illustrate how his or her management style has influenced you.

TRANSLATION:

What are your values? What character traits do you admire?

This is the curveball question. The committee isn't looking to evaluate your judgment in selecting some famous, powerful person in your firm or in the world. What they're really after, which you reveal in your selection of the person, are the qualities, attributes, and strengths you value in others, as well as in yourself. Some important qualities to address: drive, discipline, vision, ethics, and leadership. As always, provide specific examples. And avoid choosing anyone too obvious.

Since the person you select is not as important as what you say about him or her, your choices can be more humble. You might write about a current boss, business associate, or friend. Bad choices are your mother or father.

If you like, it's perfectly fine to go for a famous figure. Indeed, there may be someone whose career and style you're passionate about. Make sure your essay explains why you find this person so compelling.

On page 21, read about an applicant who chose a very intimate subject for this question—his wife.

Theme 4: Teamwork—How Do You Work with Others in a Group Setting?

At X School, a team, which consists of approximately five first-year students, is often assigned group projects and class presentations. Imagine that, one year from now, your team has a marketing class assignment due at 9:00 A.M. on Monday morning. It is now 10:00 P.M. on Sunday night; time is short, tension builds, and your team has reached an impasse. What role would you take in such a situation? How would you enable the team to meet your deadline? [Note: The specific nature of the assignment is not as important here as the team dynamic.] Feel free to draw on previous experiences, if applicable, in order to illustrate your approach.

TRANSLATION:

We need cooperative, one-for-all-and-all-for-one students here. Are you cut out to be one, or are you a take-over type who has all the answers? Are you likely to help everyone get along and arrive at solutions? (We like those kinds of students.) Can you lead others to order and synergy? (We especially like leaders.) Or do you retreat or become a follower?

This, too, is a curveball question. But you can't afford to get it wrong. After the career goals question, it probably ranks as the most critical essay you write. Here the committee isn't looking to see how you save the team (so put yourself on ego alert as you sit down to write this one); they want to see how you can create an environment in which everyone contributes so that the sum is greater than its parts. Bottom line—the admissions committee is looking to see whether you have "emotional intelligence." Understand that schools today believe that emotional intelligence, the ability to navigate emotion-laden situations, is as important as strategic and analytical skills. This question is intended to illustrate this particular type of ability.

Expect to shift gears with this essay. Almost the entire application process thus far has asked you to showcase "me-me-me." Now the focus of your story needs to be on the "we" and how you made the "we" happen.

As you write your essay, consider that when you get to school, some team members will be from different countries where cultural attitudes play into team dynamics. Your sensitivity to these cultural differences, as well as to personality types, will go a long way toward demonstrating your emotional intelligence. For example, a team member hailing from a certain culture may withhold an opinion in an attempt to foster consensus. How can you help this person make a contribution? Likewise, consider differences among team members in terms of their academic and professional strengths. If the assignment is heavy on numbers, finance students may dominate teammates from softer sciences. How can you ensure that everyone feels valued? Teams are inspired to success when everyone is motivated and taking ownership within a context of respect.

Remember, the team in this particular essay is at an impasse, as most teams are at some point in time. Write about how you "unjammed" the jam. Ideas: A change of scene, food, twenty push-ups, a quick round-the-room confessional about why you came to b-school. Introducing some *process* is also useful; ground rules such as voting, speaking times, a division of labor, and a time line all create a method from the madness. Perhaps you encourage members to adopt roles—business or otherwise. Hint: The leader or CEO in this case might be your most soft-spoken team member. Whatever you do in this essay, be careful not to present yourself as the one who single-handedly gets the team dynamic going.

THEME 5: DIVERSITY AND WHAT MAKES YOU UNIQUE

Our business school is a diverse environment. How will your experiences contribute to this?

During your years of study in the X program, you will be part of a diverse multicultural, multiethnic community within both the Business School and the larger university. What rewards and challenges do you anticipate in this environment, and how do you expect this experience to prepare you for a culturally diverse business world?

TRANSLATION:

What about you is different in terms of your background, your experience, or your cultural or geographic heritage? Can we count on your unique voice and perspective in our wide-ranging classroom discussions? How will you support the diverse cultural climate we are fostering here?

This essay gets at two concerns for the admissions committee: How will you enrich the student body at this school? And what is your attitude toward others' diverse backgrounds? Today's business leaders must be able to make decisions in situations that cut across geographic and cultural boundaries. If your essay reveals that you have dinosaur-era, only-white-males-rule thinking, you're going to close the door on your candidacy.

So what if you are a white male? Or you have no immediate point of distinction? Maybe a grandparent or relative is an immigrant to this country and you can discuss the impact of his or her values on your life. Perhaps you are the first individual in your family to attend college or to attend graduate school. What does that mean to you? Perhaps you are involved in a meaningful or unusual extracurricular activity. How has this changed your perspective? Perhaps you did a business deal with a foreign country. What did you observe about that culture, and how did it affect your decisions?

Whatever you write about need not be dramatic—maybe you take art classes, coach a little league team, or race a motorcycle. Sound goofy? It's all in the framing. Racing a motorcycle might be about the physical and mental stamina, the ability to take risks, the commitment to learning something new.

This question can be relatively easy to answer if, of course, you have diversity or some unique element in your background. If you don't have something obvious, then you're going to have to dig a bit and find something you can amplify to suggest you bring a unique voice to the school.

THEME 6: YOUR GREATEST PERSONAL ACHIEVEMENT/ACCOMPLISHMENT

Describe a personal achievement that has had a significant impact on your life. In addition to recounting this achievement, please analyze how the event has changed your understanding of yourself and how you perceive the world around you.

In reviewing the last five years, describe one or two accomplishments in which you demonstrated leadership.

TRANSLATION:

Do you know what an achievement is? Have you done anything remarkable? What made it remarkable to you? Bonus points if you showed leadership or inspired others in some way.

This is one of those maddening essay questions because on the one hand, b-schools seek out applicants whose average age is twenty-seven (a relatively young age to have achieved much of anything). On the other hand, the schools want to know what miracles you've performed. Don't pull your hair out yet. There is a way out. Like all the others, this essay is just one more prove-to-us-you-have-some-character hoop you'll have to jump through. It's less about the achievement and more about who you are and how you see yourself.

Again, this question can be easy to answer if you have some clear accomplishment or event in your background. But if you're like the rest of us—you guessed it—you'll have to rely on framing.

Let's cover bad essay topics for achievements. Getting straight A's in college is not an achievement because everyone else at b-school has probably done the same. Surviving a divorce or breakup is a bad accomplishment topic. Personal stories are acceptable, but one taboo area is romance and marriage. If this is all you can come up with, you're going to look like you're as deep as a doughnut.

The accomplishment you choose might show some of the following qualities: character, sacrifice, humility, dedication, high personal stakes, perseverance over obstacles, insight, and learning. You need not have published a business article or won an award to answer this question. This essay is not about excellence of outcome, but what it took for you to reach some personal worthy objective. Maybe you didn't lead a sports team to a victory. The victory may be just that you made it onto the team.

Modesty Matters

Kate Klepper, Director of Admissions at Babson, on how to avoid being arrogant or boastful in the achievement essay:

"Many applicants over-amplify their accomplishments and strengths. This is a common pitfall in this and other essays. But this is one of those frustrating application conundrums. First, the schools exhort you to engage in self-praise, and then you're penalized if you take it too far. But it's hard for an applicant to know where the line is between demonstrating performance and boasting.

"One way to avoid boasting is to frame the accomplishment in terms of why it was meaningful to you. There are many levels to this; one might be the opportunity you had to grow, another the privilege to be lauded by your peers. Still another level might be the chance to gain new skills, and the last might be what you felt at a deeply personal level.

"Of course, one man's accomplishment may be another person's failure. Someone might use this essay to talk about being the slugger who hits the most home runs in baseball. Someone else might use this essay to share that the mere act of making the team, even though they spent the season in the dugout, was their greatest accomplishment.

One's greatest accomplishments in life may not be the big blockbuster ones like a promotion, or acquisition of a company. The most inspiring stories here can run counter to what you think might be impressive."

THEME 7: FAILURE/WHAT MISTAKES HAVE YOU MADE?

Discuss a nonacademic personal failure. In what way were you disappointed in yourself? What did you learn from the experience?

TRANSLATION:

Can you admit to a genuine failure? Do you have enough self-awareness to know what kind of failure is real? Can you learn from your mistakes? Do they lead to greater maturity and self-awareness? Do you take responsibility when the fault is yours?

Many applicants make the mistake of answering this question with a failure that is really a positive, such as "I'm a perfectionist and so therefore I was too demanding on a friend when she was in a crisis." Or they never really answer the question, fearful that any admission of failure will throw their whole candidacy into jeopardy. The truth is, if you *don't* answer this question with a genuine failure or mistake, one that the committee will recognize as authentic, you may have jinxed your application.

In this essay you want to write about a failure that had some high stakes for you. Demonstrate what you learned from your mistake and how it helped you mature. What's the relevance to b-school here? Your ability to be honest, show accountability, and face your failures head-on reflects what kinds of decisions and judgments you will make as a business professional.

Can't think of a time you failed? Discuss the essay question with a friend or family member. An outsider's perspective may jog your memory. Remember, if your whole application has been about work, work, work, this is a great place to convince the committee you're a real person.

THEME 8: ETHICS

Describe an ethical issue you have faced in your professional life and how you dealt with it. What was the outcome?

TRANSLATION:

Do you even know what an ethical dilemma looks like? Are you tomorrow's corporate miscreant? What kinds of decisions and judgments might you make in your future practices as a business leader?

The last few years have brought attention to the ethical issues of the business world and the failure of corporate self-governance. In the aftermath of the Tyco and Enron scandals, b-schools don't want to turn out graduates who are fast into their suspenders, fast into a deal, and fast to swindle their clients and shareholders.

The above question tests your judgment, integrity, and perspective. It's most important to present a legitimate ethical dilemma here, one that has consequences. Applicants often write about the dilemma of not obeying a supervisor's orders because they wanted to do things their way, a known *better* way. But this is not an ethics problem (unless the order was improper or illegal); it's a management problem. Likewise, handing in a report to your boss that you know is full of errors is also not an ethical problem; it's a trivial, single-impact, easy-to-fix problem.

If you were thinking of telling a story like one of those mentioned above, it may be because you wanted to play it safe. This *is* one of those uncomfortable, hot-seat essays after all. But playing it safe here would only make you appear clueless or morally bereft.

This essay requires you to roll up your ethical shirtsleeves and get down in the dirt. True ethical issues are neither clean nor pretty. Don't shrink away from a discussion of failure here or present an overly optimistic, no-loose-ends solution.

It's key that you write about an ethical dilemma in which there was no easy course—one that entailed costs either way. For example, let's say you sold a product to a client and later discovered the product was faulty; your employer wanted you to keep mum. You'd built your sales relationships on trust and personal attention, so you wanted to be forthcoming. What did you do?

This essay must show that you can work through a complex ethical impasse, and it must highlight your sense of honor and conduct. This essay screams relevance. Make sure you shout back that you know right from wrong.

CHAPTER 6
SPOTLIGHT ON TUCK'S ESSAY
QUESTIONS

In the application to the Tuck School of Business at Dartmouth College, there are four short-answer questions and one major essay. The short-answer questions are as follows:

1. How would a colleague describe you?

2. What is the most important thing you have recently learned?

3. Tell us about a personal goal you recently pursued.

4. Why have you decided to pursue an MBA?

You are given a limit of 100 words or fewer for each essay.

These questions give you an opportunity to describe all your facets—though it won't be easy to do so with such strict word limits. Questions one through three allow you to illustrate your qualities as a person, discuss your professional growth, and explain what matters most to you.

TUCK'S KILLER ESSAY QUESTION

Recently, Tuck distinguished itself by getting out in front of the curve with the introduction of a new breed of essay question.

This question is about being able to operate in ambiguous, decision-making environments in short time cycles, with high stakes. It's a management question that's an ethical question that's a leadership question that's an analytical question. In other words, it's a whole lot of questions rolled into one.

QUESTION:

Please respond fully but concisely to the following essay. Although there are no restrictions for the length of your response, most applicants use 1,000 words or fewer. Your response should be typed and double-spaced, with your name on each sheet. There is no right or wrong answer.

A well-known, multinational mining company has a long-term contract to extract precious metals in an impoverished region of a developing country. Over the past decade, the operation has proven very profitable to the company. Recently, there have been peaceful, but highly disruptive, protests by members of communities adjacent to the company's property. The ruling military dictatorship has been unresponsive in meeting the local communities' needs. The local communities are now demanding a share of the mining operation's profits in the form of approximately U.S. $8 million to provide clean water and basic sanitation for the surrounding villages.

You have recently been promoted and sent to this country as the expatriate general manager responsible for the operation. The mine is assessed U.S. $20 million in annual taxes by the local government. This year you will show a U.S. $50 million after-tax profit if you elect not to address the request of the local community. Your team has worked very hard this year. A U.S. $50 million profit is the minimum level to ensure that your team meets its bonus plan.

- Provide an analysis of your options.

- Describe what you would do.

- Discuss the rationale for your choice.

- Address your plan to communicate with any constituent affected by your decision.

TRANSLATION:

The question reads like a mini–business school case. It is dense, complex, and lengthy. And it is not for the applicant faint of heart. Indeed, this might be the mother lode of all business school questions yet. It requires superior analytical skills just to get through it and intense willpower to craft a thorough response. And that's just your first hurdle.

This question challenges an applicant to respond to a highly complex, multilevel scenario in much the way a CEO or senior manager would. Make some lists: What are all the issues? What are the priorities? What are the competing priorities? What are the consequences of one course of action versus another? How will you manage the trade-offs?

Scenarios like this, with complex, opposing priorities and constituencies, are a reality of business life. Don't strive for a tidy, win-win solution here. It does not exist. Your essay should recognize that the essence of a dilemma is that there will be consequences all around. There are no right or wrong answers, just a decided-upon best path of your own creation. Kristine Laca, Director of Admissions at the Tuck School of Business, who designed this question, notes, "We were not looking for one specific approach or answer to this essay question. People we admitted answered this question in a variety of ways."

If you're in serious consideration for a school like Tuck, you'll want to pay close attention to what the question is really asking. If after several re-reads you still don't have a clue, then your candidacy here could be a waste of time. In fact, this question is designed to see if you've got the right stuff:

- Do you have the wherewithal to approach this problem?

- Can you even develop a solid course of action and defend your initiatives?

- What is your capacity for creativity and resourcefulness?

- Can you think like a businessperson? Are you even in the ballpark of thinking like a businessperson?

This question surely helps weed out applicants who just aren't ready for the challenges of b-school . . . or the complex challenges of the business world, for that matter. In Chapter 10, you'll find two responses to this question that made the cut, as well as two that didn't.

As Kristine Laca told us, "The question was designed to be a thought-provoking question that would provide us with insight into how an applicant thinks and would act in a leadership role. We use the question to gain insight into a student's ability to analyze a complex situation, to develop a specific plan and to demonstrate clear leadership. As a future business leader, many MBAs will face complex business problems that have inherently competing priorities. In most of those situations, there will not be one correct answer or approach. This question mirrors that business and leadership reality. As a leading business school, we have a responsibility to help train future business leaders who have a sense of both corporate and social responsibility."

Okay, so why would a school expect that you could analyze a scenario so complex, one you would obviously be more qualified to answer once you've attended b-school for two years?

It's true—you might answer this question more intelligently post-MBA. We hope so. But when it comes to meeting a business challenge, a b-school education can only provide you with the tools and a framework—not the solution. A basic endowment of thinking—one that spawns ethics, morality, social responsibility, and analytical skills—must already be present in any student. It is, quite simply, a business school prerequisite.

CHAPTER 7
THE PERSONAL STATEMENT:
HOW, IF, AND WHEN TO USE IT

We mentioned earlier that most applications have an optional essay question, also known as the personal statement. It can be used to fill in the blanks—to address any topic that you were unable to weave into the required essays. We'll show you how this question might best be used to your advantage, depending on what shortcomings (if any) are present in your application.

Theme: The Personal Statement

Does this application provide the opportunity to present the real you?

The admissions committee would welcome any additional comments you may wish to provide in support of your application.

What question should we have asked you?

TRANSLATION:

What did we miss? Appeal to us in any way you want; this is your last chance. Be real.

I call this the "bonus" question. If you have an experience or personal cause that says something interesting about you, and it hasn't found a place in any other essay, this is the time to stick it in. Keep in mind that you are hoping to present yourself as unique—so show some passion!

The Tuck School of Business gives you further direction on how to complete their personal statement: "Complete this section only if you feel your credentials and application do not fully represent your candidacy." This last part of the question is saying, "Okay applicant, what did we miss?" But it's also saying, "Tread carefully with your content here; don't waste our time."

How and When to Craft an Essay that Explains a Weakness (or Rebuts a Weakness with a Strength)

How does an applicant go about writing an essay that addresses his or her weaknesses? Well, it's a complex art, and the potential communication pitfalls are many. For example, how much should you tell the admissions officers? Do you apologize for the problem, or just defend its circumstances? When have you made your point without over-explaining? How do you evoke empathy, but not pity? Is there a valid excuse for bad scores?

The efficacy of your explanation is critical here. You want to make sure that the message you intend to send out is exactly what is received. When you're offering explanations, there is no room for miscommunication with style, tone, or content. Rambling or whining in this essay will kill not only the message, but also your candidacy.

Keep in mind that you are composing essays for people who have seen real hardships and real causes for performance or employment gaps. Perched at a sort of crossroads to life, the admissions board has heard it all—anything and everything that has ever happened to anyone. Chances are, they've lived through some of these things too. They don't expect you to sail through life unscathed. They do, however, expect you to own up to your shortcomings and move on with confidence.

WHAT IS LEGIT?

Before you can craft an explanation, you have to first identify what is a legitimate problem and what is a legitimate excuse. This calls into play your self-awareness, and it can be tricky. What you think is legitimate, someone else might see as lame. For example, if your explanation for bad grades in college is simply that you partied too much, well, you've just dug yourself an even bigger hole. You highlight your true personality through the topics you choose to write about, so think before you choose a foolish topic.

A general rule of thumb is this: Unless the problem has negatively impacted you in some way relevant to the application process, it may not need to be brought up at all. Ask yourself: Why am I telling the admissions officers this story? What's my point? You don't have to bring to the attention of the admissions board every misfortune or mishap you've experienced, even if its effect on you was quite dramatic.

Paid His Own Way

Here's an example of a situation that doesn't warrant an explanation or even a mention in the application. A friend of mine put himself through school and held down two part-time jobs while attending college full-time. While this could have conceivably made it more difficult for him to dedicate time to his studies, his grades did not suffer as a result of these jobs. There is consequently no weakness to address and no excuse to be given. He could have mentioned this in the personal statement as evidence of his focus and determination, but it might have sounded lame.

Loss of a Parent

Another friend of mine suffered through her mother's battle with cancer while attending an Ivy League college. Her mother passed away when my friend was a sophomore. Years later, when she applied to graduate school, she didn't focus on this. Why? She got straight A's, graduated with the highest of honors, and received good scores. She had moved on. She did not have excuses, although she did have adversity. There is a difference.

"Hold on," you say. That has the making of a great essay! And you would be right. While you could use this topic for a personal statement, as an added value it would be better-positioned front and center as a main essay. This story is so rich that she could have used it in response to a question about unique qualities or achievements, or even a question about a person you admire or three people with whom you would most like to have dinner.

Now, if this friend had received *bad* grades, it'd be a different story. In that scenario, I would advise that she write about the loss of her mother as a main essay with a theme of triumph over adversity and in a straightforward and confident tone, use the personal statement to explain why her grades were bad and why her academic performance would be different at business school. Each of these essays would support and reinforce the other.

Circumstances and Weaknesses Commonly Addressed in Business School Personal Statements:

Acts of God (flood, fire, accidents)

Bad grades

Low GMAT score (overall, Math, or Verbal)

Test anxiety

Learning disability

Handicap

Multiple college transcripts/on-and-off attendance

Birth of a child

Illness (physical or mental)

Death or loss

Divorce or marriage

Family problems

Financial hardship

Job loss

Lack of career progress/promotions

Addressing Some Common Problems

Now we'll go one step further and advise you in more detail on how to craft your personal statement to address the most common concerns.

PINK SLIPS

In this brutal economy, b-schools know that seamless resumes are a relic of the past. Many applicants may have lost not one, but two or more jobs, particularly those who have transitioned through the dot-com era; some never even secured that first job out of school. Don't worry, though; you won't automatically be penalized for a spotty resume, as long as you fill in the gaps. You won't be blamed for layoffs, and you won't be blamed for the fact that the company failed.

In order to properly address this issue in the personal statement, you'll want to share the circumstances of your departure, but avoid providing too much detail. Play up what you learned and focus on any other positive details of your experience at the company. Were you able to stay in a single industry and build upon your prior work experiences? Perhaps you were with an Internet startup that went bust. In this case, describe how you stayed at the helm to the bitter end, and focus on the leadership you demonstrated in so doing.

If you had to grab a paycheck, be honest. Don't communicate self-blame or embarrassment. Again, put it in the context of what you learned. Talk about how you used each job to acquire specific skills or contacts.

If you were fired due to work performance, that's okay; we've all been there, too. Use the suggestions above to write self-assuredly of your experience.

BAD GRADES

If you were working two full-time jobs to pay for college, or were lettering in three sports, it's fairly obvious why your grades were a casualty. This is an understandable scenario. But perhaps you perceived college as just one long party, or you're a street-smart person who doesn't shine academically. Maybe you were just lazy, and getting by was good enough for you.

Whatever the case may have been then, you are marketing yourself now, so place yourself in the best possible light. Tell them you've left behind your partying and desultory ways. Demonstrate how in your current profession you have evolved into a highly motivated, capable, and hard-working professional. Focus on who you are today. Speak to your maturity and renewed commitment to academics.

You may also wish to provide concrete examples of academic excellence in other areas. If you scored high on the GMAT, mention it as evidence of your brainpower, but be subtle; your straight-C average and 90th percentile scores may really convince the committee you're a goof-off. Don't forget to stay in tight control of your message. Emphasize the fact that the great GMAT score means you can handle the academic rigors ahead. You're not goofing off anymore. Additional examples of academic success are courses or training programs you've taken in which you've excelled.

BAD SCORES AND TEXT ANXIETY

It's okay to admit that you don't do well on standardized tests. You won't be the first one to do so. You may even want to note that you took it twice to improve your score.

Whatever you do, don't whine on this one. Own up to the weakness and give the admissions officers plenty of reasons (with supporting evidence) to admit you anyway. Convince them you have the intellectual wherewithal to perform successfully in their program. Provide them with other professional and academic examples of your brainpower.

If your Math score is weak, showcase your quantitative skills at your job and elsewhere; if your Verbal score is poor, well then, you'd better submit essays that shine and provide other evidence of your outstanding verbal skills.

Learning Disability

This is a slippery slope. If a learning disability is the reason for poor academic performance, this is quite legitimate. But you may be portraying it as a weakness that is an inherent part of your makeup. You can't frame this as something you can move on from, so this may be one of those instances where you can make things worse. The admissions committee's main concern, after all, is that you can keep pace with your b-school peers and the volume of work.

It's hard to advise whether someone in this situation should admit to it on the application, even though it's the most legitimate of explanations. If you do, put the learning disability in the context of tenacity and hard work. Highlight any areas of academic excellence.

In Summary

We'd like to offer some general recommendations for utilizing the personal statement to explain a weakness or a problem.

- Discuss problems in a forthright, straightforward manner.

- Don't make whiny, shopworn excuses. Have a legitimate point to make.

- Write confidently about your mistakes and weaknesses; don't hide behind shame. Rebut a weakness with a strength.

- Illustrate what you've learned and how you've moved on and recovered.

- Don't focus on yesterday. Talk about who you are today.

- Be positive. Emphasize that you are a can-do person.

- Don't get too intimate with the details. What works on *Oprah* is too personal for a b-school essay.

- Avoid sounding defensive, self-pitying, or self-absorbed. Showcase how you overcame adversity.

CHAPTER 8
IN CASE YOU SLEPT THROUGH ENGLISH CLASS

Hey, it can't hurt to have a little review, even if you're already a brilliant writer.

Like any good writing, your business school essays should be clear, concise, candid, structurally sound, and 100 percent grammatically accurate. Go ahead and get the story out, but then make sure to edit with a fine-tooth comb.

The Essentials

Clarity and conciseness are usually the products of a lot of reading, re-reading, and rewriting. Without question, repeated critical revision by yourself and by others is the surest way to trim, tune, and improve your prose.

Candor is the product of proper motivation. Honesty, sincerity, and authenticity cannot be superimposed after the fact; your writing must be candid from the outset. Also, let's be frank: You're probably pretty smart and pretty sophisticated. You could probably fake candor if absolutely necessary, but you shouldn't. For one thing, it's a hell of a lot more work. Moreover, no matter how good your insincere essay may be, we're brazenly confident that an honest and authentic essay will be even better.

Structural soundness is the product of a well-crafted outline. It really pays to sketch out the general themes of your essay first; worry about filling in the particulars later. Pay particularly close attention to the structure of your essay and to the fundamental message it communicates. Make sure you have a well-conceived narrative. Your essay should flow from beginning to end. Use paragraphs properly, and make sure the paragraphs are in a logical order. The sentences within each paragraph should also be complete and in logical order.

After grammatical accuracy, a thoughtful essay that offers true insight will stand out, but if it is riddled with poor grammar and misspelled words, it will not receive serious consideration. *It is critical that you avoid all grammatical errors.* We just can't stress this enough. You aren't allowed to misspell anything. You aren't allowed to use awkwardly constructed or run-on sentences. You aren't allowed to use verbs in the wrong tenses. You aren't allowed to misplace modifiers. You aren't allowed to make a single error in punctuation.

GRAMMATICAL CATEGORY	WHAT'S THE RULE?	BAD GRAMMAR	GOOD GRAMMAR
MISPLACED MODIFIER	A word or phrase that describes something should go right next to the thing it modifies.	1. Eaten in Mediterranean countries for centuries, **northern Europeans** viewed the tomato with suspicion. 2. **A former greens keeper** now about to become the Masters champion, **tears** welled up in my eyes as I hit my last miraculous shot.	1. Eaten in Mediterranean countries for centuries, **the tomato** was viewed with suspicion by Northern Europeans. 2. **I was a former greens keeper** who was now about to become the Masters champion; **tears** welled up in my eyes as I hit my last miraculous shot.
PRONOUNS	A pronoun must refer unambiguously to a noun and it must agree in number with that noun.	1. Although **brokers** are not permitted to know executive access **codes, they** are widely known. 2. The **golden retriever** is one of the smartest breeds of dogs, but **they** often **have** trouble writing **personal statements** for law school admission. 3. Unfortunately, both **candidates** for whom I worked sabotaged their own **campaigns** by accepting **a contribution** from illegal **sources.**	1. Although **brokers** are not permitted to know executive access **codes, the codes** are widely known. 2. The **golden retriever** is one of the smartest breeds of dogs, but often **it has** trouble writing **a personal statement** for law school admission. 3. Unfortunately, both **candidates** for whom I worked sabotaged their own **campaigns** by accepting **contributions** from illegal **sources.**
SUBJECT/VERB AGREEMENT	The subject must always agree in number with the verb. Make sure you don't forget what the subject of a sentence is, and don't use the object of a preposition as the subject.	1. **Each** of the men involved in the extensive renovations **were** engineers. 2. Federally imposed **restrictions** on the ability to use certain information **has** made life difficult for Martha Stewart.	1. **Each** of the men involved in the extensive renovations **was** an engineer. Federally imposed **restrictions** on the ability to use certain information **have** made life difficult for Martha Stewart.
PARALLEL CONSTRUCTION	Two or more ideas in a single sentence that are parallel need to be similar in grammatical form.	1. The two main goals of the Eisenhower presidency were a **reduction** of taxes and **to increase** military strength. 2. **To provide a child** with the skills necessary for survival in modern life is **like guaranteeing their** success.	1. The two main goals of the Eisenhower presidency were to **reduce** taxes and to **increase** military strength. 2. **Providing children** with the skills necessary for survival in modern life is **like guaranteeing their** success.
COMPARISONS	You can only compare things that are exactly the same.	1. The **rules** of written English are **more stringent than** spoken **English.** 2. The **considerations** that led many colleges to impose admissions quotas in the last few decades **are similar to the quotas** imposed in the recent past by large businesses.	1. The **rules** of written English are **more stringent than those of** spoken English. 2. The **considerations** that led many colleges to impose admissions quotas in the last few decades **are similar to those** that led large businesses to impose quotas in the recent past.
PASSIVE/ ACTIVE VOICE	Choose the active voice, in which the subject performs the action.	1. **The ball was hit by the bat.** 2. **My time and money were wasted** trying to keep www.justdillpickles.com afloat single-handedly.	1. **The bat hit the ball.** 2. **I wasted time and money trying to** keep www.justdillpickles.com afloat single-handedly.

Don't neglect your spelling and grammar check

We imagine you'll probably write your essay on a computer. It's a very good idea. Use a computer with a spell-checker. Turn on the spelling- and grammar-checking options. Your computer is only as smart as you are, so carefully consider the advice your computer offers.

Good writing is easily understood. You want to get your point across, not bury it in words. Don't talk in circles. Your prose should be clear and direct. If an admissions officer has to struggle to figure out what you are trying to say, you'll be in trouble.

Buy and read *The Elements of Style,* by William Strunk, Jr. and E. B. White.

We can't recommend it highly enough. In fact, we're surprised you don't have it already. This little book is a required investment for any writer. You will refer to it forever, and if you do what it says, your writing will definitely improve.

Have three or four people read your essay and critique it. Proofread your essay from beginning to end, then proofread it again, then proofread it some more. Read it aloud. Keep in mind, though, that the more time you spend with a piece of your own writing, the less likely you are to spot any errors. You get tunnel vision. Ask friends, boyfriends, girlfriends, professors, brothers, sisters—somebody—to read your essay and comment on it. Have friends read it. Have an English teacher read it. Have an English major read it. Have the most grammatically anal person you know read it. Hire an editor if you feel it is necessary. We don't care. Just do whatever it takes to make sure your essay is clear, concise, candid, structurally sound, and 100 percent grammatically correct.

Always consider your audience. A big part of your overall strategy ought to be to keep in mind what it would be like to be the reader. Ultimately, you are giving a portrait of yourself in words to someone who doesn't know you and who may never meet you, but who has the power to make a very important decision about the course of your life. It's a real person who will read your personal statement, though—someone with real human traits who puts on her pants one leg at a time, just like you. Keep this person interested. Make this person curious. Make this person smile. Engage this person intellectually.

Jump-Start Your Writing

Depending on where you're applying and on how prolific a writer you are, you can expect to spend anywhere from twenty-five to one hundred hours composing your stories. The process is time-consuming and maddening. Indeed, many applicants find the writing aspect of the application so unpleasant that they reach a plateau and give up. The results are mediocre, half-baked essays.

We want you to stay the full course and make every essay stand out. If you start to run out of fuel, or can't even get started, try the following for a little octane in your writing tank: Get some free feedback. There are limits and perils to self-analysis. Call a friend or colleague for a feedback session. Ask them to recount your strengths and weaknesses. Have them list your personal and professional accomplishments. They may remind you of concrete examples and provide you with fresh insights. Chat with your references, teachers, bosses—basically anyone who knows you well.

Some specific questions you may want to ask are

- What are my strengths and weaknesses? Do you remember specific examples of this?

- What do you admire most about me? Least?

- Overall, how would you describe me? What adjectives come to mind?

- Can you think of an example of where I showed leadership, even in a small way?

Look for inspiration. Read the essays in this book, but go and seek out articles in other places. Good examples of what a well-written personal essay looks like can be found in a number of national magazines and newspapers. In The *New York Times Magazine,* testimonial-like essays can be found in the vibrant "Lives" column. No one expects you to write like a *New York Times* columnist, but study these and you may find inspiration.

You don't need to consult a publication as highbrow as the *New York Times,* though; even *Reader's Digest* is full of real-life testimonials. You'll notice how people write passionately about their experiences and what matters to them. There must be something in your life that matters to you. Make a list and return to your essays.

Let the story out. If you build it, it will come. You may have some idea of what you want to write about, but your writing skills are not up to the task. Let the content lead the way. However unformed your thoughts are, just get it all down on paper. Afterward, you can prioritize and organize your points, complete half-thoughts, and delete what's extraneous. Find the central theme and keep building upon it.

If none of the above work, try clustering.

CLUSTERING (OR ORGANIZING YOUR CHAOS)

It works like this: Grab a plain piece of paper. Take a main thought or idea, and write it in the middle of the page. Then float all of your ideas around that middle concept. Write them around the perimeter of the page and make lists.

Once you've got a page full of your chaotic thoughts, begin to prioritize your ideas by numbering them in order of importance. Delete what is extraneous, and add whatever important information you have left out.

Now start to cluster your thoughts in terms of chronology. What should go first, then next, and so on and so forth? At the end of this exercise you should have found enough ideas and sentence fragments to compose a rough draft.

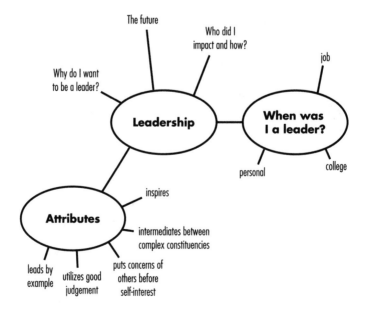

Must-Follow Checklist
for the Essays

- Communicate that you're a proactive, can-do sort of person. Leaders take initiative and aren't thwarted by roadblocks.

- Put yourself on ego alert; stress what makes you unique, not what makes you great. You want admissions officers to respect and like you.

- Position yourself as a stand-out from the crowd; emphasize your distinctiveness.

- Make sure your leadership qualities really come through. Admissions officers want to hear about skills that enabled you to rally folks around your solution.

- Communicate specific reasons why you're a "fit" for a school, (but avoid vague, fluffy statements such as "I am the ideal or perfect candidate for you program.") Do your research. Relate your specific interests to the school's academics, specific professors, culture, quality of life, and location. If you use an essay for more than one school, make sure each is tailored to be school-specific.

- Bring passion to your writing—admissions officers want to know what you're really excited about.

- Break out of your perceived mold. Use the essays to challenge any preconceived notions about who you are. Are you a numbers person or an engineer type? Challenge perceptions with unexpected portrayals that say, "There's more to me than you think." It could be that you're passionate about cooking, or that you organize a game of hoops every Saturday.

- Play up an unorthodox path to b-school. Admissions officers appreciate risk-takers. But be convincing about your ability to handle the program, especially quantitative skills that schools can take for granted in applicants in finance.

- Use your gender, ethnicity, minority, or foreign background—but only if it has affected your outlook or experiences.

- Avoid too many sentences that begin with "I." Use examples and anecdotes instead.

- Be subtle. If you call too much attention to a problem it becomes a bigger problem.

- Fill your essays with plenty of real-life examples to support your thesis and bring your story to life.

- Show a sense of humor or your vulnerability. These qualities make you likeable. They make your stories more personal.

- Don't write in a vacuum. Make sure that each of your essays reinforces and builds on the others. Think of each essay as one note in a song.

WHAT NOT TO DO: FIFTEEN SURE-FIRE WAYS TO TORPEDO YOUR APPLICATION

1. **Write about the high school glory days.**

   Unless you're right out of college, or you've got a great story to tell, resist using your high school experiences for the essays. What does it say about your maturity if all you can talk about is being editor of the yearbook or captain of the varsity team?

2. **Submit essays that don't answer the questions.**

   An essay that does no more than restate your resume frustrates the admissions committees. After reading 5,000 applications, they get irritated to see another long-winded evasive one.

   Don't lose focus. Make sure your stories answer the question.

3. **Fill essays with industry jargon and detail.**

   Many essays are burdened by business-speak and unnecessary detail. This clutters your story. Construct your essays with only enough detail about your job to frame your story and make your point. After that, put the emphasis on yourself—what you've accomplished and why you were successful.

4. **Write about a failure that's too personal or inconsequential.**

Refrain from using breakups, divorces, and other romantic calamities as examples of failures. What may work on a confessional talk show is too personal for a b-school essay.

Also, don't relate a "failure" like getting one C in college (out of an otherwise straight-A average). It calls your perspective into question. Talk about a failure that matured your judgment or changed your outlook.

5. **Reveal half-baked reasons for wanting the MBA.**

Admissions officers favor applicants who have well-defined goals. Because the school's reputation is tied to the performance of its graduates, those who know what they want are a safer investment.

If b-school is just a pit stop on the great journey of life, admissions committees would prefer you make it elsewhere. However unsure you are about your future, it's critical that you demonstrate that you have a plan.

6. **Exceed the recommended word limits.**

Poundage is not the measure of value here. Exceeding the recommended word limit suggests you don't know how to follow directions, operate within constraints, organize your thoughts, or all of the above.

Get to the crux of your story and make your points. You'll find the word limits adequate.

7. **Submit an application full of typos and grammatical errors.**

How you present yourself on the application is as important as what you present. Although typos don't necessarily knock you out of the running, they suggest a sloppy attitude. Poor grammar is also a problem. It distracts from the clean lines of your story and advertises poor writing skills.

Present your application professionally—neatly typed and proofed for typos and grammar. And forget gimmicks like a videotape. This isn't *America's Funniest Home Videos*.

8. **Send one school an essay intended for another—or forget to change the school name when using the same essay for several applications.**

Double check before you send anything out. Admissions committees are (understandably) insulted when they see another school's name or forms.

9. **Make whiny excuses for everything.**

   Admissions committees have heard it all—illness, marital difficulties, learning disabilities, test anxiety, bad grades, pink slips, putting oneself through school—anything and everything that has ever happened to anybody. Admissions officers have lived through these things, too. No one expects you to sail through life unscathed. What they do expect is that you own up to your shortcomings.

   Avoid trite, predictable explanations. If your undergraduate experience was one long party, be honest. Discuss who you were then, and who you've become today. Write confidently about your weaknesses and mistakes. Whatever the problem, it's important you show you can recover and move on.

10. **Make the wrong choice of recommenders.**

    A top-notch application can be doomed by second-rate recommendations. This can happen because you misjudged the recommendors' estimation of you or you failed to give them direction and focus.

    As we've said, recommendations from political figures, your uncle's CEO golfing buddy, and others with lifestyles of the rich and famous don't impress (and sometimes annoy) admissions folk—unless such recommenders really know you or built the school's library.

11. **Let the recommender miss the deadline.**

    Make sure you give the person writing your recommendation plenty of lead time to write and send in their recommendation. Even with advance notice, a well-meaning but forgetful person can drop the ball.

    It's your job to remind them of the deadlines. Do what you have to do to make sure your recommendations get there on time.

12. **Be impersonal in the personal statement.**

    Each school has its own version of the "Use this space to tell us anything else about yourself" personal statement question. Yet many applicants avoid the word "personal" like the plague. Instead of talking about how putting themselves through school lowered their GPA, they talk about the rising cost of tuition in America.

The personal statement is your chance to make yourself different from the other applicants, further show a personal side, or explain a problem. Take a chance and be genuine; admissions officers prefer sincerity to a song and dance.

13. Make too many generalizations.

Many applicants approach the essays as though they were writing a newspaper editorial. They make policy statements and deliver platitudes about life without giving any supporting examples from their own experiences.

Granted, these may be the kind of hot-air essays that the application appears to ask for, and probably deserves. But admissions officers dislike essays that don't say anything. An essay full of generalizations is a giveaway that you don't have anything to say, don't know what to say, or just don't know how to say whatever it is you want to say.

14. Neglect to communicate that you've researched the program and that you belong there.

B-schools take enormous pride in their programs. The rankings make them even more conscious of their academic turf and differences. While all promise an MBA, they don't all deliver it the same way. The schools have unique offerings and specialties.

Applicants need to convince the committee that the school's programs meet their needs. It's not good enough to declare prestige as the primary reason for selecting a school (even though this is the basis for many applicants' choice).

15. Fail to be courteous to employees in the admissions office.

No doubt, many admissions offices operate with the efficiency of sludge. But no matter what the problem, you need to keep your frustration in check.

If you become a pest or complainer, this may become part of your applicant profile. An offended office worker may share his or her ill feelings about you with the boss—that admissions officer you've been trying so hard to impress.

CHAPTER 9

STRAIGHT FROM THE MOUTHS OF THE EXPERTS: INTERVIEWS WITH STUDENTS AND ADMISSIONS OFFICERS

Won't take our word on b-school essays and admissions? We asked MBA students and business school admissions officers to share their thoughts on these matters. You might say we have the issue covered from every angle.

Lisa Guglielmi
First-Year Student, Haas School of Business, University of California–Berkeley

Q: Lisa, how many schools did you apply to?

A: Six. Stanford, Harvard, Berkeley, UCLA, Kellogg, and Michigan. All in the first round.

Q: So all told, how many essays did you have to write?

A: Well they all have one common essay question. It's a version of "Why do you want the MBA, why now, and why at this school?" so this was one essay with slightly different versions. Several of the schools had the "What are your three greatest accomplishments?" question. The rest of the questions were very different. I easily wrote at least ten-plus essays.

Q: Which essay did you work on first?

A: The leadership essay.

Q: Why did you choose that one first?

A: It was the easiest one for me. I had a very good example of clear leadership.

Q: How did you go about writing your stories?

A: First, I put everything down on paper. Then I reread it to see if it communicated exactly what I wanted it to. That was the hardest part, making sure that what I wanted to say actually came forth. Because sometimes you'll write and write and write, but the point you're actually trying to get across doesn't come through.

In these kinds of essays, it's easy to write too much and provide too much detail. But what you want to focus on is who you are, and not the details that capture the *exact* experience.

Q: Did you take a test-prep course?

A: Yes.

Q: When?

A: I was working as an investment banker, and my firm paid for the course. I was very busy at work, so I didn't actually take the test until almost a year after the course. When I did take the test, however, it was six months before I worked on the essays and the rest of the application. I wanted to get the GMAT out of the way and focus on the application.

Q: What made you decide to apply in the first round?

A: I did a lot of research. Everyone seemed to say your odds were better in the first round. I also think that applying early in the filing period shows admissions that you're very serious, that this is something you've thought out very thoroughly.

Q: What was the hardest part of the application for you to work on?

A: The essays, definitely. It's so difficult in just four or five essays to accurately portray yourself and capture all your unique experiences.

Q: Which was the hardest essay for you to answer? Why?

A: I would say it was one of the Berkeley essays. Berkeley has two longer essays, then mainly short questions; this was very different from the other schools I was applying to.

   The essay that I really struggled with was "Whom would you like to have over for dinner?" I found this question to be a little more creative, whereas the others had been straightforward. You don't know what the admissions committee is looking for in this question, so I found it harder.

   But if you try to write what you think the admission person wants here, you just dig yourself a hole. It's always better to come from who you really are. I've gone back and read friends' essays who are here at Berkeley and at other schools. The ones that really stand out are those that are genuine. If you pose as someone you're really not in these essays, it's very easy for the admissions committee to see through it.

But back to the "dinner" question. I guess the best way I can tell you how I answered this question is to tell you how I went about the entire essay-writing process.

I got some great advice from a friend: Before working on any [of] the essays, sit down and make a list of the five or six qualities about yourself that you absolutely want to get across to the admissions committee. Then, go through each essay and make sure that you address one of these five or six big ideas in each one so that you create a complete picture of yourself. The application should really be seen as a total package.

This particular tool really helped me, because at first I was just so overwhelmed by it all. When you have to pick five or six qualities about yourself, it requires a lot of introspection. In this way, instead of looking at each specific question in a vacuum, I focused on getting these qualities across. As I said before, I would write and write, then reread and realize I had left out that one very important characteristic or aspect that I had made a goal to highlight.

So by the time I got to the dinner question, I had covered what I wanted to in the other essays. I could have a little more fun with this one, show a different side of me.

Q: What about your recommendations? How did you handle that?

A: My schools requested only professional recommendations. I had already selected two bosses for this—one current and one past. I chose the boss from my previous position, rather than someone else supervising me in my current job, because he knew me very well, he was an excellent writer, he was honest, and I knew he would support what I was saying about myself in the essays. The person who knows you the best is the one who should write your recommendations.

Q: What advice would you give an applicant about to embark on this journey?

A: Don't get overwhelmed. Look over the entire application and, as hard as it is, get everything down on paper. Step by step, list or outline what characteristics you want to highlight.

Have someone you don't know very well read your essays and give you their take on each one. They should be able to immediately pick out the characteristic you are trying to portray. The fact that your reader doesn't know you helps because they are not as inclined to just give their perception of you as a person.

It is also good to have people who know you well read your essays. These readers would say, wait a minute, you're not giving yourself enough credit for something, or you left out some of the specifics in this story that are meaningful to the point. It's not easy to brag about yourself and your accomplishments, and people who know you well can help you draw the line between bragging enough, but not too much. So both sets of readers were especially helpful.

I probably had five different sets of eyes look at my essays to see if they got what I intended. If the feedback was that they didn't, then I knew I was off my mark. I would scrap the entire essay, no matter how hard I had worked on it, and rewrite it completely, sometimes with entirely new topics.

Jenni Winslow
First-Year Student, Haas School of Business, University of California–Berkeley

Q: Jenni, how many schools did you apply to?

A: Just four. Stanford, Berkeley, UCLA, and Kellogg.

Q: Where did you get in?

A: I got in to all four.

Q: What was the most daunting part of the application process?

A: The essays.

Q: Why?

A: The sheer quantity of the essays I needed to write was overwhelming. To deal with it, I first organized all of the applications together by creating a grid in Microsoft Excel. Then I wrote an essay question in each cell and looked for where there might be overlap.

Q: So your first strategy in the application process was to organize and examine all the essay questions for similarity?

A: Well, first I took a test-prep course. I took the class the spring before. The course ran from approximately January through March. Then I took the GMAT test in May with the knowledge that if I didn't do well as well as I wanted to, I could take it again and still have time to apply early for next year.

Q: Did you do well enough?

A: Yes, I did.

Q: How did your time line evolve from that point?

A: Well, I got to breathe a sigh of relief for the summer, which was nice. But by late August, as soon as all the applications were out, I had them in my hands—I had put my name on all the schools' lists so they would be sent to me immediately.

I also used the time in late August to contact all the admissions offices at each of the schools to schedule campus visits. I wanted to visit each of the campuses so I could figure out for myself what was different at each of these schools.

The gist of the visits was that I wanted to attend class, meet the people, meet the professors, and see the campus, so that I could write to that in my essays. Part of this process is figuring out which schools are right for you. I had figured out all were great options, but I needed to differentiate them for myself and in the essays. I also wanted to articulate what unique contributions I could make at a particular school. To do that, you need to do more than just read a brochure.

Q: So before you even put pen to paper, you had already done a tremendous amount of legwork and preparation?

A: Absolutely.

Q: Going back to the essays, how many essay questions did you have to answer?

A: Stanford [had] two. One of their questions was, "What is most important to you, and why?" and the second was, "Why do you want the MBA, and why here?" I think this last one is used at "X" school everywhere. So I got to recycle that last essay question, but I articulated unique differences at each school.

The Berkeley application was probably the most difficult in that there were six to eight short questions. Somehow that was harder than having to answer one long question. The question I found the most interesting to write—it was on Berkeley's application—was "Who would you most want to have dinner with and why?" That was fun.

Q: Whom did you pick?

A: Oprah Winfrey. She has been amazing in terms of how influential she has been. And while she is not known for this, she is an incredibly savvy businessperson.

After I got in at Berkeley, I learned that Madonna and Oprah are among the most common answers. Madonna is awesome because she, too, has built an empire. She has her public persona, as does Oprah, but these women are highly astute. They have built extraordinary businesses.

A number of people pick out a compelling figure from history as well.

Again, after I got in, I heard that with the Stanford essay, the most common answer to "What's most important to you and why?" is "balance in life."

Q: How often did you do a rewrite?

A: I probably did at least three or four rewrites of each question. Often what I would do is work on a question for a day. Then I would shelve it, leave it alone for a few days. Then I'd get perspective and go back and read it and work some more.

Another thing I did was to purchase three different books—one was a guidebook on the MBA, one was how to get into the top MBA programs, and the last one was a book with sample b-school essays, which proved very useful in getting ideas on how other people had done this.

Q: What would be your final piece of advice to someone about to start this process?

A: I applied in round one at three of my schools and round two at Kellogg. My advice is to start *early*. Figure out where you want to apply, and then map out your priorities. What needs to happen first at what school? When you say you want to apply to five schools in the first round, you might not be able to do that. I credit that I got into all four of my schools by applying early.

Don Martin
Director of Admissions,
University of Chicago Graduate School of Business

Q: Don, why are the essays so important in business school admissions?

A: Because we want to get to know who a student is outside of the typical academic and professional environment. At Chicago, some of our essay questions are designed to allow us to assess an applicant's fit with our school in several ways: One, why have you been thinking about an MBA? Two, what do you hope to accomplish? Three, how will the MBA help to move you along your career path and why here at Chicago? And four, what will you contribute if we admit you?

But to get to know the real person—what makes them tick—we also include essay questions on our application that encourage individuals to be creative, humorous, even vulnerable. One year an essay question was, "Who would you most want to have dinner with?" Another year it was, "What three personal items would you put in a box to open several years later, and why?" It's fascinating to see what students reveal about themselves as they answer these questions. This is the process that allows us to get under their layers and know them in a more personal way. Of course, we get to know them through their GMAT scores, grades, work experience; but that doesn't reveal who someone really is.

Q: But Don, those reading this book may be asking, why do business schools need to get to know the real person?

A: Other graduate programs offer a more standardized, static curriculum. Business schools are unique in pushing networking, teamwork, and the development of relationships. Business is about two things primarily— competition and relationships. More than other types of graduate schools, business schools need students who will survive and thrive in relationships and with some healthy competition.

In businesses, it's not one lone person who makes something happen. It happens in law—there's one prosecutor, one defense attorney. In medicine, it's one doctor. But it doesn't work that way in the real world of business. Yes, there are CEOs and presidents, but generally they have a large group of people working under them. That is why we want to know what makes someone tick. Our readers spend more time analyzing essays than anything else.

Q: Your questions do have a creative bent. What advice do you offer students who don't feel creative and who find these questions difficult to answer?

A: We have found that many of our applicants say our questions are a welcome relief. They're refreshing in that Chicago's questions get away from the more typical, traditional "How did you overcome a challenge?" type of questions. There are no right or wrong answers to these questions. If you have a flair for creativity or humor, you're free to express it here. If you don't, then the bottom line is this: Just be yourself.

The admissions process is about finding applicants that are a match for our program. The match goes both ways, us to them, them to us. One of the ways for applicants to find out if the match is good is to simply be themselves. If they are just themselves, these essay questions are some of the most wonderful ways for us to get an idea of who they really are. It's fine to say, "I want to have dinner with so-and-so" and not be so overly concerned that you picked the right ones. When applicants pick people with the intent to impress, you can usually tell. The more genuine, sincere essays are easy to pick out.

I'm not a psychologist, but this is a process for getting to know people for who they really are. We find it to be effective.

Q: Don, switching subjects, in the past I have advised applicants to avoid using their mother or father as the subject matter for their essay. Recently, because so many candidates are coming straight from college, I've rethought this. What's your perspective?

A: Well, reading about Dad has been a turn-off in an essay, and then again, it hasn't. If someone says, "I'm choosing my father because he's been a wonderful dad," I'm not sure that's a good business school essay. But what about someone who has been estranged from a parent, but that relationship was salvaged, or someone who became a stepchild or a stepparent? Capturing the relationship in that way makes a difference. If the essay about a parent is going to be more about "this person has been my best friend or an inspiration," that's okay, but it's not as appealing. But the other examples, or even writing about something because of a divorce, this can be very fascinating.

When you choose someone that close to you, there have to be reasons for why you chose that person. What prompted you to choose them, and how compelling does that seem?

These are reasons that make an essay like this good or bad.

Q: Have you seen more applicants with a less consistent work history because of the economy?

A: Yes, we are seeing folks whose work histories are more varied. These are folks who may have been part of the dot-com boom, who held off on getting the MBA because they thought they would get a lot of learning on the job, but now they're coming back.

When we see applicants with layoffs in their backgrounds, the way we approach this is, "This isn't the fault of the applicant." I see applicants who got one job, and then nine months later, through no fault of their own, were laid off again. These people have had a lot of adversity. To me, the tough economy has given applicants an opportunity to say, "Look, this is how I've dealt with this. Here's a hardship that happened, and here's how I handled it." This is what the admissions committee is going to focus on.

So I really see this as an opportunity in terms of applying to business school. But do the applicants? If there is a way that you can help us see how you overcame adversity, that you didn't wither up when things became difficult, then make that point.

I do think applicants need to focus as much as possible on an honest representation of themselves, as opposed to thinking, this will get me in. I say this for two reasons: First, every school has a culture, so our goal at the admissions committee is to select applicants we believe will fit into our culture. If someone misrepresents himself or herself because he or she wants to get in, then everyone loses.

Applicants also need to pay more attention to "Will I feel at home here?" They get way too caught up in having to get into a top-ten school. But, and this has to do with my second point, you succeed in life because of who you are and what you accomplish, not because of where you've gone to school. Applicants need to say to themselves, "This is who I am. If I don't get in, that's okay, life will go on." What I'm hoping I can convey is, if you are persistent and you have determination, you will get there. You may not know your whole path; you may not know what direction it will take. But if you believe in yourself, you will make it. It may not be here at Chicago GSB. But then it will be somewhere else.

Kate Klepper
Director of MBA Admissions,
Olin Graduate School of Business, Babson College

Q: Kate, what are some of the worst mistakes applicants make with their essays?

A: Some of the biggest mistakes are that they don't answer the essay question. Or they may answer the question in too tight of a vacuum. If we ask them about their having taken a leadership role for example, instead of just giving me an outline or narrative of what they've done, I'm looking for introspection. Take it to the next level and show me tenacity. Talk about how you were challenged, what you learned. What does it mean in the context of leadership? And how did this experience impact you professionally?

Another frequent mistake candidates make is getting caught up in the techno-speak of a particular industry. Instead of filling an essay with jargon that I may not understand, they need to talk about their role, how their actions led to change, what they learned from their experience. I don't necessarily need to know the code that had to be learned when someone recoded a company's computers.

Q: What about types of essays, for example, where they're asked about their greatest achievement or something?

A: When we ask about accomplishments, we want to know what made someone proud. Why did it make you proud? As I said before, we want to know what you learned from your experiences. How did you impact others? Impact the organization? This kind of introspection makes a huge difference. This is an essay in which any reader can find meaning and relate. If I've read an essay and, rather than having gained a sense of who the candidate is, I conclude with "So what?" then you've lost me and the opportunity.

Q: So if you have a feeling of, "So what?" after reading an essay, that's the death knell?

A: It can be.

Q: How else do applicants try to impress but wind up having the opposite effect?

A: A lot of times in these essays you don't hear about what didn't work. The person triumphed so magnificently. In other words, everything was a success. But my thinking is if every applicant was as magnificent as they are portraying themselves, then why do they want the MBA? The reality is that if every candidate were as perfect as they appear in their essays, I'd be out of business. All of us would. If you've never erred, if you've never had a problem, if you've already got it all, then how can the experiences here at Babson, or at any business school, be of benefit to you?

I should also add that our admissions perspective in terms of who would fit in at our school is going to be very different from another school because our environment is different from other schools'. It's important to communicate why a school is right for you. We understand that no school is perfect for everybody, so tell us why you belong at this particular one. And be convincing.

Q: If you can sum it up quickly, what makes for a successful essay?

A: Overall, the successful essays are the ones that leave me really feeling as though I know a little more about you. It gives me a true sense of the person behind the essay and the writing. That's an essay that I remember, and I can't wait to meet the person who wrote that essay. Applicants need to know we don't expect them to have dined with the president of a country, or been responsible for decoding the human genome. We have far more realistic expectations. We want you to be yourselves and let us get to know you.

Q: The economy has been brutal. How has this had an impact on the type of applicant you're seeing?

A: This wave of candidates seems to be coming to business school for the knowledge they're going to gain in a business program. They're much more highly defined in terms of what they are seeking to gain from their experience. They are acutely aware of what they don't know. They are really coming prepared to learn new ideas and thoughts. We're seeing this in both the greater number of applicants matriculating who have limited work experience and in older applicants whose work experiences have been negatively impacted by the economy. Right now we have applicants who, due to the economy, are applying to schools in 2003. On average, they have five years experience, which means they graduated in 1998, when the economy was great and you could have had virtually any job you wanted in almost any industry. Then the economy seized, the events of September 11 occurred, and many people found themselves out of work. Now instead of having worked for a Fortune 500 company with big-company know-how, we have students entirely more open to learning.

Q: Any other trends?

A: There is another mini-trend that I'm seeing, one which predates the Enron, Tyco, and WorldCom scandals. There is a great deal of talk and interest in social responsibility in corporate America. Candidates want to work with companies that are not harmful to the environment, companies that are paying attention to balance in the home and workplace. It may be the generation X-ers who have now come of age, but this cohort of young adults has brought issues about corporate responsibility and balancing family and work to the forefront. In fact, work/life balance is not considered a "women's issue" anymore. This is very different from a number of years ago. At Babson, we've hosted a number of panel discussions on this topic, and the attendance has been just about 50/50. So this generation of applicants has different expectations from previous generations. We do get a sense of this in their essays.

Linda Meehan
Assistant Dean for Admissions and Financial Aid, Columbia Business School

Q: How heavily are the essays weighted in admissions at Columbia?

A: The essays are part and parcel of the entire application; they are not weighted higher or lower. They are utilized as a means of getting information that we want to know. We use them to see how people think and how they pull together all of the pieces to come to a solution. In other words, it's as much about how they arrive at the answer as the answer itself.

For example, I'm thinking about the essay question that asks about an applicant's career goals and why they want the MBA and why at a particular school. This is without a doubt one of the most important essays they will write. Someone may say, "My short-term goal is to become an investment banker." What we want to know is how they plan on accomplishing this. This essay is meant to provide applicants with a vehicle to go through their entire thought process and bring us with them. Unfortunately, a lot of people miss that.

Q: What competencies are revealed in the questions you ask?

A: Their analytical abilities, written communication skills, organizational skills, and knowledge of themselves as well as their career paths are brought out in their essays. Assessing these competencies in their essays has become very difficult, given the amount of coaching available today.

Q: You bring up an interesting point. Is a "coached" essay easily visible to you?

A: What becomes evident are the irregularities you see among test scores and writing abilities. Those discrepancies make you more aware that they may have had help.

The analytical writing question on the GMAT helps provide a context for the skill level of the applicants' writing, though the GMAT no longer sends us the physical sample—we may request it. But generally speaking, if you have a low score, a 2 or 3 on the writing assessment, or your verbal GMAT score is very low, and we're reading an essay that is wonderful, there is a disconnect and it does raise flags.

Remember, there are so many checks and balances built into admissions. There are recommendations, which may speak of someone's communication skills; there is the GMAT we mentioned; work record; and in many cases, an interview. All of these elements help us make a decision.

Q: But what do you do when you see the irregularity?

A: Again, this is a holistic review process, and these irregularities are taken into account.

Q: Does your application ask if they have had any essay assistance?

A: No. Our application asks them to sign an honor statement that the work they present is their own. We have not asked specifically about essay help.

Q: How do you read through so many essays? What will be a "standout" to you?

A: First of all, I personally do not read each and every essay. My staff reads the essays and the entire application. They will then provide a summary of the application, which I then review. When there is something amazing or distinctive noted, I will refer back to that portion of the application.

Q: So yours are . . . another pair of highly important eyes?

A: Yes.

Q: The economy has been brutal. How would you suggest an applicant address a weak employment record? Is there less of a penalty these days?

A: I don't know that there was ever a penalty for unemployment. What's important is why you're unemployed. When you see someone not employed in good times, that's a trigger for something that may be amiss, but not always. For example, someone in the media world who is involved in production might hold four different jobs in four years. This would be normal for someone in this profession but not for someone working in marketing.

Today you see people getting laid off due to a downturn in the economy. You obviously would not hold that against them, as it is not their fault. But then we want to know, what are they are currently doing? How are they spending their time? This becomes what's important.

Q: What are some examples of good things they've been doing?

A: Pro bono work, giving their time and expertise to their communities. People have been working in unpaid internships at companies they hope to work for. There are those who have gone out on the creative side and done something they've always wanted to do. Some choose to travel, which may or may not serve their application well.

Q: What is your ideal use of the optional personal statement? What is a turn-off here?

A: The ideal is when the applicant tells us something that we need to know but they didn't have the opportunity to express earlier. Remember, this is an optional essay. If you feel you've done a great job in presenting yourself in your application, then you don't need to use the optional essay. But if there is something we failed to ask you that you wanted us to know, this is your opportunity. It is an open-ended essay not reserved for just the GMAT or GPA explanation.

Q: What's the biggest risk you saw an applicant take with an essay that worked?

A: Let me answer with this first: Sometimes people think they're being funny or cute in an essay. They don't realize that what may be funny or cute to them may be seen as inappropriate to an admissions committee. If you write very well and have the ability to use humor, then go ahead and do so. But if it's something you're trying to create but that doesn't come naturally to you, you can come off as flippant or too casual. This essay may crash and burn.

There is an example of the best essay I ever read, where the premise could have backfired, but didn't. It needs a little setup. The author of this essay was a Latin American male who was applying to Columbia a few years ago. He wrote an essay about being very macho. According to this applicant, Latinos are, by nature, a macho culture. This meant that being the male in his marriage, he was the most important member of the couple.

At the time, he was working as a banker. His wife was a psychologist. There was an important dinner for the principals at his firm, and obviously he felt it important to take his wife along. The day of the dinner, his wife received a phone call from a client in crisis. The wife worked with this client all through the day and gave thought to not going to the dinner because of the seriousness of the situation. The husband, Mr. Macho, thought this was horrible. How could his wife do something that might damage his career? The wife went to the dinner.

Q: I know what happened here. The client killed himself.

A: Yes, and sadly, this is a true story. It didn't take the applicant long to rethink his priorities and recognize that he was indeed not the center of the universe.

The part of this essay that could have gone awry was not just the macho part, but in handling the true drama of this story. What stuck with us, and still does years later, was his self-awareness. This was a very dramatic way for him to share with us his perspective. It certainly assisted him in gaining admission to Columbia Business School and several other top programs. This is an example of an essay that had a major impact on someone's life.

Many years ago, I worked in undergraduate admissions. I was speaking to an applicant's parents about their child, a young man whom they thought was the greatest. According to them, their son had everything: leadership, great grades and scores, wonderful extracurricular activities, and genuine commitment to these endeavors. So why, they wanted to know, did he get rejected from the school? Because, I had to answer, he looked like everyone else.

The point is, all of these candidates are great. At least 85 percent of the people who apply to the top ten business schools are all amazing, all are great. You just can't accept them all. That's a reality. So if applicants can distinguish themselves and let us get to know them, it may be the key to their admission.

Remember, we are trying to bring in to Columbia the most diverse and interesting class so that all may learn from one another.

Bill Sandefer
Director of Admissions and Financial Aid, Freeman School of Business, Tulane University

Q: How have things changed since you've been in MBA admissions?

A: The rankings are much more important. I started here ten years ago, and at that point you saw a lot of people referring to the rankings, but not many applications came directly from the rankings. In the last six years, business schools have seen a reduction in the number of applications but a much more focused set of applications. I think that's a function of people having a different information source. Instead of going to a professor and saying, "I'm interested in studying finance at graduate school, where do I go?" and then having the professor recommend schools they think would be good for you, prospective MBAs go to *Business Week* or *U.S. News & World Report* and say, "What's the best school in finance?" or "What's the best school in marketing?" And they'll start looking at those schools and benchmarking programs from that perspective.

Q: How has the Internet affected MBA admissions?

A: The Internet has been huge in the way people go about looking at schools. When we started offering online applications, the first year it was maybe 10 percent of our total applications. The next year, it was to the tune of 35 to 40 percent, so we're getting double-digit increases annually in online applications. That implies that the Net is also where they're gaining a lot of the information about the schools they're applying to. I think the Web has taken on a much bigger role, but not in the way that a lot of people think. People don't go online to learn about business schools in an advertising way. They tend to be much more selective when they go to the Web. They want immediate gratification related to their interests. If they're interested in financial aid or whether a school has a marketing program specifically for brand management, they want it right now in two clicks. If it's not there, they'll go to another website.

Q: Has the Internet bred a more savvy MBA shopper?

A: I was talking with a former admissions director at a top-tier school the other day. When we started, a big part of your day was spent telling people about the school or talking about very general issues—how do you apply, what materials you need, who needs to write your recommendations. Those days are gone. Very few applicants come in and say, "Who should I get to write my recommendations?" Because that information is there. Very quickly that comes across. People are increasingly self-selecting. The quality of our applicant pool is by far better than ever, and that seems to be a trend in the top-tier schools. I think that may be a real difference between schools that are nationally and internationally ranked and schools that have to inform applicants of every detail of the program.

Q: With so much information available online, what kinds of questions are applicants asking when they meet you in person?

A: Because people are much more savvy about their expectations in a school, they're asking a lot about what will be delivered in the program, about the team emphasis, about the breadth of requirements and the kind of knowledge you're going to get coming out of the program. People are much more specific: Why should I go to Tulane? What kind of experience am I going to have? What will the people I'm working with be like? How will it impact my future? Their questions are much, much more pointed.

The idea of going to business school and knowing exactly what you want is a myth. While you might look at a business school and say, "This school has a very strong finance program and so I'm going to go there," you still haven't had the experience, the contact with people from all around the world, the opportunities you get from being immersed in such a program. It's the sponge effect. When you encounter people, intellectual qualities, and academic qualities that you had no experience with before, it gives you an opportunity to see that things may be done differently in China or that things may be done the same way in Japan. So it either validates your current way of making decisions or it challenges you. And that may push you into looking at things differently. It should.

Q: How do you reconcile recruiting applicants with well-defined career goals with admitting applicants who are open to new experiences and ways of thinking?

A: If I could have any skill I don't possess, it would be clairvoyance. What you look for in applicants is a track record. Most have success written all over them, academic and professional. But what you're really looking for in an MBA applicant is not just a successful person but somebody who can recognize opportunities for change and incorporate them into his or her life. Some of our most recent essay questions seem to be very abstract and off-the-wall, and part of that is because we can already see what you're going to do with your career. Sitting where you are today, it's pretty obvious what your resume and your academic background will support. The things you can't see in an MBA application are how you go about making decisions, how you're influenced by other people, and how that influence manifests itself. In a community like the MBA program you're trying to get the exposure to diverse ways of thinking and new ideas, but it's only good if somebody is going to learn from it and walk away better because of it. Finding those applicants is the challenge.

Q: What are your essay questions?

A: We're running two right now. One is to identify the person that most influenced you in your life. That's pretty insightful not because of who it is—I would say 75 percent of the time it's Mom or Dad—but because it shows what influences people and how they react to it. That's something that has to be conveyed in the material you're presenting to the admissions committee. It's fine to say, "My mom made me honest," but was it through weekly beatings, was it through her exemplary behavior, or was it through the way she communicated with you?

Q: How long should an essay be?

A: I'm into brevity. One of the biggest challenges is to keep your essay within 200 words, which is like trying to summarize your life in a paragraph. Communicating effectively in a small space is a challenge. Not coincidentally, it's something you have to do in business school. Twenty-two-page essays are not a productive thing around here when you're trying to get through management communications.

Q: So one question is, "Who influenced you and why?"

A: Because we have a large international applicant pool, another essay question we've asked for a couple of years is to assemble a group and take them on a tour of your country. Tell us who will be in that group and what you will see. Part of what we're trying to gather there is the individual's perspective on the world. It's a twist on the old "if you could have dinner with anyone, who would it be and why?" But it's insightful for us because it gives insights into different nationalities and what those individuals would highlight about their backgrounds, history, countries, or needs in a way that is not so common to why would we admit you.

Q: Can you think of an essay response that impressed you with its unconventionality?

A: The tour essay that impressed me the most with its originality jumped across time to pull different people from history who had encountered the country and what readings about that person had influenced the applicant to think about or want to show about their country. I thought that was a really interesting way to approach the standard question.

Q: Is creativity important?

A: Creativity for its own sake is not a good thing. Most creative essays are not successful because in the essay I'm looking for some core values that are part of the person and how they're illustrating that. This is not the Faulkner Prize. We're trying to understand how you make decisions rather than how well you write. The GMAT includes two essays, so we already have a writing sample. The application essay is something you have a little more time to think about, and you should be able to produce something that is the best that's going to come out of the individual.

Q: How are the essays weighted?

A: If the applicant pool has self-selected itself to the point where they're close to qualifying academically and they're close to qualifying by their career interests, you're looking at a group of people who are fairly qualified on the objective measures. What you end up looking for are subtle skills that then get played out in the MBA program—how people interact with one another and function in an environment. So the essay and the interview tend to be more validating of how we expect people are going to function in the program and benefit from their experience.

Q: Can you think of an example where an essay made the difference, either for better or for worse?

A: We see both cases. An inconsistent application is the surest kiss of death. You want to open up an application and see that someone's resume, their recommendations, their essays, and their interview all support a set of goals that are compatible with what's going to happen to them over the next two years. Inconsistencies there raise red flags and, in a competitive pool, the red flag is what gets you taken off the table. So if somebody has a fabulous GMAT score, great verbal abilities, and an undergraduate degree in English and then his or her essay is riddled with errors, you look at that and say, "How attentive to detail is this person? How much effort was applied to writing that essay?" Something's wrong, and that will get you taken away.

On the other hand, you might look at people who were very active as undergraduates or who did something that had [a negative] impact on their GPA, but then in talking to them and looking at their recent behavior, you might be a little bit more forgiving. So an interview and an essay that are very positive can have a heavier weight with some candidates.

Q: How have candidates changed in recent years?

A: A decade ago, people's bosses and parents encouraged them to go directly into graduate school. Remember [that] an MBA is a management program. These are people who are targeted for mid-level jobs when they get out of the program. Employers are looking for people who can be groomed quickly into supervisory roles, so with no prior experience—no track record of success— you really are at a disadvantage. I think that message has really been communicated over the last six or seven years, that you need experience.

Q: Has the economy had an impact on applicants?

A: I have a counter-cyclical theory. The students in top MBA programs tend to be much more focused on managing their careers. So while the economy has a role, it's only one factor in a long-term process. We see people who have been planning on an MBA since high school. They're on a twelve-year track. They've thought about this for years. They've kept tabs on the rankings for five or six years. They have a very refined idea of what they want to accomplish. With these applicants, I don't think the economy has an effect. Last year we witnessed some dramatic economic events, but only about 10 percent of the class could be traced to having a direct correlation to the economy. The remaining 90 percent of the class was basically on target for what they had planned on doing for a long period of time.

Q: What areas are applicants most interested in?

A: Eight years ago the emphasis was on general management with a broad range of skills and then whatever other experience you got thrown in was fine. Certainly in the case of all the major MBA programs, the first year was spent on a breadth of skills. That has largely changed. When you walk through the door, you need to be focused on the industries that you're interested in and the kinds of things they want, because those opportunities are going to appear much earlier in the MBA life cycle. You're going to be taking electives in that first semester, you're going to be exposed to speakers and opportunities in that first semester that have long-term career impacts.

Q: Is industry looking for specialization rather than a generalist?

A: I think that's definitely true. A company will come in and look for someone who has the training as an MBA, who understands marketing and finance and human resources, who has some knowledge of the international marketplace, but fundamentally you're being hired to run a finance department. Or you're being hired to run a brand in the case of the brand management area. So you have to understand all of those things but you also have to have deep knowledge in your subject, and you can get that through prior experience and specialization in your program.

CHAPTER 10

THE ESSAYS

CASE EXAMPLES: ADMISSIONS OFFICERS CRITIQUE WINNING ESSAYS

To show you how some applicants have answered the essay questions, we asked the b-schools for samples of "winning" essays. To show you what worked about them, we also asked the admissions officers to provide a critique.

As you read through the essays, keep in mind that each was but one of several submitted by an applicant for admission. Moreover, they were part of a package that included other important components. One essay alone did not "win" admission.

One other reminder: The purpose of including essays in this book is to give you a nudge in the right direction, not to provide you with a script or template for your own work. It would be a mistake to use them this way.

Obviously, this collection is by no means all-encompassing. There are thousands of winning essays out there; we just couldn't include them all.

> **Editor's Note:** Personal details, such as names, companies, and institutions, have been removed from these essays to protect the identities of the applicants. The essays have not been otherwise edited since they were submitted by the applicants.

Babson College

Olin Graduate
School of Business

Essay #1

Question: a) What are your specific career goals immediately follow-ing graduation? b) What skills, competencies, and experiences do you have right now that will help you attain those goals?

Following graduation, I plan to become involved in projects that link business principals and models with innovative social programs, particularly those that support positive youth development. Most of my work life has focused on adolescents. I have worked for various youth service organizations, provided clinical services to youth and their families, and managed a program for young teens. Ultimately, I want to start a new organization that focuses on youth entrepreneurship, meaning that youth are supported in their efforts to innovate, organize and implement their plans. Learning about well-developed concepts in for-profit industries is essential for achieving my goals. The challenge will be to create ways to apply those principles in the non-profit sector.

As a social worker, the difficulties my clients face frustrate me less than the funding system within which services operate. Inefficient bureaucracy, weakly established means for linking research with service development, and turnover in funding limit my ability to expand and/or improve services. For example, the money that presently supports the program I manage was awarded to foster the development of "models" that prevent youth involvement in substance abuse and other risk behaviors. After two years of delivering services and refining the program, we have created a workable model. However, now that we have established ourselves and are capable of expansion, our contract is set to expire. In the search for new funds, there are two options: apply for one large grant or several small ones. Either option is likely to require that some parts of the current model be dropped or altered to meet the requirements of the new funders. This turnover in funding has a domino effect—management and front-line staff leave, which in turn disrupts operations. The social service organizations that house various programs are similarly effected, as staff positions come and go. The resultant organizational instability makes it nearly impossible to seek or develop alternative sources of capital, and the cycle repeats itself.

A related problem is the difficulty applying performance measures to non-profit entities. In nonprofits, results cannot be linked solely to revenue and expenses. Current tools for evaluating social service programs focus on concepts developed by social scientists. While those tools are essential for assessing clients' needs and developing programs, they are not adequate for measuring the performance of an organization over time. By combining new knowledge about various business concepts with my background in social science, I will be able to develop alternative ways to address this problem.

My MSW degree provided excellent clinical training and allowed me to gain skills in program development, evaluation, grant-writing and staff supervision. Over the last three years, I have tested those skills as a program manager. I have felt prepared to handle most youth and family concerns, staff issues and general oversight of daily activities, but I need further training in operations, marketing, application of technology, and strategy. I am obtaining an MBA to fill gaps in my current skill set, learn about venture start-up and expand my worldview. Babson's focus on entrepreneurship throughout the curriculum, and the opportunity for specialized training, will help me attain my goals.

CRITIQUE

This essay explained the clear direction that the student intends to take upon graduation. The student did a good job of connecting her prior work experience and education to future career goals. This is especially important when candidates are making a career change or are seeking employment in an environment or industry that is outside the norm for MBA recruiting. The student identified areas where MBA knowledge and skills would be an asset, recognized her lack of knowledge in certain areas, and succeeded in demonstrating to the admissions committee why the MBA—specifically the Babson MBA—was the appropriate next step in her career progression.

Essay #2

Question: a) What are your specific career goals immediately following graduation? b) What skills, competencies, and experiences do you have right now that will help you attain those goals?

For the last decade, I have helped guide the career of [Band A] from a college band into a professionally touring and recording entity with a national impact. This evolution has endured many growing pains, but the band has persevered because of my vision, passion, and work ethic. My vision of growth for the organization and for myself helped us discover and create opportunities that put us in a position to succeed. In addition, my vision of survival helped us withstand an avalanche of challenges that would have ended the careers of most other groups. Equally rewarding has been the complete nature of my involvement from the songwriting and recording to the supervision of manufacturing, distribution, promotion, and ultimately live performance itself, when the songs and the fans come together. I have always run the band like a business, adopting long-term growth strategies and learning from the management decisions that have contributed to the successes and failures of other bands that came before us. This application of professional intensity to what would otherwise be a hobby, and transforming it into something enduring and impacting, has been extremely rewarding.

Within a year of forming, [Band A] entered a radio contest and won first place out of 200 groups throughout New England, and this taste of success inspired a vision of further accomplishments. Everything started with education and elbow grease. I buried myself in every book I could find on artist management and band development. I opened a bank account and kept detailed financial records. I read *Billboard* and *Rolling Stone*, and spent time with most bands that passed through town in order to learn from their successes and failure. I developed a business plan that incorporated these lessons as well as some ideas of my own. The plan emphasized long-term and short-term growth strategies applied to recording, touring, and management. I even phoned hundreds of college venues, metro rock clubs, and studios to put the plan into action. Our collective musical ability combined with my appreciation for problem solving, my drive to succeed, and my desire to identify and face challenges has given the band a distinctive edge.

Since college, we have survived ten line-up changes, traveled more than 500,000 miles performing more than 1,200 concerts in all 48 continental states, earned a recording contract with [Record Company A], recorded three albums with some of the top producers and mix engineers in this country, and our music is featured regularly in films and on national television. [Band A] has earned its success on the strength of two underlying principles: the development of a good product, and the importance of being aware and thoroughly involved. I strive to be involved with every aspect of operations from the studio to the stage, and from the radio to the record store. A holistic understanding of how all facets of the industry come together has been an essential part of our growth and development.

Working and performing with [Band A] has been uniquely rewarding. It has allowed me to pursue an ambitious dream that blends a diversity of gratifying elements including artistic expression, self-employment, and the development and management of a business. Beyond rehearsal and performance, my responsibilities have included book keeping, cash flow management, payroll, tax preparation, maintaining the mailing list, establishing and main-taining a product distribution network, booking tours, negotiating performance contracts, coordinating recording projects, securing product endorsements, coordinating charitable concert events, conducting interviews, and making other public appearances. I feel I have an aptitude and appreciation for management, and if recognizing management ability is the first step in assembling a career in management, the next step is discovering an appropriate application of that potential. To this end, I have three specific interests that I would like to explore in graduate school.

I want to consider applying my abilities to the non-profit sector as my grandfather did with [Nonprofit Organization A], or my mother continues to do with [Nonprofit Organization B]. My personal and professional interests could be combined in museum management or involvement with an arts or social service foundation. Contributing to society and enhancing our culture by supporting the arts, in addition to helping an organization run more productively and efficiently, are important concerns of mine.

I also want to explore entrepreneurial opportunities. One of the most satisfying aspects of my tenure with [Band A] has been overseeing the evolution of the group from a college band into an enduring and financially viable entity. This was accomplished through hard work, a vision of growth and survival, and an appreciation for the ways in which the different elements of an industry combine. I would love the opportunity to foster this kind of development in another setting.

Finally, although my career in music has precluded further exploration of the international dimension of my personal and academic development, my appreciation of foreign cultures is great. I lived in France during my junior year of High School, backpacked through Europe for two months before college, and majored in International Relations at Brown. Adaptation, exploration, and communication in a foreign culture are one of the greatest challenges I have ever faced, and I look forward to doing it again. Babson would be an ideal environment for me to discover professional opportunities that are aligned with my interests.

I have enjoyed my career as a professional musician and artist manager, but I am ready for a change that would permit a more personally and financially stable lifestyle. The experience of completing Babson's MBA program would help me hone my general skills and interests into a specific field. It would enhance to my unique business background by proving to my future employers and peers that I am an experienced and well-trained leader and decision maker.

CRITIQUE

This essay demonstrated the need for business skill in an unconventional environment in a way that was believable, convincing, and persuasive. This student showed the admissions committee that although he had not worked in a large or even midsize company, his experiences could be linked to many business situations. The student demonstrated leadership abilities, teamwork experiences, and the recognized need to run his band like a business. The student's self-awareness of both skills and limitations gave the admissions committee a clear understanding of the candidate and what he would bring to the community: artistic creativity, outside-the-box thinking, flexibility, leadership skills, an understanding of running a business, and the experience of traveling throughout the country.

Essay #3

Question: a) What are your specific career goals immediately follow-ing graduation? b) What skills, competencies, and experiences do you have right now that will help you attain those goals?

In order to achieve my career goals, I have outlined my strategy for success by mapping my career goals at specific time intervals over the next fifteen years. In addition, my professional and personal experiences coupled with a Babson MBA will ensure my future professional success.

In three years, my career goals are to be a Babson MBA graduate, to attain a post-graduate entry-level position as an Associate in the credit derivatives group at [Bank A], and to begin to give back to my community by serving it. The completion of the Babson MBA program is the most critical component for achieving my career goals. As a newly graduated Babson MBA student, I will begin my new career structuring transactions in the credit derivatives group at [Bank A], as it is the number one ranked credit derivatives dealer in the world. My wife will continue to work for a few more years so that her income can allow me to accept a post-graduate entry-level salary. I know that the best place to start a new career is at a large bank with top-notch expertise in a specific area (credit derivatives). This will not only provide a challenging work environment due to high customer flow, but also will allow me to learn a new business from the best credit derivatives professionals in the industry. Additionally, to successfully attain my career goals, I need to ensure that I have the right balance with my personal life. As such, the next phase of my personal growth progression is to begin to serve my community during this time interval. My first priority is to raise money for cancer research. Initially, I will solicit sponsorship to raise money in cancer bike rides and also contribute separately from my own pocket. Also, as I was an underprivileged child without a role model at critical points in my life, I will begin my involvement as a role model for [Nonprofit Organization A]. to provide a source of guidance to children without fathers. Hopefully, I can guide a fatherless child to make the right choices by teaching him the lessons I have learned from my mistakes rather than having to learn the same lessons from his own mistakes. Also, as I am acquainted with the VP of Finance of another university from past business dealings, I will be seeking his advice (as he is well respected in his industry) on a proper strategy to gain membership to the Board of Directors or to a board of a similar university. I have a strong desire to freely lend my expertise to the VP of Finance of a university or university system to assist in minimizing interest costs and maximizing asset returns through the use of municipal debt and derivative products.

In five years, my career goals are to be promoted from Associate to SVP at [Bank A], to continue to nurture and grow my professional network, to continue my community service and to allow my wife to transition from her current career at [Bank B] to her new career as a full-time mother and part-time gymnastics judge/coach. By this time interval, I will be quickly promoted to SVP as I demonstrate my business acumen and leadership ability to management. As a SVP, I will be a senior member of the credit derivative group at [Bank A] and I will be positioning myself to manage the group in the near future. Also, I will continue to work hard to maintain and grow my existing professional network as it will be important to strengthen existing and to develop new professional allies. I will continue to be involved in raising money for cancer research and I will use my seniority at [Bank A] to make it an organizational priority to raise those funds. I will also continue to work on attaining the university board membership and to be involved with [Nonprofit Orginization A]. Most importantly, this is the time interval when my wife can choose to become a full-time mother to our children. In addition, I'll encourage her to begin the pursuit of her passion to become a gymnastics coach and judge.

In ten years, my career goals are to be promoted from SVP to MD of the credit derivatives group at [Bank A], to maintain and grow my professional network, to continue my community service and help my wife manage our family. By this time interval, I will be promoted to MD and will be managing the credit derivatives group at [Bank A]. I will continue the aforementioned community service projects and will have gained membership to the [University A] (or similar university) Board of Directors. Additionally, I will have a hands-on approach to helping my wife manage our family. I will be actively involved in every family member's life by providing encouragement, life guidance and friendship. I will be actively involved in my children's lives from their parent-teacher conferences to sporting events. I will continue to encourage my wife to pursue her gymnastics dreams.

In fifteen years, my career goals are to seek out a smaller investment bank (such as [Bank B] or [Bank C]) to change the direction of my career, to maintain and grow my professional network, to continue to provide community service and to stay actively involved in each family member's life. By this time interval, I will have excellent experience from a top-notch bank to leverage into a position at a smaller investment bank. I will strongly desire at this point to move to a smaller company because they tend to allow employees to place more emphasis on family and life balance. As such, I will be starting a new credit derivatives group or taking over the management of an existing credit derivative group (or another type of derivative group) at my new company. This new position will allow me to devote more time to my family and community service.

The work experiences that will help me to achieve my career goals have evolved from [Bank B], [Bank C] and [Company D]. At [Bank B], I had the opportunity to be a part of a municipal derivatives team of four professionals that consistently generated significant annual revenues and also improved the municipal derivatives market through constant innovation (for example, we were the first municipal derivatives desk to introduce a municipal bond option program called "MuniCHOPs"—municipal call hedging option program). From this experience I learned that I have the entrepreneurial spirit and can work well with a team under stressful circumstances. From my [Bank C] experience, I have learned that companies and employees may differ culturally. Upon my departure from [Bank C] to gain managerial experience at [Bank D], I assumed that [Bank D] was culturally similar to [Bank C]. However, I learned rather quickly that while [Bank D] was an excellent bank, it was also a conservative regional bank. In fact, [Bank D]'s conservative culture was the antithesis of [Bank C]'s entrepreneurial culture. As such, I realized that my entrepreneurial spirit and ambition were not appropriate for the culture of [Bank D]. This experience will remain with me because I have learned that companies, as well as employees, may be different and those differences must be recognized in the implementation of strategic managerial objectives. From my [Company E] experience, I have honed my entrepreneurial, communication, leadership and business relationship skills.

Also, my personal growth experience will help me to achieve my career goals. From my personal growth experience, I have learned that strong relationships are the most important component to my personal and family happiness. As such, the nurturing of strong professional relationships, thereby increasing my professional network is just as important to my professional success. As an experienced professional it is important to teach and develop younger professionals unselfishly, to foster a team-oriented environment, and to continuously maintain open lines of communication with former colleagues and business school classmates. Additionally, I have learned that balancing my life between my professional and family goals will contribute to my professional success as well. This will enable me to avoid both professional and personal regrets and pitfalls, thereby maintaining a high level of happiness. Also, as part of balancing my life, I am no longer motivated to professionally succeed by only the prospect of making money. But rather, I am motivated to succeed so that I can provide my family with the things that I never had as a child: family happiness, a comfortable home in a nice neighborhood, life guidance and a finer appreciation of life.

A Babson MBA will provide a diverse student body, an excellent selection of academic courses and the opportunity to begin a new career. The Babson MBA program offers a culturally diverse student body (38% international, 62% domestic, according to *Business*

Week Online) that is similar to today's culturally diverse workplace. This prepares the Babson MBA student to learn how to understand and accept differences among culturally different group members under stressful circumstances. Hence, the Babson MBA student is better prepared to assimilate into a team environment at a culturally diverse company. Additionally, Babson is known for the entrepreneurship program. As such, I am interested in exploring the decision making process of the student that desires to be an entrepreneur. As one who has taken risk by starting a derivatives consulting company and worked (and will in the future) in a fast-paced entrepreneurial environment (but never had time to appreciate the moment) I want to develop friendships with those that have similar interests. Thus, I will have an opportunity to study the entrepreneurial spirit through the bond of those friendships.

Additionally, I am looking forward to formally learning finance from the Babson MBA program. As I believe that having a strong technical base is important, I look forward to scheduling Valuation (FIN 7000), Risk Management (FIN 7504), Portfolio Management (FIN 7530) and Advanced Derivative Securities (FIN 7550). Also, as I will be a senior level manager, I am interested in learning about leadership and organizational behavior. As such, Strategic Management (MOB 7000), Negotiations (MOB 7120) and Implementing Strategic Change (MOB 7500) are important to my interests in learning about leadership and management. Finally, my first elective priority is to ensure that I am scheduled for the Marketing for Entrepreneurs course (EPS 7574) so that I can meet fellow entrepreneurs.

It is of paramount importance to me that a wide variety of financial services firms recruit MBAs at Babson. As such, recruitment from various financial services firms will ensure that a diversified set of career paths is available. For example, as previously discussed, my targeted employer upon graduation is [Bank A]. However, if there isn't an opportunity to join [Bank A] in my chosen field (credit derivatives), then there are other potential employers that recruit at Babson that I can explore for opportunities in credit derivatives including [Banks B, C, D, or E]. Then there are smaller financial services firms that I can also explore career opportunities (in credit derivatives or another area of derivatives) at including [Banks F, G, or H]. At the moment, I do not have entree to a career outside of the municipal industry at any of these financial services firms.

As I have been in the municipal industry since I was a junior in college (13 years), I have a strong desire to grow professionally by beginning a new career in a different segment of the financial services industry. However, due to my longevity in the municipal industry coupled with an undergraduate degree from [University F], I have found it difficult to break-through to a new career in a new industry. As such, the prestige of the Babson MBA program, the success of Babson's alumni and my successful track record will be, in combination, the mechanism that allows me to shatter the glass ceiling that I have encountered.

My carefully planned career path and professional/personal experiences in combination with a Babson MBA will ensure that I am successful in my next career.

CRITIQUE

This essay, although too long by normal standards, covered a lot of information for the candidate. It is a good example of a student with clearly defined career goals, a plan of how he intends to achieve those goals, and clear articulation of how the Babson MBA is going to assist him in attaining those goals. Due to the fact that this student had a unique situation with regard to his work and prior education, degrees of latitude were afforded with regard to the length of the essay. This is not a strategy I would recommend for candidates; try to stay within the recommended word limit. This student clearly did the necessary research and was able to weave certain details of the program that supported his goals into the essay. Again, I advise caution in taking this approach; the last thing the admissions committee wants to read in an essay is what's in their course book. However, the relevance of what is stated directly supported the student's goals and made a clear connection.

Case Western

Reserve University

Weatherhead School of Management

FROM THE SCHOOL

The Weatherhead School of Management at Case Western Reserve University is a model of innovation and diversity. From our cutting-edge, Frank Gehry-designed building, to eighteen areas of concentration, including Bioscience Entrepreneurship and Nonprofit Management, the school is noted for being 'forward-thinking' and innovative in its approach to management education. The admissions committee, therefore, keeps these hallmarks in mind when reviewing and admitting candidates to the full-time MBA program.

"The committee purposefully constructs a class profile that mirrors the school's innovative and diverse nature, considering nationality (45 percent of the class is international), gender, ethnicity, work experience, and educational background. However, beyond the rudimentary demographic information, the committee also considers the 'gray area': What makes one candidate stand apart from the others? What qualities has this person demonstrated that *guarantee* involvement in activities outside the classroom? How do you know this person will be effective in the numerous team settings? It is through the essay questions that the committee is able to 'see' the candidates—not just for what they have done academically or on a standardized test, but for the people they are and that they wish to become."

ESSAY #1

Question: Describe your motivation for pursuing an MBA degree.
How does it fit with your short- and long-term career goals?

My earliest impression of community service may have been the pins my grandmothers received for giving blood. My desire to help others was embedded by my family and manifested itself through a combination of three things: 1) my public policy education at [University A], 2) an introduction to the nonprofit sector at a seminar in D.C. through [Nonprofit Organization A], and 3) an internship at the [State A]'s 4-H Office. These experiences solidified my desire to work in the nonprofit sector.

My career thus far has entailed a rapid assumption of responsibilities. [Nonprofit Organization B], a national advocacy organization, hired me as a Development Assistant, and soon I was promoted to the newly created position of Prospect Researcher. As such, I was responsible for identifying and qualifying funding sources and setting up a "research shop." At [Nonprofit Organization C], a five-hospital system with numerous ancillary services, I conduct prospect research for twice as many Development Officers. I also have fundraising responsibility for [Program A], and I write grants for [Center A]. As a result of my career growth and increased responsibilities, my salary doubled in just under two years.

Three and a half years of nonprofit experience so far has exposed me to a variety of nonprofit organizations. Although their missions, size, and my role in them have varied dramatically, there are similarities that are current issues in nonprofit management. So focused on their missions, nonprofits often lack the qualities of a well-managed business. Some nonprofits walk a precarious financial tightrope, and others have significant human resource problems. These weaknesses compromise their effectiveness and their ability to tackle important social problems.

These kinds of administrative issues are almost always known quantities, but nonprofit managers often lack the skill sets and experience to know how to approach solving them. I believe the MBA from Weatherhead and a certificate from the Mandel Center will provide me with the unique background needed to balance the mission of an organization with its responsibility to operate effectively. The curriculum is the most comprehensive and practical of any of the schools that offer this combination, and I look forward to working with and learning from dynamic teachers and taking part in the Mentor program. Now is the right time to pursue my MBA because I believe am ready to contribute to organizational health in a strategic way, and business skills will equip me to move to this level and be effective.

With a degree from Case Western and the Mandel Center, I will gain a solid mix of business skills and understanding of the special issues nonprofits face. In the short-term I see myself as a Development Director or senior manager helping ensure both the fiscal and programmatic health of a community agency that depends on charitable dollars for its operating budget. In the long term I hope to work on the cutting edge of nonprofit management theory or become involved in the funding side of the equation as a grant maker or an advisor to high level donors looking to leverage their charitable dollars. The Weatherhead School offers me the best path to achieving the same satisfaction my grandmothers got from giving blood—helping nonprofit organizations help others more effectively.

CRITIQUE

Paragraph 1: The essay begins with a well-constructed introduction, which gives good insight into the candidate: focus on community service, importance of family, educational background, breadth of work, and internship experience. This paragraph gives a solid picture of the candidate in just a few sentences. It serves as a good foundation for the rest of the essay, which elaborates on the various facets of the candidate.

Paragraph 2: In detailing specific work experiences, the candidate is already highlighting the skills and talents she can contribute as a student in our program. Additionally, the assumption of new/different responsibilities and an increase in position and salary illustrate that her abilities are recognized and rewarded by the organizations for which she has worked.

Paragraph 3: Here, the candidate demonstrates her ability to analyze organizations with regard to basic business functions. This paragraph is also a preliminary introduction to the motivation aspect of the question.

Paragraph 4: This paragraph is the "heart" of the essay; it details the motivation for the degree, and it highlights aspects of the school program and how they fit with her goals. This paragraph has been perfectly set up by the three previous paragraphs.

Paragraph 5: This is an excellent essay summary that gives specific answers with regard to short- and long-term goals. The final sentence brings the essay full circle, back to the reference of how her desire for community service evolved.

Summary: This is a well-constructed essay that remains focused on the topic while giving the readers insight into the person behind the application. Specific examples of work experience and elements of the program that fit her goals give the impression of a candidate who has evaluated her own situation, set goals for her career, researched the options, and made an informed decision about what she is looking for in an MBA.

Essay #2

Question: How will your background and experiences enhance the quality of the entering class of Weatherhead MBA students?

Moving from rural Tennessee to suburban New York at the age of twelve was not an easy thing to do. Trying to blend in during this fragile stage of life was a challenge; "y'all" was not a part of the typical middle schooler's vocabulary in New York. However, this change in lifestyle at a young age laid the foundation for a passion to meet different types of people and experience various lifestyles and cultures. In college, I had several experiences that enriched me. From taking a class taught by Maya Angelou to scuba diving on the Great Barrier Reef during my semester abroad, [University A] provided the perfect slate for an undergraduate experience filled with meaningful experiences.

One of the most worthwhile experiences I have had, however, took place after I received my diploma from [University A]. Being chosen to serve my country for ten months in a [Nonprofit Organization B] program was one of the greatest honors I have received. Describing one of the projects that my team worked on will help illustrate the lessons I learned and the memories that I take with me into each new experience in my life.

My [Nonprofit Organization B] team, comprised of twelve individuals from eleven different states, lived for two months in a three-bedroom house that had been repossessed by [Nonprofit Organization C] after the tenants had violated the rules of living there. We lived in a neighborhood in which drug deals on the corner were common occurrences. We would build houses for [Nonprofit Organization C] during the day and return at night, exhausted and sore, to walk down the street to the community center and help the neighborhood kids with their homework. In this unique life experience, I literally lived among the people whom I was serving. I did not work all day and then return to a place of security, equipped with the amenities I was used to in my life. That was not an option.

Never before had I been so close in proximity to the very root of the problem that we sought to eliminate by building houses for the poor. No longer could I judge those on "the other side." I was one of them. They were one of us. I was reminded of the premise that Maya Angelou taught her class around—"We are more alike than we are different." Although she had made us recite that each week in her class, it was three years later when I was living it. She was more right than I had ever realized.

My background, shaped by these types of experiences, will add to the diversity of the class beginning this fall at the Weatherhead School of Management. Not only am I eager to share my own life experiences with others but I am also equally excited to be challenged by those who have had a very different past. The exchange between myself, one who wants to apply an MBA to the nonprofit sector, and another student, perhaps one who is ready to improve his managerial skills for the consulting field, has the potential to be outstanding. I know I would contribute to the diversity of a class of individuals, each from a different background with a different set of skills, all ultimately seeking the same thing.

CRITIQUE

Paragraph 1: The first sentence, simply stating a fact of her life, already draws the reader in to the essay—thinking of a twelve-year-old girl trying to "hide" her southern accent from her New York classmates. This reference point sets up nicely the following sentences, which exemplify her interest in meeting different types of people and discovering different cultures.

Paragraph 2: Here the candidate sets up the remainder of the essay. Also, as this experience is not one that many people will have shared, it reminds the reader of her uniqueness—in both pursuing the volunteer work and being selected for the program.

Paragraph 3: In describing her living conditions, the candidate speaks to her ability to be flexible and adaptive—twelve people in a three-bedroom house, living in a neighborhood far from her own life experience. The detail enhances the commitment to community involvement. She is not a "weekend" volunteer, but chose to live a lifestyle that would put her in daily contact with those she hoped to help.

Paragraph 4: This paragraph illustrates personal growth gained from her experience. The ability to enter a challenging environment, adapt to difficult surroundings, and appreciate the experience as one of growth and learning is exactly what an admissions committee would hope for with all candidates.

Paragraph 5: This summary paragraph brings the focus to the question at hand, with the candidate reiterating not only how the experience enriched her and will allow her to contribute to the class, but also her eagerness to learn from others with varying backgrounds.

Summary: The essay is effective in two ways. First, it demonstrates self-knowledge and personal growth—both of which are important for candidates to possess and embrace to fully take advantage of the MBA experience. Second, it details a nonwork experience. While the volunteer experience is certainly valuable (and valued by the admissions committee as they look for students to enrich our community), some candidates do not feel that they should write about nonwork accomplishments. They believe that because they are applying to business school, they should focus on business experiences only. However, most every school wants/ expects students to have a balance between school and their personal life, so it is beneficial to learn about what they've done in the past.

Claremont Graduate University

University

The Peter F. Drucker
Graduate School of Management

Essay #1

Personal Statement: What special contributions do you believe you will bring to the Drucker School? Why is a Drucker School MBA important to you?

What special contributions do you believe you will bring to the Drucker School?

If this is going to be a personal statement, I might as well put "me" all over this statement. So, "out" with the generic and "in" with something a little *different*. I feel that I bring the following qualities and contributions to my Drucker experience.

Leadership

How do leaders become better? By learning from those who have been where you are trying to go. These leaders can show you the way, so you may lead others. I feel that Drucker provides those experienced leaders, both teaching the classes and sitting next to me learning. The exciting idea about graduate school is the fact that you are not merely gaining experience from internships and lectures, but the most experience will probably come from my study group members and classmates. As far as I know, there isn't anyone applying to Drucker from my company. So, my experience in the retail industry will probably enlighten my classmates, hopefully, for the better.

I've been involved in leadership opportunities most of my life. From co-captain of my basketball team to VP of my chapter of [Association A], leadership has taught me responsibility, courage, and strength. I know how it feels to have the entire weight of an expensive project on your shoulders. I feel that it is very important to have leadership experience in a program that relies so heavily on group participation. In every group, you are not always the leader. But after participating in these roles, I understand the role of a leader. By understanding, I believe that I can be more effective and cooperative in a group.

Resolve/Don't Quit Attitude

There have been so many times in life that I just wanted to throw my hands in the air and say, "That's it! I can't do it!" But I have always had that voice inside pulling me back together, telling me that I can make it. "Just hold on a little longer." I know for a fact MBA programs are not easy and Drucker is no different. But I know that I have the strength and resolve to pull through. Strength also comes from those around you. My "don't quit" attitude will definitely rub off on others, encouraging them that we can do this together. With all the group projects and study groups involved in the program, there is no choice but to pull for each other.

When I was eighteen, a car accident left me paralyzed from the neck down. Doctors counted me out from the first day out. They said that I would never walk again and would have to look at buying a more permanent wheelchair. I told everyone in the room that day; "I am *walking* back to school in the fall". When everyone counted me out, I decided then and there that I couldn't give up. Why attempt to do anything in life, if you don't think you can be successful at it? Regardless of how many times you may think you have failed, barring death, you can try again with the knowledge gained from the previous attempts. I have been told that a leg that has healed after being broken is stronger than it was before. Through relentless physical therapy and prayer, I carried my own books into my dorm room to start the fall of my sophomore year of college. Broken temporarily, but stronger indefinitely.

Creativity

With the current status of the economy, creativity will be a "must-have" in whatever industry you enter. I'm glad I have it. You have to think outside of the box to figure how you will first find your niche in the job market. Product development is the area of marketing I aspire to enter, once I receive my MBA. My creativity will flow into every aspect of my Drucker experience, from group projects to on-campus organizations.

As a member of my marketing association, I helped create our theme and exhibition for the national convention. Using items laying around campus, such as street signs, pieces of tarp, and plastic tubing, we re-created a construction site in a New Orleans convention hall. I do believe that I have the ability to make something from nothing at all. I enjoy taking a look at everyday items and finding methods of improving upon them.

Sense of Responsibility to self, family, and community

Accomplishments are not simply for you. When you gain a degree, you have a responsibility to your family and community also. I feel a great need to use my knowledge to help others around me. There are so many underprivileged youth in Southern California that could use the encouragement of people like me to inspire and show them the path to greater aspirations, beyond simply sports and entertainment.

While at Drucker, I plan to participate in numerous community service activities, [Nonprofit Organization B] and [Nonprofit Organization C]. But I must use my added knowledge from a Drucker MBA to go back to those communities that gave so much to me, in South LA and Compton. I do not want to be the only person to benefit from my degree. I want the world to receive the wisdom and kindness that was passed down to me.

Sense of the Big Picture/Ability to bring people together

Have you ever met a person that could enter a conversation and understand where everyone was coming from? I feel that I have the unique ability to view issues with an open mind and relate to someone's opinion without sacrificing my own. My belief is the key to communication, in a community as diverse as Southern California, is listening. Being able to hear exactly what someone is saying and why it is being said, in the tone/fashion they are presenting that idea.

International students, statistically, dominate the graduate school arena. You find this highly affirmative in the state of California. With the diverse backgrounds and languages we come from, it is imperative effective communication is present to bring about common understanding. The Drucker program is passionate about group work and participation. I know that I can come into a group setting and be productive. Looking beyond language/cultural barriers to see the big picture, both in class and in life, to bring us all together.

Charisma

The first time I heard the word "Charisma" was watching Earving "Magic" Johnson of the LA Lakers. Sports broadcasters were amazed at the way "Magic" could begin to speak and everyone would listen. Yes, I know. I could have used great leaders of the past or present, but "Magic" was different. Outside of his great basketball ability, he was an average guy. But, even after basketball was over for him, he could lead in political, economic, and social issues with the same passion and following. That's charisma. And I believe that I've got it. When it's time to take on a project, I can light the spark within and ignite those around me. Just like "Magic".

Why is a Drucker School MBA important to you?

Importance of a name vs. UCR

When I attended college for my undergraduate studies, my priority was to attend a school that I could afford. [University D] provided me with a reputable education and a full four-year scholarship. But [University D] was one of the lesser known of the [University System] campuses. I felt that it cost me some exposure to opportunities that might have been available if I attended a more prominent school. That's where Drucker comes in.

To me, Drucker has the name and national attention that I was not able to receive in my undergraduate years. In 2001, Drucker was ranked in the top 20 of MBA programs nationwide, in US News and Reports. The opportunity to have a MBA that means a lot to

Fortune 500 companies, combined with your Claremont, Ca. location, makes Drucker a very desirable place to be.

Small school—make a BIG impact

If you throw a rock in a lake, the ripples are not quite as large as if you were to throw a stone into a small pond. I believe the previous analogy suits the effect of a counselor, a professor, and especially, an active student, in a small school environment. Given the opportunity, I think that I could both impact, and be impacted, by an education here, at the Drucker School of Management. A smaller school gives all those included greater means for interaction and learning. Simply from comparing the information sessions I attended, Claremont appeared to care more about the quality of their students and the integrity of the management program.

Coming from a small school, such as [University D], I appreciate the extra time and effort campus faculty and staff had to offer. I realize I have grown far more than my counterparts that attended larger school systems, like [University E] or [University F]. I have learned that within a smaller school lies a great opportunity to participate in multiple organizations. But when participating in those organizations, it's not just attendance in meeting or paying dues. It is not large and non-productive. You can actually accomplish projects and make an impact in the community.

Not just a Drucker MBA, a CGU graduate degree

Here's the clincher for me. I am delighted that you are able to take courses at other schools within the Consortium of Graduate Studies. Business is a field that, I believe, encompasses all other areas of study. Psychology has always been a field of study I felt was important to further my understanding of human behavior. If I could better understand human behavior, I could then determine marketing strategy based on possible consumer behavior. By taking classes in psychology or economics, I feel I could gain a more global idea of marketing and strategy. My MBA would be enhanced by the chance to not only learn from Drucker, which is great in itself. But, I can also participate in seminars and courses within the entire Consortium.

Investment with a strong return

All in all, I would be an excellent candidate for the Drucker MBA program. I possess the drive, intensity, and endurance to withstand the rigors of a semester system at full speed. Community service and social integrity are, and will always be, very important to me. My MBA degree will be part of a long journey, full of people that taught me many great things.

The rest of my journey will be spent implanting my knowledge into others that can follow our lead of creating change in boardrooms and classrooms.

I want [my] focus [to] begin in marketing with product development at a consumer product corporation. Later, use that knowledge to help struggling Los Angeles areas in community development projects. For, I believe that the two areas deal with the same thought process just different outcomes. I want to motivate more corporations to invest in their communities to spark a chain reaction of social consciousness at the business level. I hope that Drucker is the school that can help me on my way.

CRITIQUE

The Drucker MBA Academic Committee found that this personal statement accurately portrays the "real" student, who has a personal approach. Since the Drucker Graduate School of Management offers a very personal approach to educating future ethical business leaders, it is important to create a mutually beneficial match between student and classroom, and to be able to gain a sense of an applicant in the personal statement—something that gives the "between-the-lines" type of information that cannot be obtained in an application for admission.

This student portrays his knowledge of the Drucker School and its ideals as well as how he will personally contribute and adapt to the culture of the school. Through abstract traits, the student defines what those qualities (leadership, attitude, creativity, sense of responsibility, big-picture concept, and charisma) mean in the world of business. He then elaborates further to explain how, through specific examples, he will contribute those qualities to make the classroom a well-fostered learning environment.

The Drucker MBA Academic Committee is interested in knowing what strengths and skills a student will bring to the classroom, as much of the Drucker curriculum is integrative and interactive among other students and faculty. It should also be noted that as an academic committee we strive to enroll students who will not only bring much to the classroom but also gain much from the classroom. This student gives a very clear picture that his admission into the MBA program would be mutually beneficial to himself and the Drucker School.

Additionally, through his response to the importance of a Drucker MBA, it is obvious that this student understands the value of brand recognition by acknowledging the name and reputation of the Drucker MBA. As an academic committee, we want students who will be proud of their efforts during MBA course work and who will take that pride into their leadership business roles. We want alumni who will support the school in more than monetary ways. Alumni can play key roles in public relations, recruitment, and overall advancement of the Drucker reputation. This student appears to understand that we are "A Different School of Thought," and he believes those differences will be worth the investment of his education.

Essay #2

Personal Statement: What special contributions do you believe you will bring to the Drucker School? Why is a Drucker School MBA important to you?

What do I bring to the Drucker School?

As an undergraduate, there was a schism between humanities and business majors. We were completely polarized into either the pre-professional group or the liberal arts group and the most common response to hearing that my major was Comparative Literature was the question, "What are you going to do with that?" Even then, I felt strongly that the pursuit of humanities was worthwhile because, through it, I learned about life and about people. I was introduced to interdisciplinary education through [University A's Honors Program], and then was drawn to an interdisciplinary major that emphasized critical thinking. It took some time working to really answer the looming question of what I was going to do with my degree. But, after a few years, I was able to make the connection between business and my humanities education and realize that it takes a good understanding of people, as well as an interest in them, to be a good manager and effective leader.

Another challenge of this system is that there is little regular employee evaluation, which is compounded by our president living in New York. I have taken a leadership role in addressing many of the human issues, from showing appreciation to employees and customers, suggesting actions to help employees grow and develop and mediating disputes, while trying not to violate our structure and philosophies to administering benefits. Recently, we completed a job at a university in Utah in which we applied our technology to a new market for the first time building a specialized lab for an electron microscope. The timeline demands and scheduling, plus the stress of the learning curve on a new project, created a dispute between two employees who happen to be brothers. One, uncharacteristically, left the job completely and came home early, while the other finished the job. When they each came to me to tell their side and get my support, I was able to listen and be empathic without taking sides, and then suggest that they think about what they could change to make to prevent the situation from reoccurring. I was happy with how I handled the situation, and how they handled it. They have made some adjustments for subsequent jobs and I have made some suggestions for each of their continued development.

I am very proud of the manager I have matured into over the last several years. In my early twenties, I believed that career advancement was best achieved by moving around every couple of years and trying new things. More recently I have come to believe that real personal growth is achieved more by staying and putting down roots, than by moving. In a sense both perspectives are valid. By moving around and trying different positions, I gained great technical skills and an understanding of many different industries and departments. By staying in a position that offered little external structure, I learned to motivate and manage myself and to build solid relationships. Ultimately, it is the combination of technical skills with personal skills that will determine my success as a manager. At this point in my life, I can say with confidence that I have developed both skill sets and am ready to pursue a degree in management.

Why a Drucker MBA?

My interest in a Drucker MBA originated from personal recommendations of people I have greatly respected. I had initially heard of the Claremont colleges in high school. The teachers and administration of the private academy I attended strongly advocated Claremont because of the personal attention and focus on teaching. Later, when working for [Company B], one of the managers who happened to be an alumnus encouraged me to consider the program. Most recently, I consulted my boss' wife who is an Executive Vice President of Strategic Technology at [Company C]. Of all of the schools I was considering, her strongest support went to the Drucker program. I found that especially surprising since she herself had earned her Executive MBA at [University D].

After I began researching the Drucker program for myself, I was drawn to interdisciplinary approach and the concept of business management as a liberal art. I believe the philosophies of the school closely fit my own, as I do not believe that business can be successful and ethical when isolated from the human elements. Quite early in my career, I went through layoffs with three different companies. One company distinguished itself in my mind by continuing to hire up until the day prior to the layoffs with no regard for the effect on the employees. Since then I have been fortunate to work at companies such as [Company B] that took great pride in their management skills and philosophy, even when faced with difficult decisions.

Because of my liberal arts background I feel much more at home with the Drucker Program than with some other programs I have investigated. Even through the application and information gathering process, the experience has been much more personal than with other schools. The core philosophy mixed with distinguished faculty and thoughtful support programs makes the Drucker MBA program very rich. Possibly the biggest point of differentiation, and thus the biggest attractor, is the focus on leadership and management. These skills are so absolutely timeless that whatever happens in the economy, whatever changes arise over the next twenty years, they will be excellent preparation. Accounting or marketing practices may change over time, new technology comparable to the internet may emerge, and the investment to acquire leadership and management skills will still have been well worth the investment.

CRITIQUE

The academic committee is able to gain a sense of the student's personality from this essay. It is critical for the Peter F. Drucker Graduate School of Management to enroll students who are pursuing an MBA for reasons greater than increased salary and career advancement. Because the Drucker MBA has a liberal arts approach to management, the school aims to graduate students who are socially responsible and have goals of becoming leaders and managers. The Drucker School is a school of management, not just business. The student who wrote this personal statement is clearly focused on becoming a better manager, not just advancing her career or salary.

This student comes from a nonbusiness academic background but has worked in business for ten years. With this type of background, the student can bring a different perspective to the classroom that will increase its diversity and perspective. She understands the importance of building business skills to complement her nonbusiness background. The academic committee also notes that this student has given very specific examples of goals she has set and of ways she has practiced her personal leadership skills. It is valuable that she realizes that rectifying the weaknesses in her technical skills can make her a better leader and manager. Thus, the classroom will lend itself to teaching those technical skills and will give opportunities for her to practice those skills. The Drucker MBA program is a highly integrated team atmosphere both inside and outside the classroom. This student shows that she works well in a team environment by giving specific examples.

Time management is a critical skill for part-time students who also work full-time. Based on personal examples of things this student manages in her career, we recognize that she can successfully handle the demands of working full-time while attending school part-time. Additionally, she explains her understanding of the Drucker School and why we are "A Different School of Thought." This is imperative because students who enroll in the Drucker MBA program need to understand that we educate future business managers and leaders. We take a different approach to education by providing a small, personal environment taught by world-renowned faculty. Students who understand and appreciate this approach reap incredible benefits from their Drucker MBA.

DARTMOUTH

TUCK SCHOOL OF BUSINESS

Note: The four Tuck essays included are each in response to this question. See page 44 for detailed information.

Question: Please respond fully but concisely to the following essay. Although there are no restrictions for the length of your response, most applicants use 1,000 words or fewer. Your response should be typed and double-spaced, with your name on each sheet. There is no right or wrong answer.

A well-known, multinational mining company has a long-term contract to extract precious metals in an impoverished region of a developing country. Over the past decade, the operation has proven very profitable to the company. Recently, there have been peaceful, but highly disruptive, protests by members of communities adjacent to the company's property. The ruling military dictatorship has been unresponsive in meeting the local communities' needs. The local communities are now demanding a share of the mining operation's profits in the form of approximately U.S. $8 million to provide clean water and basic sanitation for the surrounding villages.

You have recently been promoted and sent to this country as the expatriate general manager responsible for the operation. The mine is assessed U.S. $20 million in annual taxes by the local government. This year you will show a U.S. $50 million after-tax profit if you elect not to address the request of the local community. Your team has worked very hard this year. A U.S. $50 million profit is the minimum level to ensure that your team meets its bonus plan.

- *Provide an analysis of your options.*

- *Describe what you would do.*

- *Discuss the rationale for your choice.*

- *Address your plan to communicate with any constituent affected by your decision.*

Essay #1

"Argue for your limitations and they're yours."—Anonymous

A great leader possesses two indispensable traits: the ability to recognize his or her own limitations, and the ability to recognize the motivations and competencies of others that can help exceed these limitations. Coupled, these traits provide a powerful capacity for problem-solving. As the manager of a mining operation in a developing country, my problem-solving skills are now challenged.

MINING OPERATION—SITUATION ANALYSIS

Assumptions

To better define the parameters within which I am working, I make the following assumptions. My team is composed primarily of ex-patriates in management, with local citizens comprising the balance of the workforce. The bonus plan allows managerial participation only. The dictator is concerned with holding onto power, and maintaining his $20M tax revenue. We are nearing the end of the fiscal year; therefore, I can forecast that the $50M minimum profit will be achieved, if unforeseen costs are not incurred. Finally, the $8M demanded by the community has been confirmed as the amount required in order to meet their priority needs, which are, in fact, basic sanitation and clean water.

Business Strengths

The operation is productive enough to achieve $50M in after-tax profit this year, allowing us to benefit from the bonus plan, which enhances management's productivity incentive. Ties to the surrounding community exist through local employees. The government is a stakeholder via its tax revenue. My team possesses managerial and cultural experience specific to operating in this community.

Business Weaknesses

The community sees relatively little benefit from the operations of this profitable foreign corporation. This inequality, combined with government disinterest, has led to operational disruptions. The government is unconcerned with community needs, yet we pay $20M in annual taxes. The bonus does not benefit most local workers, hence, they have little productivity incentive. Although they represent a tie to the community, this is not currently leveraged. A lack of clean water and sanitation results in chronic illness amongst employees, detracting from productivity. Finally, the company lacks technical knowledge and experience in community development.

Opportunities

Several significant opportunities exist. Creation of a profit-sharing plan to include the local workers could create incentive and provide added economic benefit to the community. My company is also afforded the opportunity to exercise social leadership—by making a real difference in citizens' lives. This could conceivably increase productivity through improved employee health and morale. In addition, protecting the government's tax revenue could act as leverage to induce positive government action.

Threats

Protests grow in frequency and severity, disrupting business operations. Community illness continues to threaten productivity. Bad publicity surrounding the situation leads to poor employee morale and decreased value in the eyes of shareholders. A looming threat is the potential precedent set by paying the full $8M. In this scenario, the bonus plan goes untapped, and assuming full corporate responsibility leads to further demands, by the same communities, and by different ones—in my company and in others. My operation's potential profit would already have decreased by 16%. Similar events throughout my company and others would be financially unsustainable. It could present insurmountable obstacles to doing business in developing countries, that is, if limits are not set.

Resulting Elements of Plan

—Sustain and even increase productivity by:

- Rewarding management this year with the bonus.

- Creating a profit-sharing plan to provide added incentive for local workers (contingent on increased productivity and the resulting profits).

- Improving health and morale through community development efforts.

—Decrease the risk of further operational disruption.

—Share accountability for community development amongst different stakeholders, not solely the company.

A SUSTAINABLE SOLUTION

I propose a partnership of different parties that will share accountability for addressing community needs. A pilot program will be implemented, to identify and address the highest-priority need. The stakeholders in this program will be my operation, corporate headquarters, an NGO, and the government. The company will contribute funds, as will, if at all possible, the government. The NGO will provide technical expertise. My operation will aid in project management, in conjunction with community representatives and the NGO. The community will provide an in-kind labor contribution. In addition, a profit-sharing plan will be added for the employees, starting with the new budget cycle.

Importantly, the company's initial financial contribution should come from corporate, not the local branch. This is because the financial structure does not take into account these unforeseen costs, which are necessary to operate effectively in the country. A cost-benefit analysis should be provided, showing that this contribution can increase productivity and minimize costly risks such as operational disruptions, bad press, weak employee incentive, and poor morale—all of which lead to reduced operating margins. Another selling point is the publicity possible: our corporate collaboration with the social sector, working to improve lives in the communities in which we operate. This publicity could increase employee morale and shareholder value.

Corporate action takes time. The argument to decouple the "social costs" from the financial structure was made. If the change is not fast enough, my branch will provide the first installment for the pilot, from next year's budget. Any perceived time lapse will be made palatable to the community via the expansion of the bonus plan and through strong community engagement in planning for the pilot. Initial funds will also pay for NGO selection. Once identified, the NGO will be convinced to participate because of the benefit to the community, but also the unique partnership—an opportunity to tap into the private sector to accomplish its own goals.

My branch will act quickly on several fronts. Strong links to the community will be developed through local workers, who will act as community representatives, and help identify others from outside the company. Through these links the community will be engaged. With the NGO and branch management, they will prioritize what portion of the project should first be implemented and how. The sell to the community should be based on the fact that the pilot program is a necessary first step. The community will benefit from it and the proposed profit-sharing plan. If successful, further projects may be possible.

The government must be persuaded to provide partial funding. This should be presented as an opportunity to increase government popularity, e.g. security, and ensure its continued tax revenue. The story line: their lack of participation will make country operations increasingly difficult financially, and possibly unsustainable. Diplomacy (e.g. the local US ambassador) should be used to apply cautious pressure to the government using this stance.

In the long run, corporate can decide whether to expand the program. In this case, foundations and aid organizations could be contacted as potential donors. Implementing the pilot program gives corporate time to evaluate the issues, identify other donors, and reform the financial structure appropriately. Insight will be gained from the pilot, aiding their decision-making.

This collaboration creates value beyond what I alone could have created. Each constituency contributes different, but complementary abilities. Corporate social responsibility is acknowledged, but limited by sharing accountability with other parties. Profits are maximized by quelling operational disruptions, maintaining and expanding worker incentives, and creating strong employee and community morale.

CONCLUSION

The leaders of multinational corporations have the opportunity to enhance operations, and financial performance, by addressing social issues. Partnering with social-sector organizations can be an effective model for doing so. It is a way of exceeding corporations' own limitations and effecting positive social change. Those who do not address social concerns will increasingly find their financial concerns are at risk. Kofi Annan stated this eloquently, "Thriving markets and human security go hand in hand; without one, we will not have the other."

CRITIQUE

This essay presents a clear, thoughtful analysis of the situation, with a creative, compassionate, and mutually beneficial solution. This candidate's solution depicts a realistic situation of working with the corporate headquarters, a nongovernmental organization, the government, and local citizens. Throughout the essay, the candidate maintains a serious yet optimistic tone, often referring to the dilemma as an "opportunity."

ESSAY #2

My past experiences are surprisingly relevant in my analysis of this case. As a civil engineer, I am well aware of the importance of clean water and basic sanitation infrastructure. While on active duty with the U.S. Army, I worked as an officer in [Location A], [Location B] and [Location C] in positions that involved a significant amount of community interaction. In [Location A] I was an environmental advisor to the General responsible for all U.S. Army facilities. I managed environmental programs and responded to [Location A residents'] complaints about sewage runoff into local rivers, hazardous waste spills and leaking underground oil storage tanks. The U.S. Army hires many local civilians to supplement the active duty and U.S. civilian staff, so I received more than enough feedback from local sources. In [Location B], I worked as a construction equipment maintenance officer and frequently traveled to [City A, Location B] and [City B, Location B] to purchase repair parts, which taught me the importance of maintaining good relationships with local businesspeople. In [Location C] on a peacekeeping tour, I planned future road and bridge repairs, which were often restricted by U.S. policies forbidding nation building. Each repair project had to be justified by military patrol requirements rather than local community desires, although projects that met both needs were definitely the most rewarding.

As a student of cultural anthropology, I've studied the mechanics of societies, hierarchy of needs, issues of globalization and perceptions of wealth, poverty and happiness. Although specific cultural details in this case are not presented, a relativistic analysis of the situation would yield some explanations for the conflicting views of the mining company, the local community and the dictatorship, all of which are worth considering before making any decisions. And as a current resident of [Location D] and former resident of [Location E], I've become accustomed to living and thriving in multi-cultural environments.

The following are the potential courses of action I would consider as general manager of the mine. Some are mutually exclusive while others could be performed in unison. I've divided these courses of action into three categories: those involving the company directly, those focusing on the local people and those involving outside agencies.

Company Options

- Pay for the infrastructure work directly as an operating expense. Charging the $8M as a direct expense will only decrease bonuses by 10%, given a revised pre-tax profit of $62M, therefore the monetary impact is not as severe as it initially appears. This option will give me the most control over how the money is disbursed, who gets the construction contracts and how quickly the work is accomplished. Future profits should pay back the $5M expense many times over. Conversely, this action could lead to future community demands that are increasingly outrageous.

- An extreme option is to withhold $8M in taxes and use it to fund the local community's infrastructure projects. This will most certainly enrage the country's dictatorship with potentially dire consequences for the mine, but it may also force the country to re-evaluate how its citizens' needs are being met.

- Shut down the mine temporarily or even permanently. This option will demonstrate the mining company's resolve to avoid being subjected to extortion. The obvious disadvantage is that future potential profits will be forfeited. But the ethics of the company will not be comprised and the locals may decide to work with, rather than against, future multi-national entities.

People Options

- Coordinate a meeting between local community leaders and my management team. Listen to the local leaders first and consider their ideas, but also explain that it is not the company's direct responsibility to provide for all community needs. Past company leaders may have been ignoring community complaints for years so listening now may lead to a lessening of demands. A risk is that the locals may become more frustrated, disruptive or even violent.

- Increase the wages paid to local employees of the mine so they are well above the average local wages and establish a management-training program for the best local employees. Assuming a significant percentage of the mine's labor force are local nationals, this should help placate them by injecting more money into their community and by increasing opportunities for advancement. A disadvantage is that the increased labor costs may erode profits in both the short and long term.

- Institute a community partnership initiative. Beyond basic infrastructure— schools, police forces and small business enterprises could also be improved through the mine's support. Although this option is the most expensive, it would certainly reverse the public's sentiments and will help create a new generation of qualified and cooperative workers.

- Hire a civil affairs expert to work with the local media and press agencies. Although this may be considered propaganda to some, the local community has likely not been given enough relevant information about how the mine operates. This may help the disgruntled locals to consider why the mining company cannot be expected to provide for every need.

Outside Agency Options

- Assuming the mine is owned by a parent company in the United States, I could contact the U.S. Embassy to ask for assistance from organizations such as the U.S. Agency for International Development (USAID) or the State Department's Office of Commercial and Business Affairs. These organizations could exert pressure on the dictatorship to allocate a portion of the $20M in taxes to local community projects or may be able to obtain outside funding for these projects. The potential disadvantages are that embassy bureaucracy may prove to be too slow and the organizations may be restricted by political or policy constraints.

- Coordinate for the infrastructure upgrades through donations to a non-governmental organization (NGO). This will satisfy the community's needs, while providing oversight of the project by outside agencies. The collaboration of the for-profit mine and non-profit NGOs is a win-win situation for both. Sanitation and clean water directly impact the health of the local labor pool so this investment the community's health will also lead to increased future productivity.

- Contact the local military defense attaché to ask if any foreign military construction units would be interested in performing the construction work as a training exercise, which can often be done if financing is available for the project. This would bring in a foreign military presence and allow less of the $8M to be siphoned off by potentially corrupt local nationals.

After deliberation on the above options, I've decided to pursue the following four-step course of action:

1. Initially, I would avoid taking any action in response to the protests for as long as possible after my arrival at the company. Many newly appointed leaders decide to change procedures to demonstrate their authority before they are fully aware of the impact of these decisions. I would focus on reviewing all incoming and outgoing correspondence relating to the local community and would also meet with subordinate managers and the community leaders to determine the history of partnering between the mining company and the local community.

2. Since the mine has been operating for over ten years, I would evaluate the global market for the precious metals being mined and review the mine's ten-year plan for future production. Is this a high, low or average profit and revenue year for the mine? If the market looks grim and the productivity is declining, it may be a good time to suspend operations. I would also need to confirm that company bonuses do not represent a significant percentage of total compensation, because a 10% decrease in a bonus that is half of an employee's income is much more significant that a similar decrease in a bonus that represents only a quarter.

3. After gathering the above information, I would seek advice from the corporate level of the mining company, and advise them of my plans described in the next paragraph. As part of this action I would research all company, host country and international regulations that relate to this situation so I am aware of any legal constraints.

4. Assuming the above research does not yield any surprises, I would authorize the $8M infrastructure expenditure and charge it as an operating expense. The $70M profit would be reduced to $62M; the dictatorship will be paid only $17M in taxes while the mine keeps $45M in profit. Although the military and NGO construction options are valid, in this case, with disruptive protests occurring, I think these options would be too cumbersome. Therefore, I would hire a construction manager to supervise the construction contracts from within the company.

My constituents are the mine's employees, corporate executives, stockholders and directors. I would explain to them that my decision was based on thorough research and analysis of many alternatives. No company works in a vacuum, or can afford to focus solely on maximizing profits at the expense of the corporate reputation. A local population without clean water and sanitation infrastructure is not in the company's best interest, as the spread of disease will lead to decreased productivity locally with negative publicity impacts that are potentially far greater.

Bonuses are incentives that vary based on economic and social trends, and the performance of the company, but are rarely guaranteed. The biggest immediate concern for many employees will be the 10% decrease in bonuses, resulting in negative feedback and maybe even some resignations. Based on my analysis, a confrontational rather than cooperative solution to the protests would have resulted in a greater than 10% impact on future profits and bonuses. I would strive to make this clear to all constituents.

Depending on the actual success of the infrastructure improvements, I would also propose to the corporate marketing executives that our resolution of this problem be highlighted in future marketing campaigns to demonstrate the company's attention to human welfare issues. Similar campaigns by other companies have increased market share by adding intangible value to the companies' products.

CRITIQUE

This essay utilizes the candidate's skill and experience in engineering to develop a realistic, thorough, yet simple solution. The analysis demonstrates a careful and thoughtful consideration of the pros and cons of each action from the viewpoint of the various constituencies. The essay demonstrates a keen understanding of the writer's responsibilities, but doesn't downplay the needs of the locals, validating that they affect the company's success.

WHEN BAD ESSAYS HAPPEN TO GOOD PEOPLE

The following pages contain samples of real essays submitted to the Tuck School of Business that answer their killer long question. Sometimes it's easier to learn from one's mistakes. For that reason, two of the essays we offer you are poor examples of how to respond to this question.

ESSAY #3

Notes from the flight over:

- Analysis of my options.

Positive negotiating tools:
We have the Long-term contract as an asset.
Local government receives 20 million in taxes from mine.
Local workers comprise a meaningful percentage of local residents.

Undesirable issues:
Local communities want $8 million for clean water and basic sanitation.
Local communities protesting disruptively (assume that protests affect earnings).
Military dictatorship unresponsive to local community needs.

Option 1: Do nothing

Results: Company makes $50 million

              Team hits minimum level for bonus

              Locals still unsettled

Option 2: Bribe the Dictatorship

Actions: Pay the military to crush the protests

Results: Potentially improved profits (provided that new profits exceed bribe).

              Real problem still exists, but exacerbated by force.

              Dangerous precedent of graft.

Option 3: Negotiate w/ local gov't

Actions: Taxes aren't progressive, offer them a 1-time cut of profits above 50 mil. This would be in exchange for an up-front payment to community for water, along with a percentage of the taxes going to the community for water.

              Do some goodwill PR w/ the community (not related to the water). Keep the local government identified as the source of the clean water to avoid setting the precedent of having to pay for municipal improvements.

Results: If local govt and community play along, protests subside, and after-tax profits increase. Run the risk associated w/ the precedent of paying a higher tax rate.

What's an ex-pat GM to do?

Looking back, there was so much I didn't know at the time. Yes, of course I knew our business, and I earned my promotion. I was even fairly well versed in a pseudo-expatriate lifestyle. Still, it was a situation that required a good deal of metered guesswork, instinct if you will.

I was busy fighting my way up the chain of command in the States, and I ran into an obstacle. Nepotism can be a bitch. When you lose the opportunity for up, out starts to look pretty good. I started to fish around for opportunities elsewhere, and the board caught wind of my new direction. They slapped together this package for me, what I now refer to as the Heart of Darkness deal, and sent me on my way. Jumping to General Manager created a world of new challenges, and removed any permanent obstacles to internal ascension. The expatriate element of the deal even sounded sexy at the time.

I was on a plane with my family before I could research the new locale. I was told that my predecessor had left for personal reasons, and needed to be replaced immediately. I later determined that he had been too closely tied to the country's military dictatorship, and the board wanted him out. When I grabbed the reins, my division was finishing up Q3 and getting ready to head into the home stretch. They were on path to hit the $50 million minimum level for their bonus plan, but they had been working like dogs to get there.

Local communities had been peacefully protesting for the bulk of the year. Those protests reduced the number of able-bodied workers that we had in the mines, and restricted the daily flow of material. It was clear from the start that the division had been running at 110% of their normal efficiency in order to hit 85% of their financial goal (the minimum target for bonuses). If I would last as their GM, I would have to sweeten the pot—to reflect the work that they had been doing.

When I first analyzed the situation, I came to the following conclusions: On the positive side of the table we had a long-term contract on the land, and the local community depended heavily on us for their survival ($20 million in annual taxes, and jobs for a large percentage of the population). On the negative side we had the local community protesting for $8 million of spending in cleaner water and basic sanitation, and an unresponsive military dictatorship running the state.

On the plane flight over I hashed out three basic plans on how to approach the situation. The first and simplest idea was to stay the course. Without any change in direction, my division would hit the minimal level required to receive bonuses. The protests were of a peaceful nature, and it was unlikely that the protesters would attempt any form of local coup with the national, military dictatorship in place. While this approach was the simplest to accomplish (bearing in mind that I still had a division to run), it did nothing to address the limited bonuses that my employees would receive, or the quality of water and sanitation in the local community.

My second idea was really just a childish whim. It wouldn't take much to bribe the military dictatorship into crushing the local protests. Besides my own personal compunction against using force to quell peaceful protests, there was the slippery slope of providing graft to a military dictatorship. It was not an option. I mention it only because, as I later discovered, a similar idea was the cause of my predecessor's downfall.

After more serious thought, I came to the realization that I would never find incremental success with a company that was perceived as an outsider to the local community. While the vast majority of our workforce was comprised of local workers, very few locals were employed in managerial positions. This was a reflection of the dearth of college-educated people in the local community, but nonetheless branded us as a foreign operation.

I believe that intelligence thrives in many forms. While the local community did not have many citizens with the hard quantitative knowledge that I would need for group managers, I was certain that there would be a healthy selection of locals who could positively assist the division in relations with the community. I tasked the division's management team to find a handful of entrepreneurial and politically savvy workers, and hire them as cultural liaisons between the division and the community. At the time I didn't realize how critical this decision would be.

While I was waiting for my team to hire the new liaisons, I progressed onto what I thought would be the ultimate plan. The structure of our taxes to the local government was simple. The $20 million tax was a flat fee, levied as a form of lease payment for the land that we used. I presumed that I could dangle a progressive tax carrot in front of the local government to change the rules of the game a little. My plan was to ask the local government to front the $8 million needed to improve the water and sanitation for the local community. In exchange for that up payment, I would give them a healthy 10% cut of all after-tax profits in excess of $50 million until they received a total of $10 million. I intended to have our liaisons focus on improving the community's opinion of the company, while maintaining the view that the local government paid for the improvements. I didn't want to set the precedent of our division paying for capital improvements to the local community, for fear of an annual conscription being dedicated to that cause.

All I can say is; I am damn glad that we hired those liaisons before I put the preceding plan into action. I completely misjudged the characteristic of the local environment. My liaisons keyed me into a few pertinent facts. For starters, the local government did not have the $8 million to take care of the improvements that the community was requesting. Secondly, regardless of the wording of the deal, the local government would have balked if we started progressive tax payments one year and then tried to rescind those payments after the $10 million goal was reached. Finally, without having any association to the sanitary improvements, the local community's opinion of our company would not improve at all. I would have removed the temporary obstacle of the peaceful protests in exchange for higher taxes, and we would still be viewed as outsiders.

I spent a week trying to immerse myself in local culture and customs through lunches and dinners with our newly hired liaisons (time was short). While I didn't consider myself an expert on traditional rituals or history, after that week I had a much better appreciation for how our division could work in harmony with the local government and community.

The plan that we created went as follows: Our liaisons were personally connected with many officials in the local government. Through their personal relationships, we learned that the government would respond quickly to a public challenge to match funds for the sanitary improvements. Since the local government did not maintain surplus funds from taxation, the plan was to ask for matching funds in the form of a tax cut to the corporation. Our division would then spend the matched funds on local improvements (in the name of the government). While the liaisons assisted our PR department in crafting a local campaign to issue the challenge, I worked with our accountants to free up some assets to back the challenge.

The prior year's assessment of our physical plant had revealed that much of the capital equipment in our mining process was decades old. At the time, we used an archaic effluent treatment procedure to separate waste material from rocks potentially containing valuable ore. This outdated procedure was 70% slower than modern techniques, and dumped a considerable amount of silt into a local river. While the silt was harmless to humans, it had an aesthetically undesirable muddying affect. There was also the long-term issue of the silt collecting in the river near our plant. Every three years we would have to have the river dredged just so we could continue operations.

Replacing the old process with a modern solution would cost $20 million dollars and take several years to fully implement. No one in the chain of management that preceded me had a long-term commitment to this division, and therefore, they applied capital improvements to areas that would yield faster results.

With the end of the year rapidly approaching, I realized that we could publicly commit to this capital improvement without booking any of the charges to the current fiscal year. By tying this capital improvement to the fund-matching challenge, we could get the local government to free up some of our tax money for other sanitary improvements. Best of all, the investment would increase our productivity, and the amortized cost could be spread out over a 10 year period.

Our liaisons helped us to design a powerful publicity campaign to chide the local government into the fund-matching plan. The liaisons knew the right tone to take with each local medium (e.g. TV, radio, newspapers, and community meetings). Within an extremely short period of time, the local government was making counter proposals publicly to call our bluff. The timing was perfect, as we had just received approval for the new effluent treatment plan. The rest is history. We presented the new effluent treatment plan to the public, and the government followed through with the matched funds (in the form of a tax cut).

The protest quickly subsided. My division was able to pull their numbers up to 92% of goal, which resulted in a healthy increase in bonuses. Within three years, the new process was fully implemented and the group was running a full 30% more efficiently than with the old process. Our relationship with the local community and government improved dramatically. We had created a precedent for reduced taxes and community improvements. Since such a large percentage of the local community worked for us, it was often possible to find ways to improve our infrastructure while benefiting the community. In the end, we had a more profitable and more stable division simply by becoming better integrated with the local community.

Of course now that everything is running smoothly I am starting to look for new places to grow. My kids are getting old enough that I want to bring them back to the States for school, and my success here has opened up some new opportunities at the head-office. I will probably move on to a new post soon. Looking back, I see what a great learning experience working in this environment was. I hope that whatever path my life follows next will prove at least as challenging.

CRITIQUE

I read this essay and wondered if it was a joke. The essay attempts to craft the answer in a fictional narrative, but instead depicts the writer as insensitive and thoughtless—the antithesis of the characteristics that Tuck is seeking. The fact that this candidate mentions "pay the military to crush the protests" as a potential option offers a window of insight into his character. Other tongue-in-cheek, colloquial expressions such as "nepotism can be a bitch," "sweeten the pot," and "call our bluff" are apparently meant to be humorous, but instead depict the applicant as immature—somewhere between not serious and ridiculous. This candidate's solution for the mining dilemma is based on forming a liaison with the local government to "chide the local government into the fund-matching plan"—not a very realistic or creative solution, and one that shifts the negotiations from the GM to the liaison. The essay concludes with the message that now that the problem is solved, he will be moving on, likely back to the United States and a new, advanced post. Throughout his essay, this potential candidate presents himself as not serious, vulgar, flip, arrogant, and uncommitted.

ESSAY #4

Business leaders often come across different situations with an ethical dilemma being involved. Successful leader should be able to find or to create a new choice not obvious at first sight. Besides, leader should consider ethics as a part of the equation, as an aspect of the management process.

First of all, we should identify the stakeholders. They are my team, local communities, ruling dictatorship and my company shareholders. My ultimate goal is to find an ethical and mutually beneficial solution.

In general, I see the three variants of possible action:

My first variant is to address the needs of local community by giving the money required for satisfying their needs. In this case I'm giving up the interests of my team. In fact, our excellent results this year became possible only due to our team spirit and emotional momentum built. In other words, I should do my best to satisfy my team. In fact, an esprit de corps is at stake. Besides, there is a great risk that talented employees left without appropriate incentives will leave the company for job that pays better probably in another country. This in its turn will lead to lower profits next year.

The second variant is to ignore the interests of local community and pay the bonuses to the team. But our business cannot exist without local community that is the source of workforce for the company. Moreover, our company is the part of local social environment. Ignorance of the local needs will break the harmony of our business "ecosystem." Tension will grow and our operations will become less efficient or even impossible as a result.

My third option is to decline the tax imposed by the government or to dispute the amount to be paid. However, these solutions may turn out to be dangerous both for me and for the company's property. In this case, the ruling military dictatorship is likely either to cancel the contract or to hamper the progress of our business.

To make the right decision and elaborate an action plan as well as plan of communication with all parties involved, let us consider all pros and cons.

It is usually very difficult to change the rules of team compensation in a large multi-national company. For instance, [Company A] in Russia alone profits more than U.S. $50 million per year, which is less than 1% of the company's total net profit. Certainly, nobody will change the corporate compensation policy if local team doesn't meet the goal. Having U.S. $8 million paid to communities, I can try to save the team bonus but company management will hardly compromise with me. Though there is a small probability of such an outcome. Anyway, there are two options: either team receives bonus or not. Keeping in mind my strategy to avoid dilemmas, I have to retain the profit level required for the bonus to be paid. If all this fails and my efforts turn out to be in vain, I will resort to the company's management so that the problem could be approached as an exception to the company's rules.

With just bare figures in mind, not paying money for the local needs looks very attractive. In Russia for instance, corporate management style today is far from ethical. As recently as two or three years ago there was a miner's camp in front of Russian Government House. In such a way mines workers protested against delays in wage payments which exceeded twelve month. This particular example shows that ethical dilemmas in Russia are often being resolved not in favor of ethics. Being a well-educated and intelligent person I understand very well that such social unconsciousness is one of the main problems of developing Russia. I don't want to seem cynical, but probably being ethical pays back and no doubt gives chance to sleep better. That's why I need to do my best to satisfy the demands of local community because that's my duty as a member of prospering society.

Turning back to our problem, I want to emphasize that there are lots of ways to be socially conscious without paying U.S.$8 million right now. People have been waiting for help for a long time why won't they wait for one more quarter? The good idea is negotiating with community leaders the donations plan that will assume not lump, but monthly or quarterly payments effective from the next quarter. Acting this way I'm securing my team bonuses and achieve ethical balance and harmony in the business "ecosystem." At the same time it is crucial to persuade management and shareholders that local communities should be supported to provide an effective business process of an enterprise.

To rebel against draconian taxes is not as absurdly as it may seem at first sight. Actually it is the local authorities that should take care of the people. I don't want to say that tax should not be paid, but it is necessary to discuss the purposes of the subsequent spending of the money collected. In fact, such close interaction with the government should be a part of our integration into the local social life. Being a part of the area infrastructure that gives jobs and contributes to the country's budget we have the right to influence the funds allocation. In developed countries this right is usually exercised by lobbying but under military dictatorship the only way to do this is to make a deal with the dictator.

Satisfying the local needs by the government is the most desired outcome. We have killing argument to use in our speech: we can raise the dictatorship's reputation. All we have to do is to declare that the dictatorship demonstrates exemplary social consciousness with respect to its people. This declaration will be heard as we have an authority recognized in the World community.

To summarize all said above, I see the following action plan:

First of all, I'll try to convince the government to take financial responsibility for local demands using the arguments discussed. Partial compensation of local needs is also good deal because it'll give us time—at least couple of quarters. If it fails, I will resort to the second step.

The second step is negotiation with local leaders aiming at postponing of our financial help. I can also propose different "indirect" compensations for local community. I can create more jobs for local people by opening new departments, for instance, local company for our mining machinery services. I can found joined committee for local area development that will be financed not only by our company but also by the government, and different international funds. I can implement new technologies of water and air purification for the region using the experience of our other branches worldwide.

If all this doesn't work, I'll try to obtain the bonus from the company on exceptional basis assuming that we are giving the money to satisfy the demands of the society.

After all, if all my efforts are in vain I'll pay the bonus to my team because first of all I'm the leader of the team and its normal functioning is my responsibility given by my management and shareholders.

Critique

This essay suffers from a host of problems. The candidate demonstrates an unrealistic assessment of the situation and his abilities. If the writer's initial plan, which involves delay tactics, doesn't work, he states, "I'll pay the bonus to my team." Statements such as "keeping in mind my strategy to avoid dilemmas," "not paying money for the local needs looks very attractive," "probably being ethical pays back and no doubt gives chance to sleep better," and "People have been waiting for help for a long time why won't they wait for one more quarter?" present a character who is incapable of solving problems, unethical, and insensitive.

Massachusetts Institute of Technology

of Technology

Sloan School of Management

Essay #1

Question: Please give us an example of when you exhibited creativity in a personal or professional setting. Please describe your thoughts and actions. (500-800 words)

"We have a perceptual problem around efficacy," said the packaged goods company president. It was my first day on a new assignment for their hair thickening product, and he was explaining that their launch had been followed by a year of flat sales. "Although the product has clinically-proven efficacy, centuries of snake oil salesmen have created incredible skepticism in the market." His challenge: redefine efficacy to distance ourselves from "potions and lotions" and increase market share.

After a month of brainstorming ways to convey efficacy, we conducted one-on-one interviews to test our ideas. Man after blading man expressed angst over his hair problems, but none of them had done anything more advanced than the combover. "You see, we need to convince them there's a product good enough to warrant doing something," the president said.

I was not convinced. The more we tweaked the message to stress clinical efficacy, the more we had to caveat it to satisfy the FDA; the more we touted real results, the more we sounded like a late-night Infomercial. In my mind, we were just undermining our own efficacy message. We needed to find another angle to attack this problem.

While the client continued testing messages, I took a week to reflect and explore. Looking for insights, I studied [Company A]'s success, learned the psychology of plastic surgery, and read a history of hair color marketing in *The New Yorker*. It was in the article that I found an inspiration, for it described how [Company B] refocused its marketing on emotional rather than physical benefits—hence the tag line "Why? Because I'm worth it!" Reflecting on this example, it occurred to me that perhaps we were focused too much on what was going on top of men's heads, and not enough on what was going on inside them.

Curious to explore this further, I recruited a psychologist specializing in body image to review the interview transcripts with me at my office. What we uncovered was surprising— almost all men have high levels of concern when they first notice their hair thinning. However, over a short period of time, their concern fades due to internal acceptance, external reinforcement of worth ("honey, I love you just the way you are"), and general aversion to appearing vain. As a result, most men are resigned to their fate before they have time to do any serious exploration of options.

With this information, I reframed the question from "how do we redefine efficacy" to "how do we get men to act before apathy sets in." To answer this question, I used existing research to develop a quantitative, visual description of how men flow through the entire decision process. Along with the decision steps, I showed the most frequently mentioned reinforcers or blockers of action at each step in the process.

Although this system dynamics approach is typically used for complicated industrial problems, it was perfect for this puzzle. First, it made it simple to see the apathy cycle we had identified. Second, it highlighted that men who broke the cycle most often did so because of the encouragement of a friend, not the existence of effective products. Third, it showed that the overwhelming benefit to men who had acted was a sense of control—regrowing hair was an aspiration, but taking control was their inspiration.

These findings suggested three important steps. First, we had to reach men before they became apathetic. Second, we had to assure them it was "normal" to do something about hair thinning. And third, we had to emphasize that taking action was taking control. To bastardize [Company B]—"Why? Because it beats sitting back like a defeated old man!"

When I shared this new interpretation with the president, he understood my earlier skepticism of the efficacy dilemma. Within two months we replaced the efficacy-focused advertising with a new campaign emphasizing the importance of acting early to treat thinning hair, and the associated feeling of control it creates. In addition, we adjusted our media purchases to hit younger men who were early in the recognition to resignation cycle. Finally, we developed a program encouraging existing users to share their experiences with friends.

Through creative approaches to the problem, I drove significant change. At a product level, within a year sales grew by 18% and the average customer age dropped from 33 to 28— a good indicator that we were driving men to act sooner. At a company level, I introduced new tools and disciplines which have been successfully applied to other tough marketing problems. And at a societal level, I helped thousands of men find a better hairstyle than the combover!

CRITIQUE

This one was fun to read and is a great example of working smarter, not harder. The student's task seemed like a typical consulting engagement, but he was able to look at an old problem with new eyes. As he phrased it, he "reframed the question."

Creativity is often thought of as a moment of inspiration; in this case, the candidate accompanied that moment with some impressive follow-through. He hired the right kinds of experts, modeled the decision process of the customer, and adjusted strategy based on his findings. Intuitive leaps are important, but so too is the ability to implement, and this student showed both. Wouldn't you want him on your team?

Essay #2

Question: Please describe an impact you have had on a group or organization.

I joined the Board of Directors of [Company A] in 2001 for a two-year term. [Company A] is a non-profit treatment, education and research center that provides traditional Chinese medicine health care to approximately 700 people each month. Most of the center's clients are low-income or homeless and suffer from life-threatening illnesses such as Hepatitis C, HIV, AIDS—and Cancer. The medical attention that people receive at [Company A] supplements the traditional treatments they receive and allays the severe side effects that accompany such treatments.

When I joined, [Company A] was in a dire financial situation. California's budget for AIDS research had been slashed and the public funding that had provided 45% of the organization's budget in 2000 would only cover 20% in 2001, at the same level of operation.

As a Board member, I focused on development, with the goal of ensuring the organization's long-term success. My first action was to identify and cultivate individuals and foundations capable and likely of meeting the organization's operating expenses in the short-term. After developing a list of potential investors and in collaboration with the Executive Director and founder, I developed a three-year $400,000 proposal to the California Endowment to fund ongoing initiatives.

As is the case with many community-based nonprofit organizations, the staff and board at [Company A] were unaccustomed to tailoring a pitch for their programs and had an opportunistic approach to fundraising. They had never had the bandwidth to aggressively seek funding and were unable to communicate about their work with people who weren't already familiar with Chinese medicine. With little background in the subject, I was especially sensitive to this tendency and set out to remedy it. I led an informal media and communications training for the Board to help them craft the pitch for their work and develop the proposal for [Endowment A]. The training I conducted generated incredible momentum around fundraising and jumpstarted the Board of Directors. If the proposal we developed is approved, this funding will support [Company A] after my term has expired. I f not, the process of developing a pitch and creatively raising funds will still have sparked action on the part of Board members who had long since stagnated in their roles.

At each Board meeting, I update the Board on fundraising progress and lobby for a stronger focus on fund development in this difficult economic climate. Ancillary conversations with individual Board members have ensued and I finally am seeing the results. Raising funds has become a focus for the board and long-term funding strategy has become a reality during my tenure. Since I've given them communication tools and encouragement, the Board has taken on aspects of fundraising from which they had previously shied away. Surprisingly enough, the work has become more fun as well—we have rallied around the common goal of raising money for [Company A]'s important work. In this situation, I am most proud of the fact that my impact is going beyond the immediate task at hand and is actually affecting behavioral change.

My work has also led to bringing back to life a nascent Cancer support program. The staff at [Company A] had never developed a long-term project with measurable impacts and needed guidance in order to sustain a fledgling program. I coached the Executive Director, presented a strategy to the Board, and created a map for a program that now serves cancer survivors in two low-income San Francisco neighborhoods, Bayview and the Mission, where residents have some of the highest rates of Cancer in California and the lowest rates of health care access. To date, the program has served almost 100 people and is receiving significant recognition and support from the Western medical community.

With state funding evaporating and demand for services skyrocketing, [Company A] still is in a difficult situation. I believe that strategically raising funds and developing programs are critical to surviving this challenging time and I've made it my mandate to communicate these priorities to the Board of Directors. Despite the fact that I only recently joined the Board and that my experience with Chinese medicine is minimal, I've succeeded in making the organization more financially viable and effectively managed.

CRITIQUE

This essay is a wonderful example of how people can highlight leadership and organizational skills outside their work environment. So often, applicants think of community service as a box to be checked rather than a chance to really show their stuff.

It's clear in this essay that the applicant cares deeply about the work of the group, but she doesn't spend a lot of time just talking about that; she takes us through a compelling situation and describes how her actions had an impact. We always ask ourselves, Would this situation have turned out differently if the applicant wasn't there? The answer in this case is an obvious yes. She also does a very good job of focusing on the context of the situation—the challenges faced by the organization, the ambiguity inherent in cross-cultural situations—without being accusatory. This is impressive.

I'd ask all applicants to look at how succinctly this candidate describes the situation and how much time she devotes to articulating her process. Our job as admissions officers is to search for the "how" behind the "what," and this student made the "how" very clear. You can easily imagine her leading another organization to enhanced success.

Rutgers—The State University of New Jersey,

Rutgers Business School

Essay #1

Question: Describe an ethical dilemma and how you resolved it.

Within the past year I faced a situation where I had to quickly decide whether to compromise my ethics to aid my company in its attempt to win a much-coveted new business pitch. My decision not only impacted me, but also my colleagues, and could, quite possibly, have impacted my company's reputation and revenue.

An understanding of the context and pressures involved best sets the stage for my quandary. My healthcare communications company performs project-based services for pharmaceutical clients. As such, we often participate in new business pitches where our team will present our thinking, strategies, and concepts to the potential client with the goal of winning the business. Preparation for these pitches is intense, involving many hours spent researching the product and its market, analyzing the competitive landscape and unique product issues, brainstorming strategies and tactics to meet the identified needs, crafting creative concepts, and rehearsing for the presentation itself. All the above are typically done within two weeks leading to a one- to two-hour pitch. In essence, a pitch is a high-intensity event where my team is challenged to create the most innovative solutions and present in a way that wows the client, outclasses the competition, and secures additional income for the company.

I discovered competitive intelligence at a pitch purely by chance. While the client took a break and we set up in the room, I discovered our two competitors' pitch binders on a chair. Pitch binders traditionally include a company's strategies, tactics, and, more importantly, a proposed budget for the client's consideration. Herein lay my dilemma.

My quandary was this: should I a) quickly peruse the competitors' pitch binders, allowing me to then tailor my own team's presentation, thereby gaining a competitive advantage, or b) leave the binders untouched, ignore the opportunity availed, and trust in my team's strengths to win the pitch and beat the competition? With my colleagues shortly aware of what caught my attention, the temptation and pressure to peruse the competitive binders heightened.

I faced a dilemma in a situation that did not afford lengthy consideration. I had to make a firm decision quickly and convince my colleagues of the ethics of the decision, whichever path I chose. In the end, I determined to act upon my basic instinct that it was unfair and ethically wrong for my team to review the competitors' pitch materials. I made a decision I was ethically comfortable with and my faith in our capabilities and strategies for the client won over the temptation of an easy assist. With my internal ethical conflict decided, how then to convince my colleagues not to peruse the binders themselves?

My next challenge was to state my own personal stance and call upon the ethics of my teammates to make similar decisions. Not only was I one of six presenters, but I was also not the most senior individual. My superior could have made a different decision, which would carry more weight and sway my colleagues. I therefore determined to convince my superior of the merits of my decision to create a strong voice with the team. By acknowledging the temptation, yet clearly stating my thought process and the questionable ethics, I successfully convinced my superior and the rest of the team followed our lead and concurred. I left the binders where I found them, reassured the team that we could and would win the pitch unaided, and proceeded with the presentation as planned when the client returned.

In the end, my team prevailed in winning the business—without the assistance of a peek at the competitions' materials. I have never questioned my decision, and aspire to adhere to my ethics in the future as well as I did in this situation. Had we not won the business, I would still be confident that my actions and those of my team were both ethical and fair.

CRITIQUE

The Rutgers Business School graduate admission process does not, in general, require an interview. Therefore, the essay takes on an even greater importance by providing the admissions committee with the opportunity to obtain a sense of the applicant's writing and critical thinking skills. At the same time, it offers the applicant an opportunity to showcase those talents.

The term "business ethics" was once considered an oxymoron. In today's business environment the exact opposite is true, and companies, as well as graduate programs, are looking for individuals with strong ethical and moral character. Our essay topic is by choice very broad. We are looking for not only the identification of the ethical dilemma, but also the candidate's reasons for choosing this particular example and the resolution of the problem.

The candidate in this example faced the age-old dilemma regarding the potential acquisition of competitive intelligence. In business, does the end always justify the means? Is winning the only important criterion, regardless of the cost? Clearly, for this individual, the answer was no. In making that decision, she also exhibited a strong faith in her product, her company, and the presentation skills of her colleagues and herself. This is particularly important to our program, which demands team presentations and cooperative efforts throughout the MBA.

The applicant also offered a glimpse into her leadership skills, another area that we consider important in the review process. After making her own decision as to the proper way to proceed, she also had to convince her senior colleague and the rest of her team to follow suit. This took courage and conviction, strengths that will serve her well in our rigorous program.

We also evaluate the writing skills of the candidate. Business communication is an important skill and a required element of our MBA program. This individual wrote succinctly and on-topic without overembellishment, abilities that will be appreciated by both professors and employers.

ESSAY #2

Question: Describe an ethical dilemma and how you resolved it.

One of the first lessons I learned as a consultant is to maintain the integrity of the client-consultant relationship. The relationship is a fragile one, with the client revealing the inner workings of their operations, politics, and strategies to perfect strangers. While client confidentiality rules are most times clear cut, maintaining client integrity becomes a bit more complex when the client is your own firm.

Upon graduation from [College A] in 1998, I sought to apply my economics degree and math minor in a challenging business position. I accepted a position at [Company B]'s Economic Analysis Group (EAG) in [Location C], the global headquarters for [Company B]'s transfer pricing practice. Transfer pricing is the economic principle that exploits differences in global corporate tax rates to maximize profit within multinational corporations. My role as a research analyst was to assist in justifying the prices charged across borders among subsidiaries of large multinationals and maximizing global corporate profits within the rules of global tax laws.

The EAG was a relatively small group by [Company B]'s standards, and communication was very open among the 40 professionals. It was tradition to circle the large boardroom table every Friday morning during staff meetings to share tales of complex transfer pricing issues. Most managers and partners paid little attention to the analysts as they described their projects. Six months into my tenure, however, the managers and partners began to look up from their scribbles and notes and pay close attention when it came my turn to speak. They all knew that I had been assigned a highly sensitive and "secret" project—one that directly affected their compensation.

I joined [Company B] at an interesting time in the firm's history. [Company B] and [Company D] had already announced their split, but the corporate divorce had only recently made it into arbitration. [Company B] was looking to get as much money as possible for grooming [Company D] into the firm that it had become. I became part of that unique firm history when I was assigned my most delicate project—valuing the historic split between [Company B] and [Company D].

The project itself was not much different than other transfer pricing studies that I had performed. What was different, however, was the secretive nature of the assignment. Only one manager and I knew the details of the engagement in the [Location C] office. I was instructed by the legal department in [Location E] not to discuss the matter with anyone, especially the partners within the firm.

The [Company B] partners had a personal interest in the outcome of the split. One global partner in particular, [John], was extremely interested in the effect of my research on his compensation. I had worked with [John] on multiple projects before, and by nature he was a challenging and persistent individual. During informal meetings in his office for client work he would make a passing joke or question about my secret research. For the most part these comments were easy to brush off. That all changed, however, once we left the office for a client trip.

Soon after I was assigned to the [Company B] split, I was asked to go on a client visit with [John]. Our goal was to visit the headquarters of a new client, a pharmaceutical delivery systems manufacturer in [Location F]. The client's transfer pricing issues were challenging and included valuing and shifting ownership of their intellectual property to a lower tax jurisdiction in [Location G]. This was my first on-site client trip and our goal was merely to collect facts from top management as we started the valuation process.

The train ride to [Location F] was pleasant enough. We conducted our business at the client and the interviews went extremely well. [John] even complimented me on how prepared I was and how I handled myself. Halfway through the trip home, however, [John] cornered me on the firm split, directly asking me about the details of my special research. My face turned bright red and my stomach dropped.

I initially ignored his question and tried to change the subject. He persisted and asked me to be a "team player". I responded firmly, "[John], I am not allowed to divulge client information ever, regardless of whom the client is. You know that. If you have any specific questions about this research, please ask [Mike] (the director of the tax practice in [Location B])." He was a bit stunned, but sat back and was quiet the rest of the way home.

I was nervous about how terse I had been with a partner. I was still relatively new to the firm and was already working with [John] on several projects. Upon my return, I spoke with the manager whom I was working with on the split. She shared with me [John]'s persistence in questioning her on the same issues. She commended me on my response and told me not to worry about [John]. Her counsel turned out to be true. [John] didn't get any easier to work with, but he did cease the constant pestering regarding my research on the split.

Looking back, I am proud of how I handled myself in that difficult situation. I set my own ethical precedent that integrity is essential in my professional life. Overall, this challenge has helped me mature and develop strong interpersonal skills in difficult business situations. I continue to build on this lesson in my interactions with clients and internal consulting teams.

CRITIQUE

The essay often plays a key role in the application review process. Applicants have the opportunity to showcase their skills in both writing and critical thinking. A well-written, well-conceived essay that both stays on point and offers a unique story can clearly enhance the applicant's potential for an offer of admission.

Our essay topic asks the candidate to define "ethical" from his or her own perspective; determine whether a particular incident or experience was, in fact, a dilemma; describe the thought processes that were used in resolving the issue; and identify that final solution.

The applicant in this example was faced with a number of challenges and articulated them very well. He was young and relatively inexperienced when this incident took place. However, despite his youth, he was in a position of access to sensitive, confidential information that was desired and of great personal importance to more senior members of his firm who could have a direct impact upon his future with the company. Should he use his newly found "chip" to better his own position and cross the ethical line, or should he maintain his own level of ethical behavior and risk a professional backlash?

In a concise, well-written, thoughtful essay, this candidate clearly described the thought processes he utilized in making his decision and the options that he considered. The ethical boundaries that the applicant maintained in a challenging situation identified him as the type of individual who would be a very successful MBA candidate and the type of future business leader needed in these uncertain times.

Essay #3

Question: Please submit an essay describing what you learned from your experience as a member of a team whose project was not completed successfully.

I took the job of Chief Technology Officer with a growing investment firm, as opposed to one that is fully established, in order to take part in the design of the business. With the company in its nascent stages, many processes were still developing, and my newest undertaking was no different. My task was to design an efficient procedure for creating "Wealth Plans." These plans are the trademark of the firm, and remain its best sales tool. At that time, however, they took up to a month to prepare, and each one was different in content and design. These factors made the recognition factor negligible at best, and made the design a start-from-scratch process with the commencement of each and every plan.

Having seen these plans convince clients that our firm was their best choice, I recognized the value of their prompt and thorough completion. These plans are expansive; covering everything from the clients' investment profiles to their tax and insurance needs, and the majority of developmental delays stemmed from a lack of organization and permanent design within these modules. I would take the best parts from all previous plans, put them together in an intelligent format, and streamline the process. Looking back, it seemed simple at the time.

Originally, I had started the project on my own, and, quickly, I realized that my skills alone would not suffice. My talents as Chief Technology Officer were up to the task of programming and spreadsheet design, but I learned that expertise is not valuable in a vacuum. Without assistance from other professionals, the plans would be quite lacking in terms of content outside of my proficiency. If each module had been complete, my earlier assumptions of fast closure would have been justified. Unfortunately, not only the content as a whole differed in each instance, but the actual formulas and design of individual modules changed almost randomly from plan to plan, as well. I noted the content and flaws of each module, prepared a summary and an action plan, and took them to my supervisor.

We assembled a team consisting of a CPA, a portfolio manager, an MBA, and me (a Microsoft Certified Systems Engineer) for the task of establishing plan design and protocol. Our first meeting produced a schedule for completion, an outline of what we thought would be appropriate content for each module, and the decision that would ensure our failure—our steadfast focus on function over form. By concentrating fully on the function of the plans, we ignored the pitfall of oversophistication that would have frustrated most clients.

We progressed quickly as the members contributed individually to the overall proposal and directed the design of any modules that fell under their bailiwick. As the technology guru, it was my duty to translate the ideas and needs of each section into workable spreadsheets and programs. Though intricate in design, each instance would be simple to complete and identical in order and design to the plans of other clients. While recommendations and exceptions would always be unique to a specific client's situation, the majority of the plan now only required simple data entry on the part of our employees.

With the finished program loaded on our server, we were ready to present our accomplishment. However, wanting to recoup time spent in development of this project, we decided to take it directly to our firm's sales team for use. Upon completion of the first plan (finished in five hours instead of a month), I had been ready to celebrate our success amid smiles and a few free beers. To our surprise, we were met with the sales team's look of confusion.

We failed to remember that these plans are first and foremost a sales tool. The plan itself was flawless, and we showed everyone the amazing leaps in creativity and utility that had been made. But, unless you had been working on it for a month with the experts who devised each module, I truly doubt you would be able to comprehend it. To the sales team, this was 20–30 pages of overly analytical, unnecessarily complicated material that would confuse our clients instead of closing deals. We had developed the plan with our own needs in mind and had ignored its true audience.

Stepping outside of the confines of a project, job, or even an industry is essential to true progress and a proper perspective. The sales team and I spent another two weeks enlarging the fonts, rewording jargon, and adding a bouquet of colorful graphs. We ended up with a plan that was just as technical, but far more suitable to our clients. I had thought our progress and teamwork to be remarkable, and, if we had originally focused them in the right direction, they would have been. While I learned that you need to keep your audience in mind at every step, another important lesson was that of goal setting.

We started with the objective of streamlining the production of plans. In hindsight, it would have been more intelligent to first finalize the design of the plans in terms of their end goal—bringing in new clients. Intelligent people who are willing to work hard and well are not enough to ensure success. Without a solidly thought out purpose, long term setbacks increase, and, without leadership, that purpose cannot be determined.

CRITIQUE

Identification of a successfully designed and implemented plan or project is generally simple for the business professional, faculty member, current student, or hopeful applicant. However, such a task can be difficult when asked to identify an experience that did not conclude as intended.

This essay question demands honesty and introspection. It also gives members of the admissions committee an opportunity to evaluate the applicant's attitude toward working on teams, an important component of the Rutgers Business School MBA program.

In a very readable and well-written essay, this candidate gives readers the opportunity to follow him as he assessed a new project, attempted to complete it on his own, and then realized the need to form a team of experts in order to bring the project to conclusion. We are then made aware of the steps that the members of this group took as they reviewed their new assignment, made preliminary evaluations, implemented action plans, and presented their results.

Throughout the essay, the applicant honestly points to errors in thought and process that ultimately lead to the initial lack of success. More importantly, he clearly identifies the new learning that took place and how it was immediately used to redesign the project and meet the needs of the populations for whom it was intended.

The admissions committee believes that the willingness to admit error, learn from initial mistakes, and take corrective actions, along with the critical thinking that also took place, are traits that will assist this candidate throughout the demanding MBA program.

TULANE UNIVERSITY

A. B. FREEMAN SCHOOL OF BUSINESS

FROM THE SCHOOL

"A great essay? Much like a great MBA candidate, a great essay is the right combination of excitement, interest, knowledge, focus, and ability. Essays are but one window into the person that will walk the halls of the business school for a couple of years and wear the distinction of being a Tulane alumnus for life.

"The Freeman School at Tulane is a very special place. Consequently, we are not looking for well-rounded candidates; we look for unique people that have special abilities. Here a group of about 100 students are divided into teams providing international representation from several geographies, different economic and political hemispheres, and different academic arenas. The interaction between these groups, combined with the academic challenge, is the foundation to the Freeman MBA. It is a core experience that will change the way in which one views the world.

"The Tulane MBA is all about changing the student's worldview, while equipping the individual to make decisions. Tulane students start the MBA program by learning great interaction and trusting skills.

"Tulane's team structure, in an intensive core program, builds on the diversity presented in the MBA class to shape a unique MBA experience. I bring up this point because it is insight into how one can deal with other people, cultures, and ideas that the most recent Freeman School essay considers:

> *Describe one person that has made a profound impact on your life. What skills did that person possess? How did others react to this person? What has been the outcome of your experience with this person?*

"This is not your typical 'tell me about yourself' question. We enjoy a lot of information about the applicant including resume, references, and transcripts. Frankly, we could probably tell applicants a lot about themselves that they don't know. However, the point of an admission application is to assure that you will benefit from the experience and that the group (peers) will benefit from your presence.

"We look for an applicant that can learn from the experience of another. Central to learning from another individual is the ability to recognize strengths, skills, and weaknesses. Interestingly, these skills also translate to management skills as one seeks to understand the needs of an organization—and build a coalition of people to achieve success."

Essay #1

During my tenure at [Company A], I had the opportunity to work with and learn from the company's senior executive, [James]. Inside the structure of a small firm, I was able to work closely with [James] on a daily basis and experience his management style.

[James] and I have very similar backgrounds and a similar outlook towards life. Although I am younger than [James], our lives have followed a very similar path. We both grew up in the same town, attended the same high school, and both went to [College C]. From our similar background and outlook, I was able to capitalize on [James's] management experiences and learn a management style that suited my own values and utilized my attributes.

Three principles from [James's] management philosophy have had a great impact on the development of my management abilities. The first and most frequently stressed principle was the necessity to never allow oneself to lose sight of the larger picture. The second principle was that a manager's success depends on how well they are able to utilize their colleagues' strengths and talents. The third principle was that in order to excel, you must consistently reinvent and improve yourself.

While working at [Company A], I dealt daily with the analytical side of commercial mortgage backed securitizations. In my role it was very easy to become overly focused on the technical side of a project and forget the project's overall purpose. Early in my career I had a habit of becoming too focused on a particular issue in the securitization process and would not be able work past the issue until I had it solved. After a few frustrating weeks of spending nearly all day and night in the office in order to meet simple deadlines, I met with [James] to discuss my dilemma. [James's] approach was simple and quickly became part of my decision making process. His approach was to step back from the technical dilemma, look at the project as a whole and ask, "Does this provide value to the client?". This simple question helped direct me toward the issues that mattered the most instead of wasting time on the details that were insignificant to the outcome. [James]'s big picture outlook also stressed the importance of a proper work/family balance. Even while committing himself to running the company, [James] never forgot the importance of quality family time. With the proper balance, he was able to spend significant time at work and still devote himself to the raising of his family. The family values that were demonstrated at [Company A] showed me that it is possible to find the delicate balance between work and family time.

Another one of [James's] strengths was his ability to draw from his colleagues' strengths and talents. There were multiple ways that [James] utilized his employees' talents, but there were two ways that I found particularly valuable. The first was his belief that there was only so much that could be learned from training and watching others. Under [James's] direction at [Company A], employees gained a substantial amount of authority very early in their career. His belief was that after a certain level of fundamental training, the best way to truly learn the process was to go into the field and implement the process for the client. He had a theory that if he hired good employees, they would be able to figure out the details on their own as long as he taught them the fundamentals. The [Company A] employee had substantial authority over client interaction and the final product sent to the investors. The second belief was that in order to create a stronger company, he needed to make his employees well rounded. He wanted to expose his employees to as many different situations as possible in order to find out where their talents lay. If you were interested in a different part of the securitization process, [James] tried to let you have as much exposure to it as possible. For example, when I told [James] that I would benefit from more exposure to the investment banking side of the securitization process, he contracted me out to a client in New York. He rented an apartment in [Location B] and I spent a winter working with a large investment bank learning how a deal was run from a banking perspective.

The third principle that I learned from [James] was the need for continuous self-improvement. His theory was that self-improvement was a critical factor in being successful. At [Company A] there was typically a week or two of downtime when work was slow after the end of each quarter. [James] devoted these four to eight weeks per year to training. He implemented case studies. Employees were expected to run through difficult business deal scenarios in order to sharpen their skills. Employees were encouraged to enroll in real estate training classes via the Internet. On a one to one basis, [James] enjoyed teaching employees about different aspects of the industry and about the results of his most recent revelation. No questions were considered too basic to be asked and he made sure that there was always an atmosphere where employees felt comfortable enough to walk into his office to ask a question.

[James's] patience and professionalism earned the respect of both clients and employees. His ability to give employees substantial authority and recognition resulted in a stronger team that produced a high level of success.

Both my work related and personal decision making skills have benefited from my time with [James]. Whenever I face a decision, I am now more thorough in my analysis and pay special attention to how the situation fits into the context as a whole. As a result, my decision-making abilities have not only improved, but I find myself wasting less time on insignificant details and I have gained a more macro level viewpoint. I have been able to employ a similar employee development strategy to [James's] when I was put in charge of training new analysts in the [Location D] office. The result of the strategy was that the analyst spent a significant portion of their training in the field and was able to gain a much more practical understanding of their role. Finally, I have tried and am currently trying to follow [James]'s example of consistent self-improvement. I held the same principle of self-improvement before I worked for [James], but my time with [James] certainly helped it to grow. Under [James]'s example of self-improvement I have been able to improve both my personal and work related skills. When I wanted to improve my financial skills by enrolling in the Chartered Financial Analyst program, he encouraged me by allowing me to stop traveling for the month prior to the level one and two exams so that I could both work and study out of the [Location E] office. I am fortunate to have had [James] as a mentor. The skills that I have learned from him will forever impact my personal and business life.

CRITIQUE

Getting it right: This essay illustrates some very strong writing skills, conveys a clear message, and articulates attributes that we look for in a Freeman MBA candidate. The candidate recognizes some clear traits presented by the individual he admires: "never allow oneself to lose sight of the larger picture"; "a manager's success depends on how well they are able to utilize their colleagues' strengths and talents"; "consistently reinvent and improve yourself." Wow—any of these lines would be fitting captions for a motivational poster!

The applicant also recognizes where he fails to measure up to the behaviors presented by the individual—"I had a habit of becoming too focused"; "importance of a proper work/family balance." The applicant recognizes the perspective of his peers when dealing with them professionally and socially. He further articulates the skills he has learned as a result of his relationship with this person.

While this essay is clearly structured around a person that has shaped the applicant's professional life and attitudes, it does an excellent job of conveying the applicant's ability to recognize some core skills that will be very useful in an intensive MBA experience like the one offered at the Freeman School.

ESSAY #2

One person that has made a profound impact on my life is my former manager, [John Brown]. I had the opportunity to work with [John] as he preferred to be called for fifteen months; and his personal and professional skills made a huge impression on me. I adopted him as my mentor. [John] holds a Bsc. in Electrical Engineering, and an MBA from [Country A].

[John's] tenacity of purpose and determination to succeed against all odds saw him overcome an earlier setback of three failures, before passing the entry examination into the university for his undergraduate studies. [John] taught us to take failure as a learning experience. [John] was honest in his dealings with both colleagues and subordinates. He was continuously seeking the welfare of his subordinates much to the annoyance of his colleague managers.

[John] had excellent negotiation skills, and was very adept at bringing others to his point of view. He had an extraordinary level of drive and energy—devoted equal time to the minutest detail; he have memo drafted several times to correct all the mistakes. [John] always considered various options before making a decision—he always explored the "what ifs" of all alternative decisions. His final decisions were ultimately guided by the interest of the company with an eye for the bottom line. Occasionally, he would invite us to dinner or lunch after a very stressful working time. He made it a point to know each person's family members by their names and will always inquire about their welfare. He advised us to be innovative and take decisions in his absence, but made it a point to give him the feedback at the earliest opportunity.

Most staff held him in high esteem, and treated him with a lot of dignity and respect. His opinions were highly respected by top management. It was not surprising that all requests he recommended to top management were approved.

One of the outcomes of my experience with [John] has been my decision to pursue an MBA. He always talked about the impact of MBA experience on his life and career—he fueled my desire to have the MBA experience. I have also realized that hard work, determination, and honesty pay off in the end. Most importantly, I now see failure as a learning experience—it is easier to take risk.

CRITIQUE

Short but sweet: One essay submission to the Freeman School requires the applicant to provide a true *Reader's Digest* version of the topic. In business school, students spend a lot of time learning about the executive summary—a short statement that contains only the pertinent facts. This international student conveys several important management skills in this essay. Equally important, he responds to the essay question completely.

ESSAY #3

He was born in a small town, in a small country, [Country A], in the 1920s. In those days, the locomotive could still stir excitement among the people, the extended family was still the most important social network, and farming was a way of life. Those were also turbulent days. Once again, civil wars and local generals who vied fiercely for power plagued the country. The [military] would come in and try to impose order, then they would leave, only to come back and leave again. Out of this turmoil emerged the National Guard and its controlling leader, [General B]. Between 1936 and 1979, the country remained under the thumb of the political dynasty established by this general. Civil and political liberties were violated, public graft was practiced with impunity, socioeconomic injustice increased, and in spite of all this, the economy grew and even attained a degree of modernization.

The small town boy, [my grandfather], grew up in this environment. But he grew up to be an honest man of renowned integrity and bravery. He defied the [ruling] dynasty and for this he paid a heavy price, enduring imprisonment and humiliation at the hands of his jailers. Gradually, as it became clear that opposition was futile, he turned away from politics and threw himself into his private work, gaining a reputation throughout [the continent] as a talented administrator and banker. He rescued from ruin some of the largest corporations in the country and made them thrive. He then went on to serve in the upper ranks of the [regional banking authority], helping make the region's common market a success. As his own professional successes accumulated, he was invited to join the leadership staff of [an international bank], where he played a key role in bringing developmental assistance to [the region].

I am his first grandson, and he is my role model. His shoes are too big to fill, but I will at least try to follow in his footsteps. No other individual has had a more profound impact on my life. I grew up watching this man make difficult choices that others might have avoided because they were too risky or costly from a personal perspective. In 1979, he became involved in the national struggle to overthrow the oppressive [ruling] regime, and soon thereafter left his position at the [international bank] to join the government of the [new political party]. He served as the Revolution's first president of the [government bank], later became a member of the [leading political party], and later still served as [my country's] ambassador to the United States. He shared the revolutionaries' desire for socioeconomic process and justice, but he rejected their political authoritarianism. Acting on principle, he left the [new (leading) political party] government, and returned to development banking. I respect and admire that.

By 1983 there was much discontent with the ruling government within [my country] and there was international pressure for the [new (leading) political party] to hold free elections. My grandfather was chosen to be the presidential candidate for the opposition, which was fully backed by the United States. As the campaign began, so did negotiations with the [competing party] for free and transparent elections, something my grandfather had always dreamt for [my country]. The more he campaigned around the country, the larger the masses grew and the faster his popularity rose. He also became a serious threat for the ruling party. The [competing party] sabotaged his campaign by inciting violent mobs wherever he went. His supporters would attempt to fight off the mobs to no avail, and on one occasion a mob leader managed to injure my grandfather by throwing a sharpened rock at his forehead. And yet, he pressed ahead in the face of such adversity; and continued to demand conditions that would prevent fraud on Election Day. When these conditions were not met, he decided to stand on principle yet again. He left the race. As a consequence, the [competing party] was victorious at the polls. I respect and admire that.

My grandfather returned to politics when an armed opposition movement formed to overthrow [this] regime. Known as the [opposition], this movement needed a person with integrity and public support. My grandfather was that person. He believed in the cause of freedom and accepted to be a member of the [opposition directorate]. But he soon grew disenchanted with the [opposition] leaders, whom he found to be intolerant and whose methods he found questionable. "Abuse of power," he often would say to us kids "is wrong, no matter who the abuser is whether is the [new political party] or the [opposition]." He resigned from the [opposition directorate], knowing full well that many would criticize his decision and that some would even malign him. I respect and admire that.

At every critical point, my grandfather could have had power and wealth had he chosen to play along, but instead he chose to do what he felt was the right thing. Countless times during his career in business and politics, he was offered the chance to blur the line between the two for personal gain. He resisted, and kept them separate. And countless times, people who had no power or influence appealed to him directly or through intermediaries for help. He always found the courage to give voice to their grievances. Market women who were left holding worthless currency, political prisoners doomed to rot in jail, poor farmers who had been dispossessed of their tiny plots, mothers whose sons had been wounded in battle and had no prospect of rehabilitation for lack of resources, they all knew him as the man who would listen and respond.

I often meet strangers who, when they realize [who] my grandfather is, tell me how much they relish having met him, or how grateful they are that he helped them without even knowing who they were. When I was younger, I used to wonder why every time my grandfather visited [my country], the media would seek him out and people on the streets would rush to embrace him. Now I know.

Now I also understand that my grandfather's difficult choices are his legacy to me. In a world filled with political and corporate scandals, I carry this inheritance with deep satisfaction and pride; and in my heart and mind I hear his voice, encouraging me to pursue great professional accomplishments but never at the expense of my own humanity, principles, or honor.

These days, long after the locomotive has been retired to the museum, my grandfather is using a computer to write his political biography. If this book turns out to be only half as powerful as the conversations, the advice, and the stories he gave me when I was growing up, it will be a great book indeed. And when I give this book to my children, I will tell them that I am trying to live according to the standards set by its author. I will tell them this was my grandfather, your forebear, a man who was great yet humble, brave yet wise. I will tell them that we are all at our best when we affirm that such men can still be made.

CRITIQUE

Missing the mark: It is terribly important to read the question—not only for the idea but to see what the admissions committee is asking. We purposefully imbedded some key words in the essay question to hint at the direction an applicant should take. We wanted "profound impact," "skills," "reaction," and "outcome" to be articulated in the essay response. This essay was a wonderful exposition on a clearly interesting individual; however, the focus of the essay was to convey the life story of the applicant's grandfather. It is not until the third paragraph that the reader encounters the applicant's reaction to his grandfather's actions: "I respect and admire that." The essay—although beautifully crafted—failed to provide a clear insight into skills that the applicant has learned as a result of his encounter.

University of Chicago

Graduate School of Business

Essay #1

Question: If you were a character in a book, who would it be and why? What do you admire most about this character, and how does it relate to you personally and/or professionally? (300 words maximum)

Atticus Finch, as portrayed in Harper Lee's *To Kill A Mockingbird*, most accurately exemplifies my beliefs and my code of conduct. He embodies a strong moral compass with a composed and firm disposition. Although Atticus seems mellow and even old-fashioned, many of his beliefs are quite revolutionary. He is a hard worker who is an active parent with his children as well as an active member of the community. Raising his children with his own strong sense of morality and justice, he is a strong believer in family. A lawyer by trade, he is a teacher of both his children and his community. Atticus sees people as individuals, regardless of race and background, maintains an open mind to new ideas and thoughts, and teaches through reason rather than force. He is a patient and consistent man. The code of conduct that he maintains for himself remains constant and disciplined no matter how awkward or uncomfortable the situation. His objective is not the pursuit of money and fame, but justice and truth. I respect Atticus Finch for his keen mind, his instincts, his eloquence, and his willingness to stand up to social oppression regardless of overwhelming opposition in what may seem to be a hopeless and futile situation. He is very deliberate and erudite in his actions and knows how to maximize the resources at his disposal to achieve his goals. I admire him for his courage to test the social paradigm and for his willingness to stand up for what he believes is right. Passionate, yet collected and composed, I conduct myself with beliefs which parallel those of Atticus in many respects. Using the resources at my disposal and proactively developing my skills, I work in a calculated manner to attain my future goals professionally and personally.

Critique

What makes this essay so effective is its simplicity. Within the first two words of the essay, the reader already has a positive impression of the writer. By identifying Atticus Finch as the literary character he most admires, the writer chooses someone who is easily recognizable and who is known for his strong moral character and social ideals. Before completing the first sentence, the writer has already created a strong impression in the reader's mind, and the rest of the essay serves to strengthen the association. Remember that this type of essay is designed not to educate the reader on the applicant's literary knowledge but rather to allow the applicant to create a strong association that illustrates who he or she is as a person.

ESSAY #2

Question: If you could pick three guests for a formal dinner, who would they be and why would you choose them? (300 words maximum)

If I could pick three guests for a formal dinner party, unconstrained by chronology and mortality, I would pick Theodore (Teddy) Roosevelt, Winston Churchill, and Steve Irwin, "The Crocodile Hunter". Teddy Roosevelt and Winston Churchill have always intrigued me, because apart from their enormous accomplishments in public life, they led fascinating lives beyond the realm of politics—Roosevelt the big game hunter, conservationist, and hero of San Juan Hill; Churchill the soldier, war correspondent, and Nobel Prize winning author. My third guest, the zoo director and television personality Steve Irwin, strikes me as the ideal foil for the two elder statesmen. As an Australian and non-politician, he would strike a balance between these bastions of American and British public life and focus the conversation on the personal experiences that make Roosevelt and Churchill so fascinating. Additionally, Irwin, with his cheerful self-assurance, would not be easily overwhelmed by Roosevelt and Churchill's domineering personalities.

With this triumvirate, I imagine the conversation moving from Teddy's tales of his wild game safaris in Africa and the spectacular beauty of the American West, to Winston relating his great escape from the Boer prison camp and his experiences in the British Raj, with Steve Irwin trying to one-up them as he recounts the origins of his various scars and expounds on the art of crocodile wrestling.

While the political careers of Roosevelt and Churchill can, and do, fill volumes, it is impossible to capture on the written page the passion and energy with which these men lived their lives. With this dining combination, I would hope to catch a glimpse of it. I can't think of a more interesting or remarkable evening than to be regaled by tales from these three exceptional men.

CRITIQUE FOR ESSAYS #2 AND #3

This essay and the essay that follows effectively answer a pretty common essay question. What makes these essays so effective is the way the candidates illustrate one or more elements of their personalities through the people they choose. In both instances, the reader finishes the essay knowing something about the candidates that might not have otherwise been evident in reading their applications. Steve Irwin, Teddy Roosevelt, and Winston Churchill illustrate the first applicant's thirst for adventure, while the second applicant's grandmother, political science professor, and John "Buck" O'Neill convey his strong sense of social conscience.

Essay #3

Question: If you could pick three guests for a formal dinner, who would they be and why would you choose them? (300 words maximum)

Guests at my formal dinner would be Robert Booth Fowler, John "Buck" O'Neill, and Harriet Marks. Professor Fowler is a political science professor at the University of Wisconsin—Madison who specializes in the intersection of religion and politics. He was the most passionate, creative, engaging and charismatic instructor that I have ever had. He continues to inspire me to be passionate about what I do, to act always with a determined vigor, and to devote much of my free time to the teaching and training of others.

My second guest, John "Buck" O'Neill, is a former Negro Leagues baseball player and manager who later entered the Major Leagues first as a scout for the Chicago Cubs (signing, among other players, Ernie Banks and Lou Brock), and later as Major League Baseball's first black coach (with the Cubs, in 1962). He is almost uniquely qualified to provide living testimony regarding the intersection of sports and the history of American racial relations, both of which interest me greatly. If you saw Ken Burns's documentary on baseball, you undoubtedly recognized Mr. O'Neill and his affable, gracious style, as being the show's truest star.

Third, I would invite Harriet Marks. Mrs. Marks is my grandmother, who is recently widowed and seems a bit lonely. Although she has never expressed an interest in religion and politics or in American race relations—and has little understanding of baseball—I know that she, more than anyone else, would appreciate the invitation.

Essay #4

Question: What are two attributes of your character that make you unique? How do you expect these traits to make an impact on Chicago GSB and your classmates? (300 words maximum)

Incident number one: it was a sultry August morning in Manhattan. From the 27th floor of the [office] building, the downtown skyline sprawled before us. It was the [Company A] analyst training program, and I was surrounded by a group of highly talented, driven peers from some of the best colleges in the world. We were listening to managing directors tell us wild tales about multi-billion dollar deals they had worked on.

Suddenly the words echoed in my ears. "Have any of you ever been to the god-forsaken state of Iowa?" The room of 250 was silent. My retort practically fell out of my mouth. "Yes, I'm *from Iowa*!" A huge explosion of laughter and applause. The speaker, a famed "deal maker" from our Mergers & Acquisitions group, turned red. "I am now removing my foot from my mouth," were his exact words.

Incident number two: I was in my senior year at [University B]. It was mid-December, and Wall Street recruiting season was in full swing. I trudged through the snow along 56th Street to interview with a major securities brokerage firm. To this day, I can still hear my interviewer as he took a final glance over my resume. "[Jenna], you're very qualified for this job. But one question remains in my mind: what's a nice girl like you who plays the cello wanna do on a trading floor?"

I have lived as a transplanted Iowan in New York and London for over six years, and I do play the cello. Through all the jokes and befuddled reactions I've received, I've learned that the most stimulating traits I can bring to a community are a well-rounded background and an open mind. This includes an appreciation and understanding of the rural and the urban, the domestic and the international, the artistic and the mundane. In gaining this appreciation, I've realized the overlap between these seemingly antithetic worlds and have come to understand the value of interactive diversity.

CRITIQUE

What made this essay effective was the candidate's use of the narrative. Most essays I have come across on this topic read like a laundry list: "My years of consulting experience have provided me with the tools to be an effective team player"; "My years in public relations have really strengthened my communication skills"; and so on. There is no reason to spend time further illustrating things that are already covered in detail in the application. This writer was effective because she decided to focus on two seemingly insignificant parts of her life— playing the cello and being from Iowa. As a reader reviewing her essay, I may have noticed these two things about her, but I certainly would not have associated them with her open-mindedness. By effectively using some simple narratives, she left a lasting impression of what being from Iowa and playing the cello can contribute to an MBA program.

Essay #5

Question: Why are you seeking an MBA or IMBA at the University of Chicago Graduate School of Business? What do you hope to experience and contribute? What are your plans and goals after you receive your degree?

"[Jenna], you *must* go to the U of C. The faculty, the campus, the whole environment...," raved F.H., one of my senior associates who happened to attend the GSB at the University of Chicago.

"I know," I replied. "I've been thinking about it for a long time."

You have some very convincing alumni. However, I do not need much convincing. I have known for quite a while exactly why I want to attend the University of Chicago. Let me begin by providing you with a bit of historical context in which to better understand my motivations.

For the last several years, I have worked as a financial analyst at [Company A] in New York and London. By all accounts, I have excelled in my job. I have been consistently ranked and compensated in the "star" category, was one of only a handful of second year analysts globally to be promoted to a third year position in our London office (most were laid off), and the only analyst in the global investment bank this year to be granted a third year position in our fabled fixed income division. I have also been advised that I am a "shoe-in" for promotion to the associate position. However, I am opting to seek a place at the University of Chicago GSB rather than pursue further promotion within my firm. Why?

As an undergraduate at [University B], I majored in mathematics and reveled in the theory I learned. I subsequently became interested in finance, however it was not part of [University B]'s undergraduate curriculum. I then went to work on Wall Street, but always felt there was a gap in my education. That gap has grown in my mind to the point that I do not want to continue my career without firmly grounding myself in theoretical finance and the other business disciplines.

Given my math background, I want—and indeed need—the analytical rigor of Chicago's curriculum and the practical and theoretical understanding of finance that it can provide me. While there are many other MBA programs out there, none can match Chicago's combination of prominence in economics and finance, its legendary faculty (past and present), the flexibility of its curriculum, and its location in a city that is an international business center that has as much to offer culturally as any other in the world.

I am eager to gain exposure to a very diverse and international group of classmates at the University of Chicago, as well as their insight on the industries in which they have worked. I look forward to sharing a dynamic and thought provoking classroom environment with them.

I can offer my classmates a culmination of my solid investment banking background, well-trained and analytical mind, and genuine desire to learn by working with them and forming lasting friendships.

I owe it to myself to continue to seek rewarding challenges in thoughtful and intense environments. I hope to use the knowledge I will have gained at the University of Chicago to go into corporate bond research. That is my future ambition—and an MBA education from the University of Chicago will provide me with the foundation that I need to get there.

Please accept my thanks for your time and consideration. I hope that you will enjoy reading my application as much as I have enjoyed writing it.

CRITIQUE

This essay demonstrates an effective answer to the "Why an MBA?" and "Why here?" questions. The most common pitfall that people experience when answering this question is that they do not do an effective job answering the "Why here?" question. Applicants need to keep in mind that a university admissions committee wants to know that you are interested in that university specifically and not the five other programs to which you are applying. Convincing the committee that their institution is the best fit for you is critical to answering this essay effectively.

A less common problem is not providing a clear focus for your MBA. A common response I have seen is "An MBA is the next logical step in my career." A statement like this does not answer the question. Have a clear purpose for why you want an MBA now. How is an MBA going to help you achieve your *specific* goals? Be clear about your purpose; speaking in generalities is the kiss of death.

The writer of this essay was effective because she was thorough and enthusiastic about why she wanted to go to the University of Chicago, and she was specific about the reasons she thought an MBA was important for achieving her goals. Providing an effective answer to this question is not a complicated procedure as long as you can *be specific!*

Summary

Overall there are four themes I hope you take from these essays.

1. Think simple. The most effective answers are often the most obvious.

2. Be creative. Do not use the essays to highlight attributes that are captured in other areas of your application.

3. Be specific. There are thousands of people competing for your spot, so let your readers know why you are the perfect fit for their program.

4. Let your personality be your guide. Do not try to fit your writing style to some perceived MBA student model. The readers want to know you, not Joe MBA. The more you can do to highlight your specific personality, the better your essays will be.

University of Iowa

Henry B. Tippie School
of Management

FROM THE SCHOOL

"The admissions essays serve several purposes in the application review process at the Tippie School of Management. Of course, they tell us something about the candidate's ability to compose an essay. More importantly, the essays help us to know more about the applicant as an individual and to answer questions such as: What really matters to this person? What life experiences will he/she bring to our program? What makes this person 'tick'?

"Our essay questions are quite straightforward, requesting information about the candidate's career objectives, purpose in obtaining an MBA, and leadership experiences. The best candidates use these questions as a springboard to provide a more complete picture of themselves. We recognize that not everyone writes like a best-selling author. However, we expect the admission essays to be concise, to be free of errors, and to address the questions posed.

"Two essays are required in our application. Each of the essays below was submitted as part of the application for admission to the fall 2002 entering class and are responses to the following:

> *Give an example of a situation or an action that describes your potential for success in a professional environment.*

"We selected them because each reflects the candidate's personality, fleshing out our picture of them as a real-life person."

ESSAY #1

"You have three qualities that will allow you to be successful in life: persistence, organization, and people skills."

My mother told this to me when I was young and did not fully appreciate what it meant or why it was important. I just knew that I liked to set goals for myself, have a structured environment, and be around people. Now, after years of experience through work and school, I have a complete understanding of how and why these three things are so important. They will allow me to be successful in any of life's activities and, in particular, a professional environment.

While working for [Company A], I inherited a territory that was suffering sales-wise. I knew that in order to make an immediate impact, I would have to focus my activity on the doctors and offices that would bring in the most business. One of my most important doctors, Dr. C., had a large population of patients with epilepsy in his clinic. It was my job to introduce him to the new anticonvulsant medication that I marketed and to convince him to keep it in mind for some of these patients. I knew my mission, so I prepared an initial call plan that included uncovering what his practice needs were at that time, combined with weekly visits and reminders.

At our first meeting, he took one look at me and walked the other way. After speaking with his nurse, I soon discovered that he did not believe drug reps brought value to his practice and, therefore, would not see them. At that point I knew he would be a challenge, and I was up for it. I devised a strategic plan to get myself in front of him. I decided to devote my time and energy to the "gatekeepers" by befriending the office staff and nurses.

Reverse psychology? It seemed the more attention I gave the rest of the office, the more curious Dr. C. became about me as well as my medications. Every week I would get to know each of the staff members and bring in candy or a lunch. I would always include full details about my product to prove the value I felt I could bring to the office, and also leave a friendly note for Dr. C. requesting he set aside a time for us to meet in person. The staff teased Dr. C. for not participating in my luncheon, and I believe the pressure from them (and from me) eventually broke him down. He finally invited me to sit down with him in his office to review all the details of the medication and discuss his needs at that time. The call went very well, but he did not make any commitments, so I continued with my original sales plan.

Over the next few months, I asked him to try the medicine with some of his patients. I offered examples and ideas of which patient types would make good candidates, explained the dosing schedule and potential side effects, reminded him of the numerous journal articles that praised the drug's remarkable efficacy, and kept him abreast of the competition. He remained hesitant to use the drug, but with my persistence he agreed to let me organize a conference call with a leader in the neurological community who was having wonderful results with the medication. It turned out to be a fun and educational occasion, and I felt that it afforded me the opportunity to increase my credibility with this very important physician.

Later that week, I was pleasantly surprised to receive an email from Dr. C. thanking me for the event. He said that he felt the conference was very worthwhile and that he appreciated my efforts to bring him the information. Because of this, he promised that he would try the product with the next patient who had uncontrolled seizures. It took about six months, but we were finally at a mutual understanding and able to grow the business relationship.

Throughout my life, I have discovered that knowledge and hard work will be rewarded. Add to these, determination, organized planning, and the ability to develop and maintain relationships with people, and it will make an individual very successful. It is my goal to always remember my mother's encouraging words and use these qualities in everything I do.

CRITIQUE

This candidate begins her essay with a quote stating the characteristics she demonstrates through the example provided—persistence, organization, and people skills. The level of detail she gives in her example is a little more than needed, but the essay provides insight into her approach to life that helps us evaluate her as a potential member of the Tippie MBA program.

ESSAY #2

The decimal point is a powerful little dot. With a mere step to the right or to the left, ten percent can change to one hundred percent, or to one percent. Who decided to give this amazing power to such a little speck of ink, a mere pixel on the screen? Honestly, I don't know. But if I could travel back to the time when Mr. Mathematician decided to use a small dot for the decimal, I would raise my voice and implore him to use an asterisk. Make it noticeable; make it stand out; make it BIG!

Instead, I sat on a cold metal grandstand at [Speedway A] in [City B, State B], in May of 2001. I was now in my twentieth month serving as the Systems Integration Director of [Team C]. [Team C] recruits ordinary college students, fuses them together, and challenges them to design, construct, test, and race a solar powered car across a continent. This day, the team was eagerly racking up qualifying laps at a 2.1-mile closed-course racetrack attempting to enter [Race D]—a 2,400-mile race that followed Old Route 66 from Chicago to Los Angeles. We were right on track. We had built the best car in the team's history; we had the healthiest list of sponsors the team had ever accumulated; and, we had a dedicated and eager team that had worked day and night and on weekends and holidays for almost two years to be a part of this great race.

But at that moment, as I suffered on that hard aluminum bleacher seat staring at my calculator screen, I realized that we were in serious jeopardy. The car wasn't performing like it had over the last two months during testing. The numbers just weren't adding up. My strategist murmured in my headset that things didn't look good and we should pull our driver into the pits to check things out. Ten minutes later, my fears were confirmed. It was the battery pack. We spent a full day at the track infield going over the numbers, but they all led to the same conclusion. Our battery pack engineer had made a mistake. Somehow during the design, in one of the specifications, in one of the numerous equations, a one-tenth had become a ten. Almost instantly the ability to win vanished from our dreams and we seriously doubted our ability to enter [Race D].

Just five weeks before this discovery, our battery pack engineer had developed problems in his personal life and had left the team. He was our only expert in the area. His ability and his experience were forever lost. And now, due to race regulations, the 154 laps driven out of 165 that we needed to qualify were also gone. Our $16,000 experimental battery pack was toast, and so were the hopes of every team member. The race was in five weeks.

Five weeks. I knew what had to be done, and I knew I would do it. There would have to be a new battery pack, and every team member's spirit would have to be relit. We would have to raise money, and we would need technology that had never existed before to appear, to work perfectly, and to be fully understood by our race crew. Our logistics team now had to plan for a car with unknown performance, and our public relations team had to keep our image high while still admitting the truth to our sponsors and to the public. These were the people I managed, and this was my challenge.

I volunteered to be the new battery expert, among other things. I bought French rocket launder batteries from a British company through an Australian product holder. My strategy team changed all their known values to variables; my electrical team completely redesigned the propulsion system. The mechanical design team re-built the battery enclosure. The race logistics team planned for the worst, and some key calls to compassionate corporations paid for the whole she-bang for a mere $20,000. Not a bad price considering that it took us two years to raise the other $730,000 to support the rest of the project.

We re-qualified, entered, and finished [Race D]. A mid-pack finish was more than we could have imagined. We were given the technical innovation award by the U.S. Department of Energy for our battery pack design, and our team won the award for Best Teamwork during the long stretch from Missouri through California. We were also presented with the award for best-looking vehicle design. And I am now referred to as "Captain" by my teammates. I learned to speak a little French, to become an electrical engineer, and to somehow lift high the spirits of thirty of my closest friends. For me, this was an experience of true leadership, that of bringing out the best in other people and succeeding in the common goal. If only I could just make the decimal point a little bigger.

CRITIQUE

This candidate's essay is an excellent example of a creative, interesting story that illustrates important characteristics for success in our MBA program and in business. His initiative, self-confidence, teamwork, and leadership in a unique situation come through clearly. These traits are all qualities we seek in our students. His writing style brings out his characteristics as part of an engaging story.

UNIVERSITY OF MICHIGAN
BUSINESS SCHOOL

Describe your post-graduation career plans. How will
ation, experience, and development to date support those
plans? How will an MBA from the University of Michigan Business
School help you attain your goals? (500 words)

I would like to pursue an MBA at Michigan in order to gain skills in marketing and corporate strategy for a career as a brand manager. Brand managers are the key link between the innovators in a corporation and the consumers in the marketplace. A broad knowledge of the firm, from Research and Development to logistics, is necessary in order for a brand manager to successfully develop a brand's strategy. My educational experience in economics and English has provided me with the quantitative and qualitative skills necessary for a career in brand management. From my experience as a management consultant, I have had the opportunity to work with a broad range of departments within a wide variety of firms, and I would like to synthesize this knowledge and build upon it with an MBA so as to eventually become a brand manager for a large food and/or beverage firm. My ideal specialty area would be in ready-to-eat food products because of my interest in branded food products.

Michigan is the ideal fit for my background and interests for several reasons. First, coming from [College A], I am a strong proponent for women in business, and I have continued my support for career women at [Company B] as a leader of the Women's Network in the Midwest and Canada. I highly value the Women in Business Initiative at Michigan. [Jane Doe], a fellow alum from [College A], a colleague at [Company B], and a member of the Women's Leadership Council at the University of Michigan Business School, has frequently lauded the dedicated efforts at Michigan to support women in business.

Second, my interest is to work for a large food and/or beverage company, and nearly all of the major food and beverage companies recruit at Michigan. Also, the school has produced a large number of leaders in food and beverage companies such as [Jane Doe] at [Company A] and [John Doe] at [Company B]. I would ideally like to complete a summer internship at a company such as [Company A, B, C, D, or E], all of which have actively recruited at Michigan in past years.

Third, I believe that studying business at Michigan would allow me to build upon my existing skills and enhance them with solid marketing and corporate strategy work that my liberal arts educational background lacks. The breadth and depth of courses at Michigan appeal to me as well as the exceptional faculty members. The classes which fascinate me within the marketing and corporate strategy disciplines include "Strategic Brand Management," "Consumer Behavior," and "Strategy, Technology, and the Management of Innovation." Professors for which I hold great esteem are [Professor A] in Strategy and [Professor B] in Brand Management. Lastly, I would like to get involved in the Marketing Club to learn from others with similar interests, and I would participate in the Consulting Club to share my knowledge and passion from my work at [Company B].

CRITIQUE

This is an excellent example of an essay that clearly let the admissions committee know the answers to three important questions about an applicant's background and career objectives: Where are you coming from? Where do you want to go? Why is Michigan's MBA program the most suited to help you achieve your educational and professional goals? This applicant clearly identified how she intended to build upon her liberal arts education and her professional work experiences to transition to brand management. In doing so, she showed us that she had a very good understanding of Michigan's general management focus as well as the school's relationships with recruiting companies and the prominence of our alumni in her chosen field. Further, she showed us that she has been involved in the women's network at her company and that her commitment would continue as a student by getting involved in our Women in Business Initiative.

There are several reasons admissions staff really want to understand the answers to these questions.

- Attending an MBA program is a big investment in yourself, in terms of both personal commitment and finances. We want to see how thoughtfully an applicant has approached this decision about his or her professional development.

- Your association with the business school you choose to attend is lifelong, and we want to ensure that you will gain maximum benefit from your experience in the MBA program as well as contribute to the Michigan community as a student and as an alumnus.

- We want to gain an understanding of your philosophy of management education, e.g., preferred learning style, goals for professional development, etc. Each business school has a distinct curriculum, values, and "personality," and we are looking for applicants that will be a great fit with our school now and in the future.

Essay #2

Question: Describe your post-graduation career plans. How will your education, experience, and development to date support those plans? How will an MBA from the University of Michigan Business School help you attain your goals? (500 words)

On completion of my MBA, I plan to continue my career in the investment industry by working as a buy-side discretionary trader for an institutional asset management firm. I would like to specialize in international equities, with a possible overseas assignment. Longer term, I plan to pursue a career in buy-side client portfolio management, leveraging my operations background and applying the increased knowledge of sound business theory developed through my MBA experience. More specifically, I would like to work in a senior-level business development/client service position that would allow me to utilize my cross-functional knowledge to evaluate, initiate and develop long-term sustainable relationships with large institutional clients.

My active involvement in college extracurricular activities supplemented my education by focusing on two areas of interest. I pursued my interest in asset management through my involvement in the Student Foundation as a member of the Board of Trustees, where I oversaw the investment of our club's $500,000 endowment, and through my internship with [Company A] as an assistant buy-side trader. I gained international exposure through two study-abroad experiences, minors in international business and affairs, and extensive international travel.

My work experience reflects a logical progression in an investment industry career. Working for [Company B] gave me a "big picture view" of asset management and an opportunity to discover which path I wanted to pursue. I discovered my strengths in leadership through project management, in sales through client service and sales support, and in quantitative application through research and performance data analysis. Working for [Company C] has given me invaluable experience in buy-side trading and a clear view of my near-term goal. My experience managing several significant trading relationships, ability to remain calm under pressure in a hectic environment, and confidence in trading $444 million on a daily basis will serve me well as I enter a more senior level of trading.

My education, work experiences and development to date have all prepared me well for my next challenge—that of obtaining an MBA. Six years of working in asset management has limited my exposure to other areas of business practice, and I believe a well-balanced MBA curriculum will significantly improve my knowledge base of different functional areas and provide me with essential business management skills. Michigan is my first choice because of its reputation of building deep expertise in every business function and maintaining a truly global perspective throughout the MBA program, addressing my primary goals in pursuing an MBA. I am particularly impressed with your faculty and especially look forward to taking Finance 640 with [Dr. A]. I find his research on the correlation between weather and stock returns intriguing. Michigan also demonstrates a strong commitment to providing a global education through its curriculum and international opportunities. I would like to participate in both The Global Project Courses and the William Davidson Institute summer assignment. I believe these are incredible opportunities, enhancing my education through "real world" team projects and international business experience.

CRITIQUE

This is a good example of an essay that describes the goals of someone who wants to return to the same industry after graduating from an MBA program. Most MBA applicants intend a career switch of some type, and the breadth of the MBA education allows them to make that transition. For those who want to return to the same industry, it is helpful for the admissions committee to understand why an applicant believes that getting an MBA will enhance his or her career in that industry. After all, why couldn't the candidate just progress from position to position in his or her firm without further formal education? Additionally, since Michigan's MBA curriculum is built upon a general management philosophy, the admissions committee wants to ensure that the applicant does not have too narrow a focus and will appreciate and benefit from the range of course work. For example, many MBA alumni wish they had taken more organizational behavior classes instead of those extra finance or marketing classes.

This applicant provides a very detailed description of career goals—more detailed, perhaps, than most applicants could. That is not the most important aspect of this essay, however. This applicant uses the essay to show us how her interests, skills, and goals have developed in the past few years and then describes how the logical next step is an MBA and, more specifically, a Michigan MBA.

- Extracurricular activities in college provided her with the first experiences of managing investments, trading, and international interests.

- The first career experience out of college confirmed her interest in asset management.

- The second career experience offered significant responsibility and provided her with the confidence to progress to senior levels.

- Throughout the essay, the applicant succinctly describes skills gained and then acknowledges other functional areas of limited exposure.

- The applicant describes in a detailed way, not a cookie-cutter, right-out-of-the-brochure way, the value that Michigan's MBA program will bring to her development.

University of North Carolina at Chapel Hill

Kenan-Flagler Business School

Essay #1

Question: You have recently been brought in by the CEO of your company to act as the new project lead for a high-profile team charged with bringing a new product to market. The team has become dysfunctional and risks missing the project deadline. How will you go about turning the situation around? You have one month to make the deadline. (Answer must be no more than 2 typed pages, double-spaced.)

As a project lead brought in by the CEO to lead a dysfunctional team charged with bringing a new product to market within a month, I would attack each of the following tasks to make sure that the project is completed in a timely manner and within the expectations of management:

Meeting with Management: Define Expectations

Teams can become dysfunctional due to a poor understanding of their goals and how those goals fit into the overall corporate strategy. My first task as the project lead in this situation would be to work with management to define their expectations of the team beyond the project deadline.

- *Define Purpose:* What is the purpose of the product launch? Where does this product fit in to the overall corporate strategy?

- *Define Values:* What values should be used in making decisions for the project? For example, what is more important, quality or quantity, safety or efficiency?

- *Define Consequences:* What are the consequences of the team's failure to meet its goals both for the company and for the team?

- *Define Scope:* How much flexibility do I have in requesting additional resources outside of the team?

Meeting with Project Team: Define Goals, Timelines and Roles

A team cannot function properly if there is confusion regarding the team's goals, a misunderstanding of each individual's role within the team, disorganized timelines, or poor motivation due to a lack of understanding of the importance of meeting the team's goals for both the company and the team. In order to combat these issues and get the team on the right track, I would meet with the team to organize and discuss the following:

- *Give the project context:* Discuss the goals of the team as expressed by management stressing the deadline for the project, why this deadline is important, how the product launch fits into the company's goals and the consequences of the team's failure to meet its goals both for the team and the company.

- *Define a Plan of Action:* Outline the items that have been completed for the project and which items are pending. Set a timeline for completion of the project within the one month deadline, determining exactly each task that needs to be completed, the dates each task should be completed by and which tasks are dependent on other tasks for their completion.

- *Clarify Role for Each Team Member:* Go through each action item and assign team members to each item as necessary. Where possible, ask for volunteers being careful that no one team member becomes overloaded and that tasks requiring specific expertise are assigned correctly. Give each team member the opportunity to voice any concerns over their own workload stressing that they should only volunteer for items that they can complete within the set time limits.

- *Create an "open door" policy.* Charge team members with the responsibility of letting me know about any problems that may cause project delays or reductions in the quality of work. Be sure that they understand my role as a facilitator of communication and resource allocation.

Project Management: Reinforce, Review, Reward

Projects that are not properly monitored by the project lead can quickly lose momentum. As the project lead, I would perform the following tasks on a continuing basis to be certain that each team member stays on top of their tasks:

- *Reinforce the project's goals and timelines.* After meeting with the team, communicate main points of the meeting in an email or memo. Be sure to include a detailed project plan with specific team member assignments. As appropriate, meet with the entire team or individual members throughout the project to make sure that the timeline is followed. Communicate project status and milestones to the entire team.

- *Review Team Member Performance.* Make sure that each team member meets his or her goals and timelines, reinforcing the importance of meeting management's expectations. Be flexible in changing assignments and requesting additional resources where necessary.

- *Reward Outstanding Performance.* Be sure to "give credit where credit is due" by praising those team members who display above average performance and passing on this information to management.

In the past eight years, I have worked on teams with goals as diverse as designing a global specialized IP management system for [Company A], re-branding a corporation to reinforce a position as a market leader and creating a new sick leave policy better suited to a growing company. The most effective teams have project leaders who act as facilitators by providing the necessary infrastructure so that the individual team members can effectively contribute to the overall success of the project. In my experience, teams who understand their goals and values, are organized and communicative and are empowered by management, outperform all others.

CRITIQUE

The layout of this essay immediately conveys a sense of organization, professionalism, and purpose. The candidate outlines her task by first prioritizing and defining the problem. Proper problem definition is necessary for proper problem resolution. The use of subheads is effective because the reader is drawn to the key points. It highlights how well thought out her approach is.

Her diagnosis and assessment is thorough. She considers the consequences of her action plan and the roles of her team members. This essay conveys keen business acumen and sensitivity to team dynamics. It reads like an executive summary, and an impressive one at that. In her last paragraph, she jumps out of her role and wisely tells us of her real-life experience in leading and working on diverse teams. We're convinced she'd be an asset to any team and to our school.

Essay #2

Question: You have recently been brought in by the CEO of your company to act as the new project lead for a high profile team charged with bringing a new product to market. The team has become dysfunctional and risks missing the project deadline. How will you go about turning the situation around? You have one month to make the deadline. (Answer must be no more than 2 typed pages, double spaced.)

"Mr. [Smith], thank you for agreeing to introduce me to the New Product Development team. Effective leadership will bring this product to the market in the next month. As the new project lead, I believe that it is important to establish quickly my credibility, trust, and respect with this high profile team. By clearly defining my role and authority, your support will help ensure our success.

"However, before we meet with the team, I would like to review my action plan with you. First, I intend to triage the situation. I do not need to understand all of the reasons for the team's dysfunction, but it is essential that the team recognizes a problem exists. I want to hear from them, both individually and as a team, that we have hit rock-bottom and it is time to pull together. I want to see their commitment and know they are willing to put forth the extra effort. If necessary, the team members may need to be changed and I will consider that option when I review the project's resource requirements.

"Secondly, I believe that it is vital for everybody to be on the same page with respect to the scope and amount of work that must be completed in the next 30 days. In other words, our expectations must be the same. Since they are the experts with this new product, we will develop a strategy to meet the original deadline as a group. We will define new tasks and due dates. We will reconstruct the original timeline, establish new milestones and determine the critical path necessary for project completion.

"Given the workload, I will review our staffing levels and determine whether additional resources will be required. Assignments will be based on competence and area of expertise; responsibility will be delegated based on experience and performance. Some of the activities may be channeled to outside services or different teams, but I will try to keep the work in-house and the launch costs to a minimum.

"The re-organization process will take a few days. Once we are re-focused I will establish an improved system of communication. Effective communication can prevent unnecessary delays and stimulate team cohesiveness. Based on my past experiences, a visual system works best. People can quickly identify action items and response dates without spending extra time replying to emails or reading memos. I will develop charts, timelines, and a message board that will be displayed in my office and the team center. These visuals will also serve as good reminders for the team and they will be updated daily.

"Additionally, there will be a weekly review to measure progress and address new issues. The review will be brief, but highly focused. Each team member will be required to update the team on his or her activities, as well as provide feedback for the other team members. I will moderate the discussion to ensure that a healthy measure of creativity and collaboration exists. Often with high profile teams, this meeting becomes very dynamic and stimulating. You are invited to attend any one of the four reviews.

"Finally, throughout the week I will follow up with each team member to provide encouragement, motivation and accountability. I recognize that this action plan borders on micro-management, but until the team proves that they are capable of functioning together, or the deadline is met, I will monitor this project launch closely. You have asked me to bring this new product to market in less than a month. Thank you for your confidence in my abilities and our team. We will not let you down."

*The people and events described in this essay are more real than fiction. [Mr. Smith] is the President/CEO of [Smith & Co.], my current employer, and I was recently hired to coordinate activities between the New Product Development group and several manufacturing locations.

CRITIQUE

The art of telling a great story is, of course, in the way it is told. The wonderful twist to this essay is the ending where the candidate inserts a footnote that reveals that his well-scripted fiction is based on real events. It is all the more impressive that Mr. [Smith] is the CEO of the corporation and that the applicant is his direct report. As for the style of this essay, the use of fictional dialogue is fairly commonplace, so while it adds drama and interest, it is not standout.

Overall this essay communicates a strong sense of purpose, the ability to set priorities, and a keen talent for managing detail and execution. To ensure that the process is as rewarding as it is rigorous, the applicant also tells us that as team leader, he will emphasize creativity and collaboration.

It's particularly impressive that this applicant immediately sets the team on a constructive path forward. The past failures of the team, and any griping about those failures or past dysfunction, he establishes as irrelevant, thereby creating a team culture that is performance-based and not focused on placing blame. He then sets up a system designed to create results—an agenda that aligns team incentives so individuals are not working across purposes, clearly defined objectives broken into discreet long- and short-term steps, and resources appropriately matched to objectives. He outlines a remarkable plan for a team turnaround.

ESSAY #3

Question: You have recently been brought in by the CEO of your company to act as the new project lead for a high profile team charged with bringing a new product to market. The team has become dysfunctional and risks missing the project deadline. How will you go about turning the situation around? You have one month to make the deadline. (Answer must be no more than 2 typed pages, double spaced.)

I am very confident that my extensive exposure to team oriented initiatives during the course of my academic and professional careers will strongly support my ability to fulfill the expectations of the CEO and of the team itself in bringing the project back on track and with renewed enthusiasm, coordination and creativity.

The first move would be to acquaint myself with both the product and the team by calling the team together for an initial briefing to familiarize myself with their backgrounds and the progress that the project has made. I would seek to instill a sense of professionalism and confidence in our collective ability to overcome the encountered problems and to achieve a very rewarding goal in the remaining time.

My approach in speaking with my new teammates would tend towards the informal side, but I would remain firm in my commitment to bringing this product to fruition and to serving the initial goals of the company. I would assert an air of authority but equally let my team know that I am approachable and that open communication between us would reduce confusion and enable the greater sharing of ideas through brainstorming and a fair criticism and discussion of views.

I would spend a considerable amount of my free time to evaluate the remaining work to be covered and set a plan to evaluate the quality and success of work already completed. Time is of the essence and progress cannot be stalled while I familiarize myself with the team's, circumstances, but I would ask for more caution and interaction between team members to ensure that time was not wasted through rash decision-making. My plan would be make up for lost time through greater efficiency and cooperation between team members in the final weeks and I would break the team into its various divisions such as sales, marketing, manufacturing and logistics. By enhancing the team's knowledge of the importance of interaction between various divisions each member will learn about how their work interacts with one another and when to seek assistance from other divisions when matters concern them, instead of blindly making decisions that could be ineffective and undermine the work of other divisions with which they are unfamiliar.

Taking each division in turn I would swiftly assess its strategy to meet the goal of the project and its time plan and if necessary I would revise this through suggestion to the division leader. At all times during the project I would seek to maintain constant motivation over the team by praising initiative and achievement. I would invite advice and comment from all members and see to set aside some time each week for relaxation and to strengthen the interpersonal development between team members. I demand 100% commitment from my colleagues because the company expects and demands nothing less, therefore I would ensure that the individual goals for sales initiatives, delivery and logistics networks and marketing promotions were all reached to the highest standards. My experiences of product launches have taught me that human interaction and mutual respect and understanding are key to the success of such interdisciplinary endeavors and I believe that I have the capability to instill such a characteristic to this team initiative. My firm yet approachable leadership will, I am confident, bring about an effective, enthusiastic and innovative response from the team and lead it to a solid and professional conclusion within the deadline, therefore ensuring a commendable product launch.

CRITIQUE

This applicant focuses on the interpersonal dynamics involved in leading a team to success. A primary goal in his plan is to motivate his team members and build mutual respect. He proposes facilitating a series of informal discussions to create a culture of open communication, build sensitivity to different work styles, establish a collegial atmosphere, and establish common goals. He identifies himself as being an open and accessible leader, one who intends to motivate his team with frequent praise for achievement. Overall, he communicates that he understands the key conditions under which teams achieve optimum results. Since teamwork is absolutely critical in business school, the essay communicates that this applicant is the kind of person we want to bring into our community and who will distinguish himself as a leader.

Essay #4

Question: What obstacles or major challenges have you overcome to achieve your goals? How do these life experiences distinguish you from other applicants? (one page maximum)

My most difficult challenge has been overcoming the habits and behaviors which were integral to my early successes but which ultimately were keeping me from becoming a better leader.

The overwhelming success of my first five years at [Company A] left me to believe that anything I touched would turn to gold. By the age of 25, I was a top engineer at the hottest company in Silicon Valley, with a fortune in stock options and seemingly limitless potential. My approach, which was echoed throughout the company, was brash, arrogant, and very technically focused.

As the company started to struggle and I joined a group of co-workers to study the root of our problems, I started to realize how the negative patterns in the company as a whole were reflected in my own behaviors. We were so confident in our ideas that we drowned out the quieter voices of our customers and non-technical employees. My involvement in this group not only gave me the chance to help the company, it gave me the chance to reflect on and change my own patterns. I learned that is just as important to listen to the opinions of others as it is to express my own. Through facilitation training, I learned how to be respectful and inclusive rather than aggressive and confrontational.

As a result of this transformation, I now possess a unique combination of skills I believe will benefit my fellow classmates: on one hand, I have very strong analytical skills and can present a strong case for my ideas. On the other, I have similarly strong facilitation skills and am able to bring together the diverse ideas of both strong-willed and less assertive members.

Critique

This is a wonderful example of an essay that runs counter to what most of us regard as obstacles to overcome in life: poverty, undereducated parents, broken homes, illnesses, career setbacks, etc. In fact, this essay wows with the unconventionality of the obstacle presented: the arrogance and ego of a twenty-five-year-old Silicon Valley hotshot, whose style (and that of his peers) had begun to create what he calls "negative patterns" of operation in his company. He writes of his transformation into someone who becomes more sensitive to other's ideas and ultimately excels at facilitation and consensus. The self-awareness demonstrated in this essay and willingness to admit to this committee that he was once brash and inward-focused are truly refreshing and genuine.

Essay #5

Question: Please describe your career progression to date, high-lighting leadership and management positions and reasons for changing employers or career paths, if applicable. How will an MBA assist you in achieving your short- and long-term career goals? (Answer must be no more than 2 typed pages, double-spaced.)

Having been exposed to various science and math after-school programs as a young child, it came as no surprise that I would enjoy the challenges of engineering as an adult. After successfully completing undergraduate and graduate degrees in Electrical Engineering, as well as six summer internships ([Company A], [Company B]), I decided to join [Company C] in [Location D] as an optical networking system engineer. [Company C] was a company known for its innovation, creativity, and great work environment, all of which made it an ideal place for me to begin my professional career. As a system engineer, I designed and developed requirements for fiber-optic communications systems targeted at the growing demand for integrated voice and data traffic.

At [Company C], I contributed to the success of my team beyond the average system engineer and my efforts were quickly recognized and rewarded. As a result of my effective communication skills and technical contributions, I was nominated to become an International Standards Representative (ISR), representing the strategic interests of [Company C] and the U.S. State Department at international telecommunications standards meetings. In addition to being one of only 15 ISR's at [Company C], I also developed programs to aid the transition of new college graduates to the [Company C] culture and was nominated to the Corporate Review Board within our division.

After two successful years at [Company C], I had the desire to join an exciting start-up company, expand my leadership role, and return to the Bay Area, and thus I joined [Company E], an early stage optical communications company. At [Company E], I took on several leadership roles, including leading the system software requirements development, managing optical component vendor relationships, and becoming their U.S. Standards Liaison. I also was selected as one of their external technical conference speakers. Unfortunately, despite our team's efforts and achievements, the [Company E] optics program was cancelled due to 2001 telecommunications collapse.

Due to my strong personal network and motivation to continue my career development path, I was able to join another optical start-up in the Bay Area, despite the limited positions and intense competition resulting from the telecom downturn. I joined [Company F] as a system engineer and product manager for optical sub-systems. This role provided the unique challenge of serving as the lead system engineer as well as managing the product development of five [Company F] products.

Throughout my career, I have served in leadership and contributing roles at both large corporations and small technology startups. A Kenan-Flagler MBA will be of great value to me as I make the natural transition to become a consultant and private equity investor, specializing in technology innovation and value creation. This short-term goal will serve as a vehicle to achieve my long-term interests. System engineering has allowed me to apply exciting technology to solve fascinating problems, but it is my involvement in community programs, including teaching engineering to kids and sharing the joy of problem solving with others, that truly motivates me. In the long-term, I will use the skills developed during my Kenan-Flagler MBA, combined with my own professional and teaching experiences, to develop, own and operate an international network of technology consulting and learning centers, focused on exposing youth in underserved communities to potential careers in engineering and science.

The UNC Center for Entrepreneurship and Venture Innovation will provide an excellent curriculum that will prepare me for my future as a global entrepreneur and successful technology consultant. Kenan-Flagler will afford me the opportunity to share my own unique professional experiences as well as to learn from a diverse group of bankers, brand managers, entrepreneurs and consultants from fields in which I may have had limited exposure. In summary, the Kenan-Flagler emphasis on teamwork and practical experience, coupled with the opportunity to interact with leaders from around the world, will help me to develop skills for long-term business success.

CRITIQUE

Overall, this essay is written in a very positive, open tone. The writer's thoughts flow well and cohesively. There is not too much detail or business jargon. This essay also does a good job of giving insight into what has motivated the student's career to date. There is a nice summary (in the next-to-last paragraph) of his main theme or proposition to the committee: that he is a proven leader in both large-company and start-up business environments. Not only does he clearly communicate why he is a good candidate, but he actively and successfully answers the question "Why UNC?" He tells us that UNC is a fit for him because our Center for Entrepreneurship will provide the targeted education and resources he is seeking.

Essay #6

Question: Please describe your career progression to date, high-lighting leadership and management positions and reasons for changing employers or career paths, if applicable. How will an MBA assist you in achieving your short- and long-term career goals? (Answer must be no more than 2 typed pages, double-spaced.)

There is nothing as exhilarating as racing down the slopes, feeling the wind whip your hair and cheeks, and the warm satisfaction of reaching the bottom with your body pumping full of adrenaline. At the tender age of eight, I experienced my first ski-induced adrenaline rush and this feeling has only magnified over the past eighteen years. Because of my fantastic experiences with Pacific Northwest winter sports and my love of the outdoors, my long-term goal is to build and manage my own winter sports company. Whether my enterprise takes the form of a service business or a manufacturing company, I'm excited by the idea of partnering my life-long passion with my career. But I need stronger business skills to make my company a success. I want to pursue management consulting in the short term to develop my strategic thinking. A Kenan-Flagler MBA is critical to my success as I move into consulting and then into my own business. Only at Kenan-Flagler can I get the skills and perspective I need to pursue both of these career goals.

My experience working for [Company A] laid the foundation for my interest in management consulting. I enjoyed the camaraderie, the challenging work, and the ever-changing clients and working groups. Managing multiple engagements energized me while I developed a broad understanding of business practices. Consulting will offer these same positives with more emphasis on general business strategy. At [Company A], I dedicated myself to exceeding expectations. As a result, I received responsibilities and promotions ahead of the usual tenure track pace. The abilities to prioritize my work, focus on results, and present findings to senior management that I learned there will contribute to my future in management consulting and beyond.

Because I wanted to grow my accounting and finance skills, I accepted a position with [Company B], a hedge fund manager. After my introduction to multiple business areas at [Company A], I have found that focusing on a single industry has strengthened my research and technological skills. I have gained an intimate understanding of the hedge fund industry and my technical and analytical abilities have significantly matured in this fast-paced, team-oriented environment. Because I was recognized as a leader with strong interpersonal skills, [Company B] selected me to develop and implement a company-wide formalized training program. Sharing my knowledge and learning from others continues to be a highlight of my days. I mentor new hires, interact with many departments and levels of employees, and take an active role in recruiting. My variety of past work experiences will help me contribute to class discussions and to my peers' career decisions while I learn at Kenan-Flagler.

I am at a crossroads in my career. An MBA will allow me to radically expand my business knowledge while developing the networking relationships to take me into management consulting and ultimately my entrepreneurial venture. I'm particularly drawn to Kenan-Flagler's program because it offers a unique chance for me to pursue my dual goals. The knowledge base, case competitions and interactive classroom discussions will prepare me for consulting. Yet Kenan-Flagler is also noted for its Entrepreneurship and Venture Development Studies. I am particularly interested in the classes that will allow me to analyze and consider my own ideas for new businesses. On a more personal level, I'm drawn to the intangible aspects of the Kenan-Flagler experience. The diversity of experiences that students bring is second to none. I am also excited by its focus on teamwork and the unusually strong emphasis on study groups. I look forward to working with my fellow classmates to explore ideas and support each other's endeavors.

I'm shocked when I look at the map and discover how far Kenan-Flagler is from the big ski slopes that I love. How can a place so far from the mountains offer such a perfect lift back to the slopes where I belong? Though I'll miss my snow, I'm convinced that Kenan-Flagler offers the ideal place for me to grow as a person while getting the perfect preparation for my business endeavors.

CRITIQUE

This essay begins with an exciting opening that relates to her main topic. This opening works because it grabs attention, yet because of its relevance to what follows, it is not a case of being just catchy or cute. She also immediately ties her opening to her stated goal and thesis—to build and manage a winter sports company. This links her passion with future career plans and is compelling.

This candidate also makes sure we know about her strong consulting and business background, which is helpful in convincing us that she has the credentials to succeed in the academic program. She highlights her achievements by talking about her dedication to excellence. Finally, this candidate makes a strong case for UNC by noting specific curriculum offerings and the "intangible aspects" of our community, such as our close-knit group of students and emphasis on group study. By pointing out the attributes of our program to which she is attracted, she gives us insight into how she might fit in it.

Essay #7

Question: Please describe your career progression to date, highlighting leadership and management positions and reasons for changing employers or career paths, if applicable. How will an MBA assist you in achieving your short- and long-term career goals? (Answer must be no more than 2 typed pages, double-spaced.)

While witnessing my father's fight against liver cirrhosis, I encountered many patients who were suffering, like he was, because they had been not been diagnosed early enough. These patients often relied on useless or even dangerous folk medicines, due to the lack of information they possessed about their illnesses. At [University A], I majored in pharmacy, and upon graduating, I decided to pursue a career in marketing so that I would be able to improve public awareness of illnesses and treatment options.

I began my career as a sales representative at [Company B]. My outstanding performance earned me a quick promotion to brand manager of a key schizophrenia medication. As the company's youngest brand manager, I worked with a sales team of twenty employees. Through focusing on the message that schizophrenics could lead productive lives if properly medicated, my team significantly increased sales revenues of our product.

My achievements attracted the attention of another pharmaceutical company, [Company C], and I accepted a position there marketing insulin, one of the company's top products. At [Company C], I worked to apply innovative marketing programs to raise awareness of diabetic diagnosis and blood glucose control, doubling the company's insulin sales in two years. Based on this success, I was promoted to the position of New Product Planning Manager, and am currently responsible for all aspects of new product launches, including analyzing the profitability and feasibility of new products, as well as checking the progress of clinical trials and submitting related documentation to the [Country A] Food & Drug Administration.

Looking toward the future, my short-term objective is to become a global marketing manager at a multinational pharmaceutical company, which would allow me to deepen my insight into the international pharmaceutical market. After spending several years working as a marketing executive, I plan to select a company producing new medications vital to the health of [Country A]'s patients, and become the founder and general manager of its [Country A] affiliate. Serving in this capacity would allow me to contribute to [Country A]'s healthcare system, provide patients with needed medication, and conduct campaigns to improve diagnosis and treatment rates.

Through my work at [Company B] and [Company C], I have accumulated extensive knowledge of sales and marketing; however, I will need to strengthen my understanding of essential business functions if I am to achieve my ambitious career goals. The MBA program at Kenan-Flagler Business School matches my career goals seamlessly, offering a world-renowned business curriculum that would allow me to acquire the theoretical fundamentals of finance, management, and marketing. Additionally, the school offers courses that match my specific interests, including Brand Strategy and Implementation, Data, Tools, and Decisions, and Marketing Issues. Participating in Kenan-Flagler's MBA program would enable me to build a foundation of business skills while delving deeper into issues concerning healthcare, on my way toward fulfilling my goal of improving [Country A]'s healthcare system.

CRITIQUE

This essay begins in an unusual and dramatic way, yet it is extremely effective in explaining the candidate's passion for her chosen career. Her words immediately captivate the reader. This essay very clearly communicates her unique heritage, background, and professional experiences. You leave this essay wanting to meet this person and learn more about her perspective.

This is an example of how a relatively brief essay can still be very effective. This writer makes her points clearly and effectively. Her story and interests speak for themselves. The goals are realistic, the style of writing straightforward. The overall result is very genuine.

ESSAY #8

Question: Describe your three greatest accomplishments. What does each demonstrate about your personality? (Answer must be no more than 2 typed pages, double-spaced.)

Despite growing up in Detroit, a city known more for its high crime rate and poor public school system, I was blessed with family, friends and mentors that exposed me to great learning opportunities. Whether it was in my Dad's dental office in middle school, or engaging colleagues in the workplace, it seemed like someone was always encouraging me to set high goals to achieve. Throughout my career, there are many accomplishments of which I am proud. To make progress, I defined two main criteria to help with determining which is greatest: (1) it must have had a larger impact on the community, and (2) it must have resulted in substantial personal growth. Using these criteria, I have identified a leadership experience, a professional appointment, and an academic award as my three greatest accomplishments.

In the middle of what is now referred to as the "Telecom Nuclear Winter", I had one of my greatest accomplishments while leading the product development and engineering teams at [Company A]. After joining [Company A], a small fiber-optic communications startup, I quickly learned that the current product architecture was seriously flawed, the management structure was in disarray with the abrupt departure of the VP of Marketing, and even worse, the lead investors were losing interest. Faced with the decision to either try to make the situation work or leave the company for having misled me about their situation, I took the road that builds character and helped enable the company's turnaround.

To add stability, I established a document control policy, met with potential customers to understand their product needs, and led many internal discussions to ensure that the engineering team was on the same page with the marketing team with regard to our product architecture. Based on the efforts of myself, along with the engineering staff, [Company A] established a new strategic direction within 1 month of my joining the company, developed new prototypes within 4 months, and regained the firm support of our Board of Directors within 6 months. Through this experience, I gained the confidence that I can produce results under pressure, build consensus among team members, set realistic team goals, and overcome my personal apprehension to lead a new team during a time of great uncertainty.

Secondly, I would like to discuss an accomplishment during my tenure as a system engineer at [Company B]. I was selected to become one of [Company B]'s Standards Representatives, negotiating the technical and strategic merits of fiber-optic transmission standards with other telecommunications companies. Prior to this appointment, I never realized the significant importance of technical standards, but now I know how they lower equipment costs, allow interoperability and provide customers with increased flexibility. Requiring significant international travel, deep technical expertise, and being key to the protection of [Company B]'s strategic interest, this role afforded me an opportunity to be a leader at an early stage of my career. Despite being less experienced, by an average of 20 years, than other standards representatives, my history of negotiating key international agreements led to an appointment with the U.S. State Department, representing the interest of U.S. companies within the International Telecommunication Union. In this role, I was able to exchange ideas with my peers from other countries, to work with others to establish telecommunications standards that impact our daily lives, and to expand my knowledge through impromptu discussions of global issues that reached far beyond optics.

Lastly, receiving the prestigious [Award C], given annually by students and faculty to the most outstanding teaching assistant (TA) in the [University D] Department of Electrical Engineering, is the third of my greatest achievements. During my year as Head TA, in charge of lecture, labs and office hours, I overcame some growing pains to find that I enjoyed teaching and excelled at communicating complex engineering concepts to students. I received rave reviews from students for my constant enthusiasm and commitment to teaching engineering in a way that made the learning experience more than just about solving problems. Helping over 600 students learn fundamental engineering concepts while sharing a passion for teaching, resulted in my nomination as the 1998 [Award C] Recipient. This award demonstrates my effective communication skills, ability to establish positive working relationships with colleagues, and willingness to share my knowledge with others.

CRITIQUE

Like other successful essays we've seen, this one immediately draws the reader in by creating a good impression in the first paragraph. The candidate identifies two main criteria that define his core values for an accomplishment: that it has a larger impact on the community and that it results in personal growth. He comes off as self-aware, mature, and driven by high personal values.

The fact that in this essay the writer attributes his success to the encouragement he received from others tells us a lot about what kind of person he is and clearly says that he's not arrogant. Our relatively small program prides itself on an enrollment that is team-oriented and focused on people helping one another. That he would present his accomplishments as products of the help he has received along the way indicates that he's the type of person we'd like to have in our program. Finally, that he won an award for being one of the most outstanding teaching assistants at a prestigious university (in the department of electrical engineering) speaks volumes about the high regard in which he is held by both peers and students.

ESSAY #9

Question: Describe your three greatest accomplishments. What does each demonstrate about your personality? (Answer must be no more than 2 typed pages, double spaced.)

I was born modest; not all over, but in spots.
—A Connecticut Yankee in King Arthur's Court

My three greatest accomplishments to date cover the three major areas of my life: my career, my relationships with others and my personal development. In my career, my greatest accomplishment has been my successful leadership of [Company A]'s Sales and Marketing

Department. When I took over the marketing and sales department, morale on the team was very low. The former director had been very reluctant to try new marketing and sales strategies and the performance of many team members had stagnated. In the beginning, I had very little experience developing sales and marketing strategy, however I knew that I had a team with a great deal of combined experience and intelligence. I organized brainstorming meetings for the department often including senior members from other teams. The rich discussion and debate that these meetings provoked provided me with some of the best and most successful programs that I have undertaken as a director. Some of these projects include a re-branding effort that re-positioned [Company A] as the market leader, contract standardization procedures that improved communication of client customizations between the sales and programming departments, and suggestions for several new products as well as modifications to existing products. I learned that by getting more people on my team involved in these projects, they developed a sense of ownership of the corporate strategies and implemented those strategies more effectively in their day-to-day activities. I also worked individually with each member of my team to set specific goals and worked with them continually to help them meet those goals. As a result of these measures, many members of my team have expressed a greater satisfaction with their positions and have become better and more productive employees. I am most proud of the fact that every member of my team has shown marked improvement in productivity, quality of work and initiative during my tenure as director. In leading this team, I have learned the value of teamwork, initiative, strong management and leadership not only as a means to success for myself, my company and my department but also as a means of creating a pleasant and productive work environment for all concerned.

My greatest accomplishment in my personal life has been my development of strong and diverse relationships with family and friends providing my life with great meaning and depth. Each of these relationships with my mother, sister, two closest friends and my husband adds a totally different outlook to my life and experiences. Their openness and honesty as well as their unique intelligences and talents adds so much color and depth to my perspective, giving me the ability to be more tolerant and to empathize with people who lead lives very different from my own. I have had the privilege of supporting each of these individuals when they needed me and have learned how much joy can be gained by a life filled with such acts. I have also learned to lean on each one of them and gain strength from their support and confidence in me when I have needed it most. Each of these relationships has required a good amount of work to reach their current level. I have had to learn the value of compromise and flexibility and have had to swallow my pride more than once. However, the rewards have far outweighed the sacrifices and I cannot imagine my life without these people in it. I believe that these relationships say a great deal about who I am as a person. They demonstrate the value that I place on diversity, honesty, flexibility and tolerance as well as the importance of forming a strong network of people who you can count on and who feel confident that they can count on you.

My greatest accomplishment in my personal development has been my transformation from a shy and somewhat directionless young woman to a confident, happy and very focused adult. Growing up in suburban Louisiana, I never felt that I fit in. I was bright in a culture that did not value intelligence in girls and I felt constrained by my very insular and homogenous environment. Consequently, I grew up shy and very unsure of myself. I knew that I wanted to see what else the world had to offer and college was the perfect opportunity to explore. At [University B], I was exposed to some of the best and brightest people from all over the world and to many new ideas, both in and out of class. However, I was unprepared academically, emotionally and financially for the rigors of life at a large, highly competitive university and my grades suffered. When I started my undergraduate career, I had little idea of what I wanted to do with my life. I thought that I wanted to be a physician because, frankly, I thought that is what intelligent and ambitious people did. When I realized that I did not want to enter the medical field, I felt somewhat lost. I graduated from college with a degree that I was unsure that I would use but also with a larger view of the world, a sharper mind and an interest in technology that eventually led me to [Company A]. If was during my time at [Company A] that I really "came out of my shell" so to speak. My experience working with clients and later, acting as a manager and a company leader, gave me the communication skills that I needed to work in a team environment and succeed in each of my positions. This was also the time in which I formed stronger relationships with my family and friends and when my relationship with my future husband developed. All of this gave me confidence both in myself and in my abilities. The little girl who used to hide behind her mother's legs at neighborhood parties now feels comfortable mingling with 5,000 strangers at a business reception. At [Company A], I found that I had a real talent for working with teams, managing and motivating people and offering ideas that would lead to a company's success. In the last three years as Director of Sales and Marketing for [Company A], I have developed a strong interest in corporate and marketing strategy. This has given my career a focus that I have never had before. I finally know what I want to do with my life and I now have the confidence, the skills and the determination to achieve anything that I set my mind to.

CRITIQUE

This essay is particularly compelling because of the honesty and eloquence with which this candidate writes about her feelings and experiences. None of her accomplishments is extraordinary, but each is admirable. In each story of accomplishment, what resonates is her core character and perspective. She communicates that she is open, humble, honest, flexible, and self-aware. You read this essay and think to yourself, I'd like this person as a friend, as a classmate, as a colleague.

She also communicates strong business experience. In her first accomplishment, as head of her team's sales and marketing effort, the applicant shows an innate knowledge of how teams operate and progress to success. She has a solid grasp of brand marketing and management principles. That acumen combined with her interpersonal strengths leads her to a successful outcome and a great learning experience.

In her second accomplishment she chooses to focus on a personal experience, the relationships she has with her immediate family and two friends. In this case, her essay might have been better served with another example. Writing about one's family is so clichéd and overdone, it's hard to get an admissions officer's interest. The challenge is to express that what she learned from these relationships is genuine, vital, and most important, relevant. She clearly does this.

What is truly refreshing about this essay however, is the last example. The candidate gives us true insights into who she was and who she has become by sharing her background with us. Having grown up in a culture where she felt that women's intelligence was devalued, she reveals the personal hurdles she cleared to get where she is. She is not afraid to admit that she was lost and directionless, that she was shy and overwhelmed by college, and that her grades suffered. But she doesn't make excuses; she takes us on her journey. In the end, she communicates that she has emerged as an individual with a talent for team leadership and a strong interest in strategy.

ESSAY #10

Optional Question: Please tell us about any international experiences you have had, either living or working abroad, and how it has impacted your global perspective. (one page maximum)

In more than two years of travel through almost 50 countries, I have both shared in the wonders of diverse cultures and witnessed the despair of poverty and political instability that often lurk within: I have scaled 18,000 ft. peaks in Kenya and Nepal; been beaten by thugs while bicycle touring through Nicaragua; watched in awe as tribesmen is Papua dressed in nothing but penis gourds slaughtered pigs for ceremony; and dodged paramilitaries armed with grenade launchers in Colombia. My international exposure also includes briefly living and working in Italy, becoming proficient in Spanish, and growing up as a first generation American with dual U.S. and British citizenship.

These experiences have had a profound influence on my thinking. First, they have made me realize how quickly and easily commerce and culture flow across international borders. The pervasiveness of Coca-Cola and American pop music are just two indications of how small the world has become.

Second, I now understand how global the product life cycle truly is, from materials, to manufacturing, and finally retirement. Nothing drove this home better than when, in a small village in Tanzania, I noticed a man wearing a promotional t-shirt from my old employer that only a few dozen people in California had been given. It had been donated, sold in bulk, shipped to Africa, and resold in a town market!

Finally, traveling abroad has given me insights into our own American culture. I can now see that the US is a nation of individuals, rather than a community. As each person reaches for their own piece of the American dream, something gets left behind --community, a sense of a greater good, sound infrastructure. Exposure to diverse cultures is necessary to gain the perspective needed to grow beyond one's own limited cultural bounds. With this in mind, I now spend more time working in my own community.

CRITIQUE

"Wow," is what comes to mind after reading this essay. This applicant is an extraordinary and gifted writer. He seems as much an essayist or columnist for a newspaper as he does a candidate for business school. What makes his essay soar is that he has not only had remarkable experiences across different cultures, but that he is able to extract valuable insights that are relevant to business and the human condition.

He writes captivatingly of his experiences in Kenya, Papua, and Nicaragua not to impress us (though who wouldn't stand in awe of someone who has scaled mountain peaks in Nepal—the stuff movies are made of—and ventured to distant and conflict-ridden areas). He is deeply impacted by his travels and what he sees. He emerges as someone both aware of self and reflective. As if that is not enough, we also learn that he speaks fluent Spanish and has dual citizenship in the U.S. and Great Britain.

His anecdote about the T-shirt is a wonderful example of his ability to tell a great story, because he links a seemingly inconsequential item, the T-shirt, to something that becomes highly symbolic. His observation of "how global the product life cycle is" demonstrates astute insight that's clearly relevant for someone who plans to study business.

His last paragraph gives us a final sense of the breadth and depth of his thinking by relating the American Dream to the loss of ideals and the greater good of the world. He then advocates exposure to diverse cultures to compensate for cultural limitations. To achieve this, he'll be staying close to home, an ending that is both ironic and whimsical. We're wowed all over again.

UNIVERSITY OF ROCHESTER
WILLIAM E. SIMON GRADUATE SCHOOL
OF BUSINESS ADMINISTRATION

ESSAY #1

Question: Describe your post-MBA career plans. How will a degree from the Simon School help you to achieve these goals? How does your past education and experience support your career objectives?

After completing my MBA I plan on pursuing a position as a buy side research analyst with the long-term goal of running my own fund. Spending the last few years analyzing the performance of client companies as an auditor has helped me to discover my passion of financial analysis. Auditing, however, does not provide the challenges that a career in investment management offers. The challenge of combining advanced financial tools with economic analysis for the purpose of making investment decisions motivates me to pursue a career in investment management.

Over the past few years I have worked to refine my interest in financial analysis and markets including recent coursework in Intermediate Portfolio Management at [University A]. This coursework, in addition to my independent research, has reinforced my desire to enter the field of investment management. I plan on further pursuing this interest by sitting for level I of the CFA exam this coming May.

My accounting education and career have given me an in-depth understanding of business transactions and financial reporting. However, I lack a detailed understanding of, and the quantitative tools necessary to perform, security analysis. Accounting has provided me with an understanding of the relationship between corporate performance and financial information. The Simon MBA program will help me make the link between financial information and security prices.

The majority of problems faced by business today require a collaboration of ideas from a variety of management disciplines. The economics based, cross-functional approach at Rochester will enhance my understanding of the fundamentals of business. The finance curriculum and innovative faculty will expose me to the latest developments in equity valuation and financial markets, while the core coursework will provide me with the broad foundation necessary to excel in today's business world. Access to resources outside of the classroom, especially the Investment Club and the Simon Meliora Fund, will provide me with further opportunities for growth and networking.

I am confident that the Simon MBA program can offer me the best business education and access to the greatest network of resources. I am incredibly excited at the prospect of studying at Rochester. Its exceptional finance curriculum, innovative faculty, and tight-knit community make the Simon School the perfect fit for me.

CRITIQUE

The admissions committee feels that this is a high-quality essay. The applicant paints a clear picture as to why he wants to pursue his MBA at this time given his past work experience and personal preferences. He states how a Simon MBA would help him achieve his post-MBA goals in both the short and long term. He also does an excellent job of tying in current business trends in his particular field of interest with Simon's economics-based, cross-functional approach as well as its strengths in finance, renowned faculty, and small class size. This clearly demonstrates that the candidate has done sufficient research to identify Simon as a strong fit for the type of MBA program that he is seeking.

ESSAY #2

Question: Discuss three professional accomplishments that demon-strate your potential for a successful managerial career.

I set the goal of becoming a CPA during my undergraduate studies at [University A] because I felt that it would distinguish me as someone with the knowledge, skills and abilities to succeed in the business world.

After months of intense studying, I passed the challenging exam. Earning my CPA license proved my mastery of accounting and dedication to a career in business. With this certification, I am identified as an ethical person with a broad based business understanding.

Recently, I was assigned to lead an audit team at one of the largest steel distributors in the world. The prior year's audit was plagued with inefficiencies and as a result there was a significant delay in issuing financial statements. The client was left frustrated with the level of service received from the firm.

From the start of the engagement it was apparent that I would need to regain the client's trust. I was able to develop this trust by maintaining a high level of communication. By keeping the client continually informed of the progression of the audit, I was able to avoid the bottlenecks that led to the delays in the prior year.

The client was pleased that the audit was completed ahead of schedule. Additionally, the senior manager and partner recognized me for my efforts in rebuilding the relationship.

In less than three years at [Company B] I have been promoted twice. My last promotion, to senior associate, came despite an extended absence from the audit group.

In the fall of 2001, I made the decision to pursue a special project run by [Company B]'s Forensic Consulting Group at the site of the World Trade Center terrorist attacks. I chose to participate in this project despite the fact that my departure from the audit group would jeopardize my chance for promotion.

Upon returning to the audit group, I consulted with my performance manager to determine how I could better position myself for a promotion. With his guidance, I was able to secure a place on an engagement that would enable me to demonstrate my leadership skills. By excelling in this role, I was able to prove in a short period of time that I was capable of handling the responsibilities of a senior associate.

CRITIQUE

This applicant does a great job in highlighting his three greatest accomplishments. While obtaining the CPA is clearly a more academic accomplishment, he is able to successfuly tie this achievement to his ability to succeed professionally. He also gives an example of how he was able to take the initiative to successfully mend relations with a frustrated client by completing an engagement ahead of schedule through proactive communications. Finally, he demonstrates leadership potential through his successful promotion to the senior associate level.

Overall, the applicant has demonstrated his knowledge of the Simon MBA program and has shown that he would be a good fit within the University of Rochester community. His past experiences demonstrate his ability to succeed, and he has openly communicated how a Simon MBA would help him to achieve his future goals. Finally, he has clearly and succinctly answered the question asked, providing appropriate details while remaining within the standard essay length.

UNIVERSITY OF TEXAS
McCOMBS SCHOOL OF BUSINESS

Essay #1

Question: Explain how obtaining an MBA at the McCombs School of Business will assist you in achieving your personal and/or professional life goals. Why is now the best time for you to pursue this degree? Your explanation should include, but is not necessarily limited to, a description of both your intermediate and long-term goals, as well as a current vision of your desired employment upon graduation.

I am pursuing an MBA for two reasons: to facilitate transition from the non-profit to the for-profit sector, and to earn skills that place me in an international corporation allowing me to work and live abroad. The realization that my career goals will be best facilitated by an MBA did not come easily, but the road I have taken makes me more certain that business school is the right decision, and McCombs is the right school for me.

I have worked in three industries: publishing, hospitality, and affordable housing. In each, I relished the opportunity to learn about a particular area of interest. However, intimidated by my own lack of technical skills in the business, I limited myself to entry level positions, but quickly discovered that my abilities and interests stretch farther that those opportunities could provide.

I recently left a job at a non-profit that provides below-market loans and technical assistance to nonprofits creating affordable housing. During my tenure at [Company A], the organization underwent a significant consolidation. Participating in this merger and the constant reorganization of our staff structure, I realized my passions for business run deep, and I perform best when large issues are at stake. At [Company A], we continually struggle to improve product delivery to our clients. At my publishing job, success frequently depended on the support of current legal issues, from bills passing legislature to protected access to public information. I taught myself to negotiate this access delicately but firmly with protective public information officers, then tailored that skill to fit my job in hospitality, mediating conflicts with guests or managers. In every case, I was happiest when calmly negotiating a contentious situation. Such cases, common during [Company A]'s merger negotiations, were rare in its return to everyday business.

In business school, I want to learn the environment and issues endemic to a larger corporation. Eventually, I would like to take these skills and use them in a return to the non-profit sector. This desire is similar to that of someone raised in a small town who is ready to see the city. The benefits of a close-knit community are many, but one is well-served by moving beyond this security to a larger city to see what it has to offer. In the city, the pace is faster, the options are different, the people are new and diverse. Eventually, one returns to the small town with skills, knowledge, and point of view that allow one to solve small town problems with big city solutions. This, for me, is what education is about: closing the gap between the bigs and the littles, the haves and have-nots.

A practical application of this theory could be working as a strategic management consultant in a large corporation in Mexico after graduation, then using connections I make through that position to start a nonprofit providing job training, placing participants in internships within organizations where I've worked. This plan would allow me to exercise skills I could learn in the Spanish Language Track and in such classes as Business in Latin America or Nonprofit Strategic Management, and use my experience to increase another's opportunities.

McCombs has demonstrated a strong commitment to global management education. As someone who will live in Mexico after I graduate, I'm attracted to a school that has a large and active Hispanic population and can support my desire to understand the business climate of Latin America. That McCombs was rated by Hispanics, and that UT Austin houses a stellar institute for Latin American studies, means the school takes my areas of interest seriously. McCombs's location in Texas, its Texas Plus and study abroad programs, and connections to businesses in Mexico provide the opportunity to apply what I learn in the classroom to a challenging internship and a suitable post-graduate position.

McCombs is a fast track to a high quality of learning, from more dedicated teachers, than I could find in any on-the-job training. I have the intellectual ability and curiosity to take a lesson and run with it; what I need now is the right lesson. McCombs can provide me with a framework for the business community: a standard of how things work and what trends are prevalent. In return, I can use those skills to manipulate that standard and create outstanding exceptions to it. I will succeed wherever I go to business school, but I believe that success will be greater if I can take advantage of all that McCombs has to offer.

CRITIQUE

In this essay, we appreciated the overall writing style and we particularly liked some of the comparisons drawn and the essay's creativity. It was clear and convincing, and it showed that the candidate did research about our school and how it fits with her professional goals.

Essay #2

Question: Explain how obtaining an MBA at the McCombs School of Business will assist you in achieving your personal and/or professional life goals. Why is now the best time for you to pursue this degree? Your explanation should include, but is not necessarily limited to, a description of both your intermediate and long-term goals, as well as a current vision of your desired employment upon graduation.

Sumimasen (excuse me), *arigato* (thank you), and *konnichiwa* (hello) were the only Japanese words that I knew when I first landed in Hiroshima, Japan, for a six-month work assignment. By the time I left, I had not only learned conversational Japanese but I also had a clearer vision of my career goals. My experience in Asia, combined with an e-commerce leadership position at [Company A], led me to realize the necessity of an MBA as I move toward my ultimate goal of creating a global corporation.

When I began my career with [Company A], I structured my assignments to develop both my engineering and business skills. The opportunity to develop these skills on a global scale presented itself in the form of the [Company A]/[Company B] [vehicle program]. During the vehicle development phase at the [Company B] Headquarters in Hiroshima, I served as a Powertrain Systems Team Leader. My primary task was to facilitate the issue-resolution process for the Powertrain Quality Team, a diverse group of engineers and managers from [Company B] and [Company A], as well as suppliers. For each of the numerous challenges our team faced, my tasks included leading the resolution process and presenting the solution to upper-level management.

My experience in Japan broadened my understanding of global business and led me to begin envisioning ways I could operate a company in the global marketplace. My assignment at [Company A].com further influences the development of my goals. This assignment unexpectedly catapulted me into a leadership position. When my supervisor suddenly left the department to join a joint venture ([Company C]), a huge chunk of his responsibilities fell onto my shoulders. My primary task was to lead and manage the [Company A].com "eMarketing Media Partnership Forum," a group of approximately 30 members. I conducted meetings with managers of various [Company A] consumer business groups to review prospective companies for possible partnerships. Restructuring the core Partnership Forum process, I helped achieve a 200% faster deal flow. I communicated with multiple emerging dot-com companies daily, who in each case claimed to have the best business model since sliced bread. This assignment made me realize how much I needed a business education to further develop my business acumen.

Working at [Company A].com helped me develop my long-term goal of managing a large-scale global company. With an eye toward this goal, I launched my own e-commerce company, [Company D].com in July of 2000, primarily as a means of learning more about the industry and how to manage a business. While my limited project management skills help me successfully launch this company, a business education would help me acquire the full array of business management skills I need to ensure that my company succeeds. My short-term goal after attaining my MBA is to work for a management consulting company. Understanding how different companies operate and strategize will provide invaluable experience to apply towards my goal of operating a large-scale company.

My engineering education alone is not sufficient to succeed in this fierce business environment. My experience in Hiroshima, for example, revealed to me the technical and business expertise required to lead and manage a multi-cultural team responsible for two vehicles that are manufactured on two continents and sold in 130 countries. Through such experiences I have started to develop the global management, technical, and interpersonal skills necessary to manage people and projects. To successfully overcome the challenges I will face in the global marketplace, I need an MBA.

McCombs' dynamic curriculum and international affiliations make it the ideal environment for me to develop the management and leadership skills required to lead an international company. I can develop these critical skills through innovative courses such as "Management and Marketing in the Global Arena." To achieve my career goal, I intend to specialize in entrepreneurship and to gain international experience, ideally through McCombs' affiliation with the Center for International Business Education and Research (CIBER) program. I attribute the success of such alumni as [Alumni A] and [Alumni B] (both '98) with their startup, [Company F], to McCombs' innovative faculty and international scope. I look forward to taking advantage of these opportunities at the McCombs School of Business to ensure that I develop the skills necessary to effectively establish and operate a world-class operation.

CRITIQUE

In this essay, we were impressed by the creative opening that is immediately relevant to the candidate's career and his reasons for wanting to go to b-school. Furthermore, the essay, while offering details about professional achievements, doesn't get too bogged down in those details. In the professional summary, the essay provides signposts (words like "tasks," "leadership position," and "my understanding") that really help the reader grasp the main points quickly. Many poorly written essays are missing these conventions, and hence it's sometimes hard to understand where the essay is going and why.

ESSAY #3

Question: All students bring a unique personal background to the classroom and study team that can prove to be as enlightening to fellow classmates as their professional skills. Describe what, outside of work, most distinguishes you as an individual and will most enrich the experience of your peers at McCombs from your background, life experiences, values, or interests.

As a brick crashed through our living room window, I quickly ran into the kitchen to get my mother. I can still picture the look on her face as she read the racist remarks written with chalk on the brick. The day afterward, our landlord gave us an eviction notice. I was six years old, and this was the first time that my mother had to explain to me how nasty and violent hatred could be. With a Caucasian mother and an African-American father, I received the hatred of whites who didn't like blacks and of anyone who didn't like to see the races mix.

Growing up in a multi-cultural family has allowed me to view society from many different angles. At a young age I found it extremely difficult to relate to either race. Both sides of my family expressed prejudices and hatred. Living in Detroit, where many neighborhoods are segregated, I didn't know how or where I was supposed to fit in. Not until my teenage years did I begin to appreciate my ethnicity. Over time, I began to use it to my advantage. My early life experiences as a racially mixed child have led me to look for ways to build bridges between people of different backgrounds, colors, and cultures.

My ability to reach across cultural divides was tested while I was in Hiroshima for a six-month [Company A]/[Company B] joint-venture work assignment. There, where I rarely came across other African Americans, I clearly stood out from the crowd. Given my color and my height (6'3"), some people assumed that I was a famous athlete, and they often asked me to sign autographs and pose for pictures. A few times I was even mistaken for MBA-star Grant Hill. To function in such an environment, I drew on my ability to overcome others' assumptions and stereotypes. I proved that I can smoothly integrate into any team setting. For instance, I recognized the need to build a relationship with both my Japanese and American team members in order to create a productive team environment. Unlike the average *gaijin* (foreigner), I learned and adopted the [Company B] working style (which included participating in morning calisthenics), followed by Japanese cultural practices (such as slurping

Ramen noodles), and studied diligently to learn conversational Japanese. Being racially mixed has taught me the skills necessary in a multi-cultural setting. Applying this skill set to my professional life has enabled me to bridge cultural gaps and develop strong relationships with my colleagues, enabling us to become friends.

For the second phase of the [Company A]/[Company B] joint venture, our team relocated to [Company A]'s Kansas City Assembly Plant. Immediately, I noticed that my Japanese counterparts faced some of the same difficulties that I had faced while in Japan (ordering food, banking, etc.). Recognizing their struggles, I tried to help them bridge the cultural gap. One way I facilitated this process was by hosting "cultural exchange" dinner parties. I would prepare a "soul food", Italian, or American entrée for my Japanese and American teammates. This would be the first time that some of the team members would taste collard greens, risotto, or Salisbury steak. After dinner, the group would socialize while playing UNO or Yahtzee. The team began to genuinely enjoy each other's company and wanted to learn more about one another. The Japanese members also felt comfortable enough to begin inviting the team to their homes to share traditional Japanese food and to sing karaoke. Acceptance laid the foundation for friendships that we carried into the work place and have maintained well beyond the vehicle launch in Kansas City. My ability to create friendships that cross cultural gaps will, above all else, enable me to contribute to the McCombs environment.

The McCombs community consists of people from around the globe. What has attracted me to McCombs is what *Business Week* describes as "a strong cooperative environment." My experience has taught me benefits of cooperation among people with differing backgrounds and perspectives. I anticipate learning from my peers at McCombs—in the classroom; through clubs, such as the International MBA Student Association; and through activities, such as barbecues at my residence. I will do my part to help foster "cultural exchanges" among my peers, allowing us to develop a global mindset and enjoy the McCombs experience.

CRITIQUE

We appreciated the strong, eye-opening introduction to this essay that wasn't gratuitous, but sincerely relevant to answering the question. The essay had a strong structure and relevant connections to another essay in the application, which led us to believe it probably wasn't cut and pasted from another school's application. The third paragraph was particularly powerful as it demonstrated that the applicant took the extra step to understand the "learning" that took place. It answered questions such as: Why is all of this relevant? How did it change me? How will it contribute to my success at McCombs?

CHAPTER 11

ESSAYS FROM THE STUDENT SIDE

Now that you've read the critiques by admissions officers of anonymous student essays, it's time to critique the essays of ten profiled students who believe their essays made the difference in their b-school application. We have added this new section this year to give added insight to real candidates—their undergraduate schools, GPAs, their GMAT scores, their work experience. These applicants reveal all so you can see an essay in its true context. With this method of full disclosure, you have the chance to gain a clear picture of the whole candidate and what it took for each one to gain entry at a top business school.

These applicants wrote on a variety of topics, from living abroad to launching their own businesses, from rock climbing and ice skating to deciding to leave a beloved college due to poor undergraduate grades. They constructed careful answers to some of the toughest questions posed by business schools and shared stories of both success and failure. But most of all, the authors showed their human side. These essays tell a story of the applicant that goes beyond a resume-driven list of achievements to delve into the person as a whole. This might include why they made the decisions that they have or where they plan to go in the future. In creating the new class for an MBA program, admissions officers like to know the people behind the standard impressive list of accomplishments. And we believe these essays have made that possible.

Ideally, this section of the book will provide you with inspiration, organizational structures, themes, new ways of expressing yourself, and renewed confidence that your essay can indeed make the crucial impact that you certainly seek. Take note, however, that we are not touting these essays as perfect—if there even is such a thing. Many of these students did not make it into every school to which they applied, though all are pleased with the school they chose to attend. That's the reality of the application process for the majority of applicants. It's not unusual to be accepted at Yale and denied by Harvard, accepted to Darden but denied by Haas. This is all the more reason these essays paint a valuable picture of a candidate's quest for a matching school.

Just in case you're wondering why these students would allow us to publish their essays, test scores, grades, and personal info, here's the answer to that: They realize the intrinsic value of sharing their experiences. Many said they were honored to have been chosen for publication and to have the chance to help others, like you, who may follow in their business school footsteps. Best of luck to you with your essays and beyond.

Anne Brewster

"I believe that my entrepreneurial work experience in starting up and running my own small business combined with my other work experiences in marketing and logistics helped me get in to the University of Washington MBA program. My passion for my work, along with a strong GMAT score and undergraduate GPA, also helped me catch the attention of the admissions committee. Because of the quality of my application, I received The Neal and Jan Dempsey Endowed MBA Fellowship to cover half of my first-year tuition. This fellowship is awarded to 'top students in each year's MBA class, with preference given to . . .applicants with technology backgrounds or entrepreneurial experience... These fellowships are to help the UW business school attract and support MBA students who will become future leaders as managers or entrepreneurs."

Stats

GMAT Score: 690
Undergraduate GPA: 3.52
College attended: Tufts University
Year of college graduation: 2003
Graduate school attended: N/A
Hometown: Whidbey Island, WA
Gender: Female
Race: White/Hispanic

ess school attended: University of Washington Business School
Accepted: University of Washington Business School
Denied: N/A
Wait-listed: N/A

Essay Prompt:

Goals Statement: Applicants with a plan for their future and with a good grasp of what is expected of them as MBA students are the most successful students in our program. We know plans change, and we know people often pursue an MBA to create new career options. Please tell us about your plans. Ideally, your essay should answer all the following questions: Why are you pursuing an MBA degree? What do you expect to do immediately after completing the MBA program? What is your primary lifetime career goal? How do your life and work experiences to date move you closer to these personal objectives? What specific things will the MBA experience contribute to your post-MBA and lifetime career goals? What unique aspects of the University of Washington MBA Program, if any, would contribute the most to achieving your goals? (750 words maximum)

A mentor once gave me this sound advice: to get where you want to go in life you must model the present on the future you desire. When I envision myself fifteen years from now, I see the owner of a successful apparel company and a business leader with strong ties to the Seattle community. At this point in my life, my challenge is to move quickly and effectively in order to transform my vision into reality; I view the MBA program at the University of Washington as the next step on the path to the future I see before me.

I was fortunate to be raised in a family where my creative side was nurtured by my mother, a seamstress, while tempered by the practicality of my father, a lawyer. I began to design clothing early on, and by age 11 started to sell my work to teachers and classmates, demonstrating an entrepreneurial drive that continued into high school. I found my niche in a college job as a costumer in the Tufts drama department, where I deepened my understanding of design, rounding out my work experience with summer jobs at a fabric store one year and an upscale bridal boutique the next. By senior year, I appreciated the value of my economics major to my future endeavors, but was eager to apply the concepts I had been learning in the classroom. My coursework and life experience up to this point culminated in the debut of my clothing line, Osorio, a month before graduation in an on-campus sales event. The sale was a success, and I expanded the framework of that initial project into a small business when I moved back home to the Northwest.

Since graduating I have sought out different experiences that would move me closer to my goals while building on my past achievements. Working at an ad agency, and then at a public relations firm, I learned valuable skills that I put to use immediately with Osorio, as well as long-term lessons that changed the way I viewed the business world. I felt like I was on the technical crew again in the Tufts drama department, helping run the show backstage. I was behind the curtain once more, meeting with clients and working with colleagues to develop new branding strategies and marketing campaigns. This exposure to business on a grander scale gave me additional impetus to pursue an MBA, both as a way to study how successful companies are run while learning business fundamentals in a structured setting.

Seeking a challenging, prestigious program with all the features I felt were necessary, I only had to look as far as my own hometown. The University of Washington MBA program's realistic and experiential style of learning speaks more to me than the one-dimensional academics I outgrew as an undergraduate, as well as the chance to personalize a flexible study plan. During a classroom visit I watched Jennifer Koski lead a class of completely engaged students and realized what a privilege it would be to work in this team-based setting, alongside such talented and passionate classmates, guided by intelligent and experienced professors. Outside of the classroom, the alumni network and mentoring program would be a valuable introduction to the Seattle business community of which I hope to become a member.

The career center might help me achieve my goal of a summer internship at Nordstrom, which, combined with my course work and program experience, might make me an attractive candidate for a position with the company. There, I could gain experience working for a major retailer in my desired industry and receive a grounding in the details of what it takes to succeed in the apparel business. Before I strike out on my own, I would have this career experience coupled with an MBA background to help me advance towards my long-term goals.

Now is the time to pursue an MBA, as I have reached a point where my business does not require the same input it did in its early stages. To take it to the next level I need the knowledge of business fundamentals, hands-on experience and ties to a business network of alumni and peers that the MBA program offers. In pursing an MBA at the University of Washington, I see both a means and an end: a logical and pragmatic step towards my lifelong goal of owning my own clothing business and an invaluable way to spend the next two years of my life.

Chris Kozup

"International MBAs, such as the program at Instituto de Empresa, value diversity. I consider my background to be a perfect fit with the selection criteria of the school. I have lived and worked in four continents; speak four languages and have traveled extensively. Career wise, I have been focused on the technology industry in emerging areas of wireless communications. My role as Program Director within the networking communications analyst team at META Group allowed me to develop experience in IT strategy dealing with all types of companies and levels of employees from nontechnical to CIO. Outside of work I am an avid music fan with a strong love for electronic music. I am a marathon runner and have a goal of completing a marathon on all seven continents—only four to go!"

Stats

GMAT Score: 590
Undergraduate GPA: 4.00
College attended: Ohio University
Year of college graduation: 1997
Graduate school attended: N/A
Hometown: Warren, OH
Gender: Male
Race: Caucasian

Admissions Information

Business school attended: Instituto de Empresa, Madrid, Spain

Accepted: Instituto de Empresa, Rotterdam School of Management

Denied: N/A

Wait-listed: N/A

Essay Prompt:

What was the most difficult problem you have faced in your life, and how did you deal with it?

I can not characterize the most difficult time in my life as one specific event or problem; rather it was a series of events that occurred over a period of several years. I was born and raised in Australia to teacher parents who enjoyed the laid-back lifestyle offered by rural bush communities. While the wanderlust of my parents ensured that I was well traveled as a boy, I always had the comfort of returning to my home in the northern Australian outback. But at the age of 14, my parents moved for good; to Ohio. I was not ready for the change of lifestyle that a permanent relocation would bring.

In my early teens, I identified culturally with Australia and had never considered myself anything but an Australian. I could recite the Australian national anthem; I had traveled the continent north, south, east and west; I had studied Aboriginal traditions and cultures. My mannerisms, accent and vernacular were all Australian. Yet, after four years living in the United States, I had become so acculturated that people perceived me to be an American. The problem I now faced was reconciling these two identities and becoming comfortable with my new surroundings without letting go of my heritage. I had done such a good job adjusting to the American way of life that I was now fighting to hold on to my original identity.

The struggle with my identity was exacerbated during a year spent abroad in France as a Rotary exchange student in 1992. As part of the exchange program, I spent time with a host of international students, including those from Australia. It became painfully clear that I was caught between two cultures as even the Australians perceived me as American. We spent many evenings discussing Australian popular culture, television and historical events. I discovered that even though I had the same experiences and could relate culturally and socially, the fact that I no longer spoke with an Australian accent left me on the outside.

While it was my initial time spent in France that highlighted my insecurity and lack of identity, it was ultimately time spent living in Paris that helped me to reconcile these emotions. During a subsequent summer spent interning at an advisory firm, Cambridge Energy Research Associates, I had the good fortune to become friends with a group of expatriates. I learned from their experiences as all of them possessed dual citizenship and were essentially living across two cultures. I remember quite vividly a conversation I had with one friend who had grown up in Sweden but was also French. Over a glass of wine we shared similar thoughts and experiences of how in one country we didn't identify with the culture, yet while in the other, we were perceived as foreign. It was this discussion that was the turning point for me. Having met a group of people who could empathize and understand my situation was exactly what I needed to realize that my multicultural background was a blessing.

I consider myself privileged to be both American and Australian. As a result of having lived in both countries, I find that I am able to identify with a broader array of people and can examine issues from a multitude of perspectives. I no longer worry about the root of my identity as I have come to grips with the fact that it is my experience with both cultures that has given me such a unique perspective on life. Ironically, it took time spent outside of both countries to allow me to realize the importance of each.

Erik Lam

"Given my sub-par undergraduate GPA, I faced what many believed to be insurmountable odds when applying to the top business schools. Nevertheless, with my non-traditional background in non-profit management as well as my experience in equity research on Wall Street and my solid result on the GMAT—topped off with countless hours of mirth and misery writing the essays that I believe made the difference—I was fortunate enough to have had the opportunity to attend NYU Stern, a truly invaluable experience. Bottom line to all you 'imperfect' candidates: never give up hope!"

Stats

GMAT Score: 710

Undergraduate GPA: 2.71

College attended: University of California—Los Angeles

Year of college graduation: 1998

Graduate school attended: N/A

Hometown: Bellrose Village, NY

Gender: Male

Race: Asian-American

Admissions Information

Business school attended: New York University Stern School of Business

Accepted: New York University Stern School of Business; University of Texas—Austin, McCombs School of Business

Denied: Cornell University Johnson School of Business; Duke University Fuqua School of Business; University of California—Berkeley Haas School of Business; University of Chicago Graduate Business Program; University of Pennsylvania Wharton School of Business;

Wait-listed: N/A

Essay Prompt:

Think about the decisions you have made in your life. Describe the following:

PAST: What choices have you made that led you to your current position?

PRESENT: Why is a Stern MBA necessary at this point in your life?

FUTURE: What is your desired position upon graduation from the Stern School?

"You're going to spend two years doing what? What about your future?" Those are the words I heard over and over four years ago.

I had just graduated from UCLA and turned down a lucrative consulting position in Silicon Valley to work for a nonprofit organization instead. While those around me didn't understand (I admit, I had a few doubts myself), I determined that the program at the Living Stream Ministry was a rare opportunity to participate in something genuinely special—an opportunity to make a meaningful difference in the lives of others.

As it turned out, those were the two best years of my life. It seemed like every day, I learned something new about life, about dedication to others, and about dependency on others. I am still amazed at the breadth of experiences I had during this time. My duties ranged from helping a struggling community college student become the first in his family to attend a four-year university to traveling overseas to provide relief for disaster victims. Following the 1999 earthquake that ravaged the island of Taiwan, I was sent with a group of 25 colleagues to assist in repairing and restoring the affected areas. I was also chosen to wake up at 5:30 a.m. to manage a kitchen staff of 12 and prepare breakfast for over two hundred people (given my past culinary attempts, this was no small feat). These and countless other experiences have revolutionized my view of teamwork and given me an understanding of all that can be accomplished through the coordinated efforts of a few. I came away from those two years with a resolve in my life to do more, be more, and give back to society.

Looking back, I couldn't have made a better decision. In fact, my experience in the nonprofit sector working with individuals from around the world has actually been a great help to my work at Prudential Securities. At Prudential, I work in a tightly-knit sell-side research team whose focus is on one thing: providing unmatched coverage of the food, beverage and tobacco industries. Whether that means spending all night creating a presentation for a portfolio manager in London, going over valuation metrics with the sales force in Boston, or helping the senior analyst write a research report, my role on this team has been to maintain a peaceful dynamic in an often frenetic environment.

Now, four years later, I find myself once again standing at the crossroads, knowing that it is time to move on and choose where to go from here. After much consideration, I believe what would enrich both my life and my career at this stage is further business education and leadership training. Education and training not only gained in the classroom, but also through meaningful campus interactions and community and social work.

In short, I know that this is the right time for me to get my MBA. Spending the past two years researching the food, beverage, and tobacco industries with some of the best analysts on Wall Street, I've had the privilege of meeting top management and forming an understanding of how the world keeps score of publicly traded consumer staples companies. My goal in business school is to take what I've learned both in the corporate and non-profit worlds and supplement it with a rigorous training in finance and marketing so that I can piece it all together and extend my reach to effect change both in business and in society.

There is no better place to pursue my MBA studies than at the Stern School of Business at NYU. I'm drawn by its renowned finance and marketing programs, allowing me to focus on courses like International Financial Management and Consumer Behavior, which are tailored to my interests. Even outside of academics, I'm excited by all the clubs Stern has to offer. Recent discussions with Lauren Torres (Stern '99) have already sparked my interest in the Stern Community Service Committee, Association of Investment Management, Graduate Marketing Association, and the Stern Golf Club. In return, I am confident that my diverse background and interests will be a most colorful addition to the Stern student body.

After graduation, my plans are to return to investment research covering the consumer goods industry—only this time, at a leading buy-side shop such as Fidelity Investments or Credit Suisse First Boston. In the long-term, my goal is to combine my experience in analysis with my knowledge of the consumer industry and become a brand management leader at a global consumer company such as Kraft Foods or Unilever. Regardless where I may end up, I intend to become more actively involved, both in social enterprise as well as in philanthropy.

My desire to attend business school at this time represents the same underlying motivations I had when deciding to spend two years at the Living Stream Ministry: a chance to expand my vision of the possible, a challenge to face the unfamiliar, and a choice to grasp the opportunity to make decisions that will have a lasting impact in society.

Erik Penney

"I had some good work experience for a business school application (three years at Morgan Stanley) and I had been a very involved alumni volunteer since I graduated several years before. In fact, I won an award from the school as the top alumni volunteer in the country in 2002. It was through this interaction with the school as an alumni that I met one of the deans of Rochester's business school, and he encouraged me to apply. At other alumni events I attended, I met other administrators and faculty of the business school, as well as several generally influential alumni. This was important because I knew I had a below-average GPA to compensate for, and I felt like if I was able to meet some 'decision-makers' at the school face-to-face, I might be able to improve my chances. I thought the best strategy would be to be honest about my academic past, provide a solid explanation for my grades, and hope that the admissions committee would be able make a decision based on my other attributes. To that end, I used an entire essay to explain all of my dirty laundry and think I did a good job of minimizing the negative effect it could have on my application. It was this essay, combined with a name-brand company in my work history, and probably, most importantly, the fact that people at the school knew me apart from my 'on paper' application, that got me in. After graduation, I found a great job with Jefferies & Company in New York City in Equity Sales and Trading."

Stats

GMAT Score: 680

Undergraduate GPA: 2.50

College attended: University of Rochester

Year of college graduation: 1996

Graduate school attended: N/A

Hometown: Brooklyn, NY

Gender: Male

Race: Caucasian

Admissions Information

Business school attended: University of Rochester William E. Simon
   Graduate School of Business

Accepted: University of Rochester William E. Simon Graduate School of
   Business

Denied: N/A

Wait-listed: N/A

Essay Prompt

Describe a failure or setback that you have experienced. How did you overcome this setback? What, if anything, would you do differently if confronted with this situation again?

The transition period between high school and college is often difficult for adolescents to make. The typical student goes from a very regimented existence with much parental oversight to one with a much more elastic structure. New freedoms abound, and a high level of maturity and discipline in the face of this is required in order to succeed. Many students succeed, while many stumble. I did not find the transition from high school to college to be all that easy to manage, and for a period of time I struggled. Having left the University of Rochester after two years and faced with the possibility of not returning, I could have given up and resigned myself to a different kind of life and education than the one I had always wanted.

Without question, I would consider my first two years as an undergraduate at the University of Rochester an unqualified academic failure. Although I passed all my classes, I struggled in virtually every class I took. I was unaccustomed to failure, and ever more so to the rigors of strenuous study, and didn't really know how to react. My parents were, in retrospect, very understanding and supportive, and were willing to give me myriad second chances to turn things around, none of which I took advantage of. Finally, after financing my inauspicious grade-point average for two years, it was strongly suggested to my by my parents that I return home and take classes at the local college, get my feet back on the ground, and see where that left me in a year.

My year at Brooklyn College was an eye-opener. I grew up a lot during that year, and made better grades. My study habits improved and I came to realize the value of the type of education that I had almost wasted. I swore, at that point, that I would do whatever it took to get back to Rochester and finish my degree. I returned to the U of R in September of 1995, and completed my degree in December of 1996. I regret the time I wasted during my earlier years in college, but I have never been more proud of myself than I am when I think of how I achieved the goal of a Rochester diploma after coming so close to losing it.

That experience has shaped me more than any other, and I have come to appreciate my relationship with my alma mater more, I think, than many of my classmates who didn't have as bumpy a road as I. Since then, I have become a dedicated alumni, volunteering my time and energies to regional alumni programming events in Washington, DC, culminating with being given a Meliora Award in 2002 for best regional alumni volunteer. The odd thing is, given the chance, I don't think I'd change a thing about my past. I believe that a person is the sum of his past experiences, and I truly believe that I wouldn't be the kind of person I am today had it not been for all the things I have been through. Maybe having a better undergraduate GPA would be nice, but I think I have learned more about life and about myself given what I have gone through, and if all that costs is a few points off my GPA, so be it.

Najeeb Yaser

"The major thing that helped in getting my acceptance was the essay that I have attached. I also sent a copy of my CV to the university with my application to explain my work experience. That experience includes executive manager of the largest and most prestigious restaurant in both Palestine and Israel, and working in the treasury Department of Cairo Amman Bank as a foreign exchange dealer— buying and selling foreign currency, margin trading, foreign investment, deposits and overall bank money transactions. While there, I took a training course at bank headquarters in the stock market and foreign exchange."

Stats

GMAT Score: 460
Undergraduate GPA: 3.02
College attended: Birzeit University, West Bank, Palestine
Year of college graduation: 2000
Graduate school attended: N/A
Hometown: *Palestine, Israel*
Gender: Male
Race: Middle Eastern

Admissions Information

Business school attended: University of North Carolina—Greensboro
Bryan School of Business and Economics

Accepted: University of North Carolina—Greensboro Bryan School of
Business and Economics; John Brown University MBA Program
Denied: N/A
Wait-listed: N/A

Essay Prompt:

Submit a 1,000-word personal essay describing your reason for pursuing a Bryan MBA.

8:00 AM, barely awake, a strong cup of Turkish coffee in one hand and two phones in the other, I sat down awaiting the call. It came. The First transaction of the day, money exchange between Bank Hapoalim in Jerusalem, and Cairo Amman Bank; I am to authorize this deal between the two banks from the living room of my house! Everything else is closed down. There is an official curfew enforced by the incursion of more than 160 military tanks into my town, Ramallah. The early morning hours came accompanied by the ringing sounds of phones, and blasting sounds of missiles striking various places in the city. My fear was not in being harmed by the attacks, but that the nearby Markava 3 tank would not knock down the phone posts in the area. I had work to finish, and for several weeks to come! The year of 2002 was full of political unrest in my country, and due to the many days of closure, Cairo Amman Bank, the bank I worked for then, decided to entrust me with the operations of its treasury department. Practically I had to run the operations from home for the duration of the incursions, which lasted several weeks, over the phone, with no bank notes or computers, just my word for all the operations. This particular experience gave me a great deal of confidence.

Growing up in a country like Palestine meant that life was full of surprises and roadblocks. Sometimes it is peace and other times it is war and frustration. Some days we were able to go to schools and others we had to go to underground gatherings to get some education. At times it seemed that our lives did not have hope, and dreaming of a bright future was just out of the question. Yet in some ways this uncertainty and frustration propelled me to strive for a better life, while still living in Palestine.

When I graduated from high school, peace was underway, at least for a short while, and things started to look hopeful for my generation. In addition to a major in accounting, I was active in the student body. Several times I participated in student congress, which challenged and boosted my self-confidence, and taught me many important lessons in life, especially commitment and loyalty. Later, this experience enhanced my position at Cairo Amman Bank, where I got my first job after graduating from university.

Though life in Palestine is at the least challenging, I learned that nothing in life comes easy, and that one has to work hard for accomplish dreams. I appreciate my life background especially that it did not stop me from continuing to aspire for a better future for myself and those around me. I believe that in order for a nation to flourish, its members have to take up the challenge of the present to create a different future for themselves and the generations to come. This is what I intend to do with my life. Thus, my decision to return to university, to pursue an MBA program at The University of North Carolina at Greensboro after several years of work in the professional world, will broaden my knowledge. The practical work experience gained from 3.5 years of work at the bank, coupled with an advanced degree in business will no doubt better equip me to refine my business skills, and prepare me to excel in the business world.

Rob Place

"While pursuing a degree in architecture at Penn, I excelled. Once out of grad school, however, I worked in an entry-level architecture position that required little creativity or ambition. While most accepted the production-centered role as a rite of passage, I realized that it didn't appeal to my entrepreneurial or social desire. I joined the Peace Corps and within a few months of living in Kenya, I had found work that I felt passionate about—an unconventional place where I could utilize my innovative skills, yet in a socially beneficial way. I plan to use the skill set I take with me from a Yale MBA as a tremendous asset to the foundation I have created back in Kenya, and which I wrote about for my application essay."

I knew my application would be one labeled two ways: "Wow!!!!" or "Risky." My biggest challenge was to clearly describe the consistencies between my diverse and seemingly unconnected stories. My goal was to convey who I was through my essays and have my resume back up the story with tangible/practical results.

I chose a theme that at once spoke to the strengths of my target school and described my consistent, linear career progression. My application focused on my passion for building and creation: launching a nonprofit; designing and constructing buildings; creating lasting, social change in developing economies.

I had to weave together a story that depicted my progression from architecture school to poor people and how these experiences brought me to the point of wanting an MBA. I wrote a unique application by creating an allusion to Howard Roark from the classic The Fountainhead by Ayn Rand. My essays created the visual of a noncompromising visionary such as Roark and I think the admissions staff made the connection as well. Three suggestions for b-school applicants...

1. Understand who you are. Start positioning yourself years in advance. This will allow you to look at the big picture and to start filling in the pieces naturally.

2. Understand who you are competing against. I wasn't competing against the engineers and consultants with 3.5 GPAs and 750 GMATs. I competed with other non-traditional students not armed with high test scores but unique experiences and skills.

3. Don't hide...highlight. If you are more comfortable outside the classroom or office, go whitewater rafting down the Zambezi, backpack across Asia, or play on a local sports team. Instead of hiding my un-corporate attitude, I simply highlighted how much adventure meant to me."

Stats

GMAT Score: 650
Undergraduate GPA: 2.88
College attended: Lehigh University
Year of college graduation: 1995
Graduate school attended: University of Pennsylvania
Grad school GPA: TKTK
Year of graduate school graduation: 1998
Hometown: TKTK
Gender: Male
Race: White

Admissions Information

Business school attended: Yale University School of Management

Accepted: Yale University School of Management

Denied: University of California—Berkeley Haas School of Business; University of Michigan Business School

Wait-listed: Columbia University Business School

Essay Prompt:

Why an MBA? Please describe your short and long term goals and how your previous experience and an MBA will help you to achieve these goals. (500 words maximum)

It only took me a moment to realize my long-term goals. When I walked onto Kolunga Beach, Kenya, I witnessed a most alarming site, and instantly, an amazing opportunity to help. Naked children, emaciated with the distended bellies signifying their malnutrition, fished in Lake Victoria in hopes of feeding themselves and their siblings. Alongside these AIDS orphans, women bartered sex for food. Small children carried infants on their backs while pillaging through piles of trash strewn with human feces. It was at this moment, my first in Kolunga Beach, that I realized the imminent need of a venture to address such suffering.

Immediately, I diagrammed a matrix of these problems. For example, I saw that AIDS awareness could not be expected to lower AIDS incidence without job creation or healthcare improvement; reforestation could improve soil conditions providing better harvests; income from jobs could pay for alternative fuel sources. I showed a team of volunteers that I assembled the countless connections between these problems and then mapped out a rough guide on how we could improve lives by building infrastructure and starting programs that empower people. Over the last few years, I have led a group of Kenyan volunteers to implement such a vision to improve living local living standards.

I am in the process of co-launching an international philanthropy, Kageno, which means, A Place of Hope in local *Dholuo*. It will serve as the umbrella 501(c)(3) organization to subsidiaries such as the pilot project I launched, Kageno Kenya. Kageno will assist genocide survivors, AIDS orphans, refugees, and exploited women by helping them transform communities whose resources will afford them opportunities previously unobtainable. These micro-communities are basically multi-structure complexes within said community that house a variety of projects that build infrastructure and address the financial, environmental and health needs of the given population.

I wish to get an MBA to build my personal skill set and available resources to help graft and improve the formula of Kageno Kenya onto other sites in the world and build capacity of the umbrella NGO. I would enter into Yale with an operating startup that serves as a platform to immediately apply the skills that I will be learning. I want to draw knowledge from Yale's emphasis on non-profit management. Furthermore, courses in international business and entrepreneurship will help develop expertise on economies of developing nations, international marketing, as well as launching and growing the community projects.

I have proven through my academic studies and professional activities that I can handle the intellectual and interpersonal demands that Yale requires. I offer to the Yale program a different perspective and an interesting skill set. For three years, I have worked with Kenyan volunteers to build a community project. I led this venture without computers, electricity, or any relevant experience. Instead, I have employed technical and motivational skills to implement my vision. These experiences have broadened my understanding of development issues and have shown me the challenges of working in a different culture. I would like to attend Yale to build my business skills and resources so that I may lead a dynamic organization that launches such socially driven projects around the world.

Ryan Masterson Payne

"I had worked at a private equity firm that focused on small lever-aged buyouts and I had worked as a commercial insurance broker in my family's business before applying to business school. Both businesses were heavily dependent on government regulation and contract negotiation and were major influences in my decision to pursue a JD/MBA. Once accepted at Emory's law school, I immediately switched gears and began applying to its business school, and I had completed the application by August to its business school prior to my matriculation to law school. I applied so early, in fact, that I ended up using the prior year's application. It was aggressive, but that's what they wanted to see. I was accepted by December and even got a partial scholarship without asking for one."

Stats

GMAT Score: 740

Undergraduate GPA: 3.30

College attended: University of California—Los Angeles

Year of college graduation: 1999

Graduate school attended: N/A

Hometown: Malibu, CA

Gender: Male

Race: White

Admissions Information

Business school attended: Emory University (applied as a JD/MBA after being accepted to law school)

Accepted: Emory University

Denied: N/A

Wait-listed: N/A

Essay Prompt:

The greatest challenge I have ever faced...

The greatest challenge I have ever faced was a distance of ten vertical feet. I was rock climbing, a sport that epitomizes to me both the physical and metaphorical struggle of life – scaling a vertical face while constantly searching for a decent toehold. This time, it was Ryan versus the mountain, round one, and the likelihood of a round two was quickly disappearing.

A failure to climb the rock would be simple. However, a failure to best the metaphor would be viscerally devastating. My mind had already made the logical leap of imagining the grotesquely dramatized slow-motion mental video of me sliding down the rock face while desperately clawing to fight the fall. I had traveled a mere ten feet from the ground and stood frozen still in the sun, panicked and looking down at the waiting, impatient eyes of my friends, coworkers, judgmental future boss, future wife and an entire pack of hungry, salivating wild dogs, or so it seemed. In reality, beneath me were a few of my closest friends, all honest and encouraging people who would understand completely if I decided to climb back down, if only they were willing to let that happen.

There I stood, the shirtless wonder that, before beginning the climb, had been only too eager to confidently show off his athletic, gym-chiseled physique. Now I could not help thinking to myself what an idiot I must look like to the onlookers below. No excuse went unused by me: the shoes are too tight, I need to start over, I am out of chalk, I need sunscreen, I think I am cramping...this event was not going to make my highlight reel.

My obstinate friends below were deaf to my complaints. Their encouragement was loud and emphatic, with the chatty zest of a Russian gymnastics coach. Others below sensed my plight and a crowd began to gather – all to watch a guy who hadn't moved an inch in at least 15 minutes. There was no longer a "down" option (had there ever been?) and I gathered myself to search for any nook in the rock. Each timid reach and step for a finger hold or toehold took an eternity to find, a step of pure faith and a suspension of my knowledge of the effects of gravity. Small ripples and inconsistencies in the rock the width of an ant supported my entire body weight, but I was slowly moving up.

Later upon reflection, I realized that it was never the height itself that I feared or even the falling – I could have jumped from that height and I knew it. What stopped my ascent was the thought that I had just witnessed another person climb the same rock face as proof that I was confronted with a conquerable obstacle. This thought compounded into fear as my own inability to solve the same riddle of rock nooks and folds materialized. Horrific, public failure while attempting to scale this already conquered metaphor was my most real fear. I knew definitively that the rock held all the answers to my attempts to climb it, yet I was at an impasse staring blankly at what looked like a flat face of solid rock.

As the chant from the crowd below began, I again felt like an idiot, this time with the pity of the masses on my side. Tentatively, I began to trust the rock and the crowd, inching upward. My speed increased with my confidence until I was practically walking up the rock face. When I finally reached the peak, relief washed over me in an awesome way. I had done it.

Later that day I climbed several more peaks including one that was three times the height of the first, sans any story-worthy drama. However, if not for the encouragement of my friends to confront my fear and reject my cries for rock-climbing clemency, I might still be clinging to that first rock paralyzed at a mere ten feet.

Sean Michael Holloway

"Along with my essay, my work experience and career path most likely helped my MBA application. I did not travel the normal route, spending most of my career before business school working for non-profits and spending one year as a volunteer teaching English in St. Petersburg, Russia. While I was not saving the world 24 hours a day, it was clear that I also was genuinely concerned with issues that I believed were important and was willing to take action to address them. This, in combination with my experience overseas and language skills, helped me immensely. Many programs do very well in attracting overseas talent, but I had spent four years in Russia and knew the language fluently. Few others in my class had this overseas and cultural experience, and I believe this gave me an advantage against other American students applying. Also important was the fact that I was older than most in my class, and I believe that the program seeks out those perceived to have a level of maturity that will allow them to be an 'anchor' amongst the student body."

Stats

GMAT Score: 700

Undergraduate GPA: 3.23

College attended: Michigan State University

Year of college graduation: 1990

Graduate school attended: Georgetown University

Graduate GPA: 3.7

Year of graduate school graduation: 1994

Hometown: Detroit, MI

Gender: Male

Race: White

Admissions Information

Business school attended: College of William and Mary Mason School of Business

Accepted: College of William and Mary Mason School of Business

Denied: N/A

Wait-listed: N/A

Essay Prompt:

What is the most creative solution you have ever used to meet a challenge? Was it successful? If yes, how so? If not, what will you do if confronted with a similar situation in the future?

When I was employed at the International Research & Exchanges Board (IREX – a non-profit educational exchange and technical assistance organization) as the CIS Field Coordinator, I oversaw all activities in the former Soviet Union on two academic exchange projects. Within the guise of these projects, I was directly responsible for programmatic issues in Western Russia, Belarus, and Moldova. Since the organization had no local office that could help me in either Belarus or Moldova, I spent most of my time traveling on a never-ending commute.

After spending nine weeks of a three-month period on the road, I realized that I could not keep doing this without hurting aspects of the projects in other countries. The best case scenario would be to have local staff on the ground, and I approached upper management with my concerns and ideas. Unfortunately, I was told that there was no need to have full-time staff in either country for these projects until a source of outside funding was found. Not to be easily dismayed, I argued that this meant our organization would never receive outside financial support funding. The lack of an office and knowledgeable, full-time local staff cast a bad light on our organization, showing it to be reactive – not proactive – and unwilling to create its own business and markets. I also firmly believed there was ample yet untapped interest – both in these countries and in the US – which a new office could tap into and leverage.

After several meetings with the CFO, I convinced him to at least look at a strategic business plan for the possibility of opening one office in one country. During my time with IREX in Washington, DC, I knew and talked to many organizations in the US that were interested in doing some type of project in Moldova, so I decided to focus my efforts on an office in the capital city of Chisinau. Immediately after receiving the CFO's approval, I found an alumnus of one of IREX's academic exchange programs and began to work with him during week-long trips to Chisinau, first conducting a rough, seat-of-the-pants market research study to determine just what issues and areas the office would address. Furthermore, we tried to define how synergies could be made with what IREX was doing in other countries of the former Soviet Union at the moment, and where other potential sources of funding could be found. Next we searched for office space, researched tax, banking, and other legal issues, and created a business plan ranging from initial start-up costs to a strategic plan to ensure the office would be mostly self-sufficient within three years.

Eventually, upper management decided to make the initial capital outlay in an office in Moldova. The office was opened in 1998 with one full-time employee, one part-time receptionist, and two generally seasonal projects. Now, five years later, the office is still headed by the Director I hired and staffed by ten full-time employees, with another 35 in provincial cities; all working on nine projects that are constantly running year round. IREX's new presence in the region greatly improved its reputation with clients and business partners, dramatically increased operational efficiency and created new areas of business for the company.

Professionally and personally, this experience further reinforced my belief in my ability to proactively attack a problem, quickly analyze and research it, and then come up with a creative, viable solution. I effectively worked within American corporate business culture and locally in Moldova, a place where the culture, language, and standard business procedures were all drastically different from those in America. Additionally, I believe my leadership, communication skills, and perseverance shone throughout the entire episode, as I was the initiator and driving force behind this plan. Finally, this experience reaffirmed my belief that my future lay in the field of international business, an area where I can best use these abilities I possess.

Trevor Winn

"I find the business school application process similar in many respects to the job application process and this is intentional. B-schools are judged by their ability to place students in high profile careers and the more apt your are at selling yourself as an applicant, the easier you will be for the career center to find a job. Keep an eye on the big three: GMAT, GPA, and work experience. If they are in the meaty range of accepted applicants from prior years, it makes the admissions officer's job much easier. In addition, visiting the campus to get a feel for the school community (professors, students, and administration) and an understanding of what makes the school worthwhile to you. For me it was easy, I fell in love with Darden during one of many business school visits.

The crucial factors for my application were completing and excelling in business coursework (to compensate for my undergrad GPA) and weaving together a compelling story as to why an MBA would be a fit for me in the context of my past and future goals. Minor points include that I was applying to a Southern school as a history major from California with non-traditional work experience (for business school that translate into not banking or consulting). These factors allowed me to fill diversity needs for geography, experience, and undergraduate majors that admissions offices hope to fill in every accepted class. Good luck!"

Stats

GMAT Score: 670
Undergraduate GPA: 3.10
College attended: University of California—Riverside
Year of college graduation: 2001
Graduate school attended: N/A
Hometown: Redlands, CA
Gender: Male
Race: Caucasian

Admissions Information

Business school attended: University of Virginia Darden School of Business

Accepted: University of Virginia Darden School of Business

Denied: University of California—Berkeley Haas School of Business

Wait-listed: N/A

Essay Prompt:

Describe your most rewarding leadership experience and what it means to your development as a potential leader.

Growing up in the home of a single mother in a blue-collar area was challenging. In spite of this adversity, I was the first person in my family to have attended college after completing high school. During college, I landed a teaching position with the Princeton Review that eventually led to full-time work. Most Princeton Review instructors were teaching affluent upper class students how to improve their test scores for college admission. During my full-time tenure at The Princeton Review, I was able to pursue a population of students that no one had served before and address two false notions. The first was that these students were disengaged regarding their college futures and the second was that we would damage our brand by helping the disadvantaged kids. We were able to offer students from the poorest schools in Southern California SAT preparation. It was commonly believed that these students were not interested in being helped. These two issues had prevented Princeton Review from pursuing an aggressive marketing strategy in this market space and I was amongst the few who challenged this notion. I helped to design a program that helped over six thousand students over three years throughout Riverside and San Bernardino Counties significantly improve their SAT scores. Our after-school program had a 95% completion rate that was the highest in history of almost every school we worked with. Two years after the inception of this program, the average number of college-going students from these high schools had risen by twenty percent. I had a tangible impact on the community I grew up in.

In order to accomplish this, I have become a business generalist, forced to master both the intricacies and the holistic nature of my business. I sell the product myself, I train others to deliver the product, I visit the customers, I order the materials, I write the brochures, and I am required to manage the finances of my division. Working with each functional area has taught me that personal commitment and the articulation of a vision do affect great change.

Working with disadvantaged students and underserved schools has been uplifting and, at the same time, a living parable for me. A business that does right will anchor itself within the community. Harvesting the wealth of your surroundings without an appropriate outlet to show your concern for the greater good can create a tenuous relationship with your marketplace. By aligning a business's goals with the improvement of its surroundings, a business intertwines its own fate with that of the community. I learned the relevance and understand the value of making my marketplace better because of my presence.

William Gangi

"At the time I applied to b-school, I had seven years of experience in the pharmaceutical/biotechnology industry, spending the first four years working my way up in a small biopharmaceutical company from the laboratory over to the business side (started as Quality Control Technician, promoted to Research Associate, then promoted again to Project Manager). I spent the next two and half years working as a Pharmaceutical Consultant for Deloitte Consulting. I think I was accepted because I had a great story—my needs for b-school were real and believable and Kellogg was clearly a natural choice for me given their focus on healthcare and biotechnology."

Stats

GMAT Score: 660
Undergraduate GPA: 3.30
College attended: St. John's University
Year of college graduation: 1996
Graduate school attended: St. John's University
Graduate degree: Master's of Science in Biology
Graduate School GPA: 3.80
Year of graduate school graduation: 1999
Hometown: Rockville Center, NY
Gender: Male
Race: White

Business school attended: Kellogg School of Management at North-
western University
Accepted: Kellogg School of Management at Northwestern University
Denied: Duke University Fuqua School of Business
Wait-listed: N/A

Essay Prompt:

**Each of our applicants is unique. Describe how your background, values, academics,
activities and/or leadership skills will enhance the experience of other Kellogg students.**

With my strong scientific credentials and passion for improving things around me, I
could have pursued a career in pure science. Or my love of business and my strong leadership
skills could have taken me down a strictly commercial, entrepreneurial pathway—just as my
desire to help others learn, coupled with my solid interpersonal skills, could have led me to
teaching. But each of these interests defines only a part of me; it is the blend that makes me
both unique and an asset to my fellow Kellogg students.

The guidance and support I received while growing up provided the motivation I needed
to continue with my studies. At the time, I took it for granted, but now as an adult, I realize
that too many children are missing that guidance and support, resulting in a lack of motivation
that limits their opportunities. At Deloitte Consulting (DC), I am trying to chip away at the
drop-out rate of New York City high school students by helping to launch a Mentor Program
that will offer guidance and support to underprivileged students to motivate them in their
studies. In this program, we will answer questions and provide advice via weekly e-mails and
phone conversations, offer a variety of workshops and also take the children on educational
trips.

Also at DC, I have initiated a Health Care Practitioner Orientation Program to help
assimilate new industry hires to both their new career and the firm. To aid this program, I
helped develop an in-depth orientation manual and persuaded the Human Resources
department to begin assigning a Health Care "coach" to each new industry hire. Similarly,
I conceived and developed a Life Sciences newsletter and knowledge repository. Realizing
that many Life Sciences practitioners at DC were not up-to-date with industry current events,
I initiated a monthly newsletter of recent news, events and reports collected from websites,
newspapers and journals as well as created a database to increase the efficiency of our
research efforts. It is this kind of initiative and vitality that I will bring to Kellogg.

My experience in both laboratories and corporate boardrooms have provided me with a
unique, blended perspective—one gleaned from graduate studies in biology, hours spent in

the laboratory, disputes negotiated and resolved with vendors and contractors, and strategizing with teams on a variety of projects. The diversity of my experiences will broaden and deepen my classmates' understanding of the unique challenges awaiting them in the Health Care industry, and provide insight in how to manage and interact with both scientists and non-scientists.

The experiences I have to share, however, do not end there. The camaraderie and collegial-based culture at Kellogg, so evident on campus, is one I have been thriving in for the past two years. At Deloitte, I am known as much for my approachability and ability to get along with different personalities as I am for my sense of humor. My fellow students will find themselves up to the challenge of golfing with their future bosses after I share golfing etiquette—knowledge obtained from four grueling seasons as Assistant Manager at an exclusive golf club. I can also teach them the finer points of diplomacy—a skill I found prudent to employ while critiquing the management decisions made by the CEO of a Top 5 pharmaceutical company. And every student will be on guard and ready to assist a choking victim after I conduct my workshop in the Heimlich maneuver—invaluable knowledge that helped me save the life of my project manager at Deloitte. Incidentally, the '89 Château Cantemerle Red Bordeaux given to me in thanks, tweaked my interest in wine tasting – a new hobby I will enjoy pursuing with my fellow students.

As a student of Kellogg, my goal will be to contribute to the learning experience of my fellow students and lead and organize extracurricular activities that will make our two years together as much fun as they are intellectually rewarding, in exchange for the benefit of being in a learning environment with over 600 unique and diverse backgrounds.

ABOUT THE AUTHOR

Nedda Gilbert is a graduate of the University of Pennsylvania and holds a master's degree from Columbia University. She has worked for The Princeton Review since 1985. In 1987, she created The Princeton Review corporate test preparation service, which provides Wall Street firms and premier companies tailored educational programs for their employees. She currently resides in New Jersey.

NOTES

NOTES

NOTES

NOTES

More expert advice from The Princeton Review

G ive yourself the best chances for getting into the business school of your choice with The Princeton Review. We can help you get higher test scores, make the most informed choices, and make the most of your experience once you get there. We can also help you make the career move that will let you use your skills and education to their best advantage.